A Portrait of
JESUS

A Portrait of JESUS

Steve Wyatt

College Press Publishing Co., Joplin, Mo.

Library of Congress Catalog Card Number: 92-75787
International Standard Book Number: 0-89900-601-9

These pages are lovingly dedicated to my family.

To my parents, who etched His profile
into the fiber of my heart, teaching me from birth what
it meant to live like Jesus lived.

To my wife, who sketched His features,
especially the eyes –
eyes of mercy, eyes of understanding and limitless love.

And to my children, who gave my Jesus
a chuckle in His voice
and a look of trust so absolute it could melt granite.

You gave my portrait of Jesus its beauty. I love you all.

Table of Contents

Preface

No other personality has impacted the world quite like Jesus. So monumental was His impact that the entire planet dates its calendar according to His arrival. And even though He died nearly 2,000 years ago, His life and ministry continue to cast an all-inclusive shadow across the horizon of man's history.

Songwriters still compose lyrics which extol His virtues. Poets continue to laud Him. Educators still point to Him as the ultimate personality of history. Authors continue their quest to plumb the depths of His teachings. And multiplied millions across the globe claim Him as their closest companion.

The current of our emotions runs deep when it comes to Jesus. You've never heard a student of the New Age sing,

"Oh, How I Love Shirley!" But we sing that phrase to Jesus. You've never heard a Wall Street broker look at his bank book and sing, "I Need Thee Every Hour." No, that song is reserved for Jesus and Jesus only.

This book is not intended to plow new territory. I have neither the desire nor the ability to declare some new truth. I want to simply tell you about my Jesus. The Jesus of Scripture. The Jesus Who desires to be known, demands to be followed and delights in our discovery of Him.

But first, a personal note. As this is my first attempt to write a book, I have become acutely aware that I am merely a composite of many others' investments. Steve Wyatt is a not a separate entity; he is the sum of many, many parts. It's only fitting that I now acknowledge their contribution to this effort.

I spent the first 18 years of my life listening to a man that I considered then and now to be a master pulpiteer – my father. To this day, Dad continues to command attention whenever he ascends into the "holy desk." I cherish his example.

There have been others. Ben Merold, E. Leroy Lawson and Don Nash – to name just a few. As I think of these men, I'm reminded of Spurgeon's comment about borrowing the axe of a friend. He said it's OK to borrow his axe, as long as the strokes you give with it are your own. These men have, in years past, provided me the use of their well-honed axes. Their faithful ministries – through pulpit excellence, thoughtful analysis or powerful writings – gave me the encouragement I needed to take a few swings myself.

Speaking of Spurgeon, I was so relieved, some time ago, to hear the comments of Dwight L. Moody concerning Spurgeon's impact on his life. Now anyone who knows church history knows that Moody was certainly not chopped liver.

Yet he freely confessed that the fire of His preaching came from two sources: The Bible and Charles Spurgeon. "Everything he ever said, I read," said Moody. "My eyes just feast on him."

That's the way I feel about Charles Swindoll. If he's written it, I've read it. If he'd publish his grocery list, I'd devour it. I came to know and respect him very early in my pulpit ministry, and my respect and admiration for him continue to this day. He has no idea who I am, but his is an indelible mark on my life. There are others. John Stott, Thomas Watson, Howard Hendricks, John MacArthur – these and others have made an invaluable investment in my life. My heart and mind are so saturated with their influence that many of their commitments and perspectives have become my own.

That's why, even now, when I peruse this text, I see the shadow of Swindoll. Or I would re-write a few lines, then pause and think, "That sounds just like Dad! But then, it sounds like me, too! Because it is me now!" The influence of my father, of a Swindoll or a Spurgeon has been wholly absorbed into my system.

So my friend, the Word that is made manifest in this life is really a composite of the Word made manifest in countless others. To those I have mentioned, and countless others, I thank God for your ministry in my life. If a line from these pages sounds vaguely familiar, thanks for your insight. And if my ministry has any impact on others, then please – share in my joy.

There are others who can claim their share of joy as well. The Elders of Cullen Avenue Church have encouraged me for eleven years. This book is a result of their vision for my ministry. Shirley Blackburn, herself a wonderful writer, lovingly poured over these pages, correcting my faulty grammar and suggesting what proved to be powerful improvements to this text. My wife and children faithfully supported this effort, even when their loving husband and father turned into a terrific ogre. Enough of this. It's time to get started. The goal of this book is quite simple. I want to sketch a likeness of the One Whose mark on this world outshines all others. May your journey through these pages help you paint a mental likeness of Jesus, so that as you see Him more clearly, you will seek to follow Him more closely.

We Call Him Lord!

1

Shakespeare asked, "What's in a name?" And If I could answer him, I would tell him that a name is far more than a mere title or label. I would tell him that a name describes the very essence of a person. This is why wise are the parents who give careful thought and consideration to the selection of the name which their child will bear for a lifetime.

Goethe put it like this:

A man's name is not like a mantle which merely hangs about him . . . but a perfectly fitting garment, which, like the skin, has grown over him, at which one cannot rake and scrape without injuring the man himself.

In our Anglo-Saxon tradition, names have historically been

assigned rather pragmatically. For example, ancestral heritage often resulted in family names such as Johnson or Peterson or Robertson. Often one's occupation became the identifying label. Thus Miller or Smith or Farmer. Religious heritage is another factor. Most of us know at least one woman named, "Joy" or "Hope" or "Faith." Or how about a man named "David" or "Paul?" Those who bear such names move through life with a daily reminder of their Christian heritage.

It may interest you to know that God has also placed high value on the careful selection and use of names. In fact, such has been the case from the beginning. Remember what happened at creation?

> In the beginning, God created the heavens and the earth (Gen. 1:1).

But God's creative energy was not limited to the mere construction of the heavens and the earth – He also named them! For example, when God made light, He "called the light 'day' and the darkness he called 'night' (Gen. 1:5a). When He "made the expanse" which would separate the waters "God called the expanse 'sky.' " (Gen. 1:8a). When He gathered the waters, He "called the dry ground 'land,' and the gathered waters He called 'seas.'" (Gen. 1:10).

I could go on, but I won't, except to say that on the final day of creation, God created a human being. And He called that human being, "man" – "Adam." Then God put the man into a garden and gave him two assignments.

His first assignment was to cultivate and care for the land.

> The Lord God took the man and put him in the Garden of Eden to work it and take care of it (Gen. 2:15).

14

His second assignment?

Now the Lord God had formed out of the ground all the beasts of the field and all the birds of the air. He brought them to the man to see what he would name them; and whatever the man called each living creature, that was its name. So the man gave names to all the livestock, the birds of the air and all the beasts of the field (Gen. 2:19,20a).

Can you imagine such an assignment? What a blast! "He, looks like an elephant to me! And him? He's a rhinoceros, if I've ever seen one – which I haven't, but if I had, that's what he'd have looked like!"

The job completed, God put Adam to sleep, and later, when Adam woke up, he saw standing before him *another* human being – slightly altered in design, but basically a human being! And Adam was ecstatic! He shouted, "This is now bone of my bones and flesh of my flesh" (Gen. 2:23a). Then he did what he had been doing with all God's animals. He gave her a name! "She shall be called 'woman!'" ' (Gen. 2:23b).

Do you find it intriguing that from the very beginning God sought to describe the essence of a person or a thing by assigning to that person or thing a name? And each name was chosen for a very specific reason.

As the tradition of naming continued, families would often name their child after a specific event which had occurred on or about the time of the baby's birth.

Consider Isaac. In Hebrew, Isaac's name literally means "laughter." God named the boy "Laughter" because his mother, 90 years old at the time of his birth, laughed out loud when she was told that she would bear a child! She couldn't imagine an old woman like herself becoming pregnant, so she cackled in mock disbelief! So God said, "Sarah, I'm going to name him "Laughter," so that for the rest of your life, you will be reminded that I make good on My promises." Can you imagine yelling outside, "Laughter! Come in! It's time to practice your timbrel!" Every time she spoke his name she was reminded of the laughter God had given to her heart.

Then there's Moses, whose name means "to draw out of." It was the name the Egyptian princess gave to him when she found him in the bulrushes. She said, "Let's call him, Moshe (Moses), because I've drawn him out of the water." (See Exod. 2:10).

And do you know what Moses called *his* first-born, born to him while he was herding sheep in the wilderness? He called him Gershom, which means, "alien in a foreign land."

Most of us are aware that the Hebrew word "shalom" means peace. But did you know that "shalom" is the root word behind the name David gave his son, Solomon? You see, David had been a man of war, but his son was to be a man of peace. Hence, shalom.

Hannah's womb was barren. For years she pled, "O Lord, look upon your servant's misery and give me a son." (See I Sam. 1:11ff). Finally, God answered her prayer and she named her son, Samuel, which means, "Heard by God."

Often names were added later as a result of a person's lifestyle or some other significant identifying mark. For example, there was John the Baptizer. Simon the Zealot. Judas the Traitor. James the Less (not less in importance, but less because he was shorter than the other James), Saul of Tarsus and, of course, Thomas the Doubter.

There were also occasions when a person's name was often due to a change in either character or assignment.

When Abram entered into his covenant with God, his name

16

was changed to Abraham, which means, "Father of a multi-tude."

Jacob's birth name literally meant, "One who takes by the heel." We might call him a "chiseler." And all through life that's the way Jacob lived. He was always grabbing for the things he wanted to have or do. He grabbed his brother's birthright. He grabbed for his mother's attention. Finally, God turned the tables on Jacob and grabbed his attention through a wrestling match at a place called Peniel. And from that point forward, Jacob was a changed man. So dramatic was the change that from Peniel to the time of his death, he was known not as "Señor Chiseler," but as "Israel," which means "Prince of God."

In the New Testament, Simon, one of the Lord's disciples, was always vacillating. He'd say one thing, but do another. He'd claim undying loyalty; then, when the heat was turned up, he'd turn tail and run. But one day Jesus said, "Simon, I'm going to change your name. You used to be a spineless, lily-livered wimp. But no more. From now on you will be called, "Rocky" – Peter. Instead of being as solid as a bowl of Jell-O, you're going to become rock-like in your character. You will become bold, strong and courageous."

And who could forget Saul of Tarsus, the Christian-killer turned soulwinner? Immediately after his dramatic conversion, Saul stopped stalking believers and started preaching the Gospel. The transformation was so dramatic that he assumed a new name. His name? Paul.

Now as interesting (or uninteresting) as all of that may be, it is no exaggeration to say that of all the names in history, not one compares to the beauty, the power and the simplicity of the name JESUS.

But the truth is, Jesus has many names. "Jesus" is merely

one among many descriptive labels assigned to our Savior. In fact, one commentator has counted more than *700 descriptive names and titles of Jesus* in Scripture. I didn't count them myself, mind you. I'll just accept it by faith. But certainly, many names for Jesus have been revealed to us. And I think there's a reason.

Personally, I believe that one of the best ways to really come to know Jesus and to understand Him is to paint a mental portrait of Him using only the mosaic of the many names and titles which are assigned to Him in Scripture. And that's what this book is all about. I want you to know up front that in these pages, I intend to rivet your attention squarely and unapologetically into the face of Jesus. And I dare you to take your eyes off Him.

But I challenge you to observe, not His actions, nor His sayings, but His names. Please understand, the Gospels do a wonderful job presenting four accurate and moving biographies of Jesus – they reveal to us His emotions, His compassion, His humanity, His relentless love. *But I know of no study which will force you to examine Jesus more intimately and more dramatically than a careful, thoughtful study of His names.* Most are assigned to Him by the Father. Some are ascribed to him by his contemporaries. A few are assumed by Himself personally. All are designed to help us understand Him more clearly.

As I write that, I'm reminded of a little pre-schooler named Timmy. His class had been given an assignment to do a drawing, and Timmy had been feverishly working on his drawing, but when the time was up, he still wasn't finished. His teacher leaned over Timmy's desk and said, "What are you drawing, Timmy?" He said, "I'm drawing a picture of God!" The teacher wisely said, "But Timmy, the Bible says that 'No man has ever seen God.' Nobody knows what God looks like, Timmy." Timmy replied, "They will when I'm through."

Please understand, I have no delusions of grandeur. We will not plumb the depths of Jesus' identity in these few pages," as if we could understand what we saw if we could! And even though we have, and will continue to talk "portrait," neither will we have any idea what Jesus looked like when we're through. But then, that's not my ambition. No, like Paul, I simply want to "know Christ" (Phil. 3:10a). In fact,

> I consider everything else I have learned to be rubbish compared to the surpassing greatness of knowing Christ Jesus my Lord (Phil. 3:8a).

Do you know why I feel that way? Because Christianity — when you boil it down to its essence — is Jesus. That's it. Christianity, in its pristine purity, is nothing more than living like Jesus lived. Thinking like Jesus thought. Doing as Jesus did. And if a study of His names will help me know Him better, so that I can imitate Him more perfectly, then there is not any other subject we could address that is more significant than this.

Let's begin our portrait in the Old Testament prophecy of Isaiah 7. This verse is one of the earliest prophecies of the Messiah, and wouldn't you know it? One of Jesus' names is included in Jehovah's announcement:

> Therefore, the Lord himself will give you a sign: The virgin will be with child and will give birth to a son, and will call him Immanuel (Isa. 7:14).

In that single verse, God not only prophesies that a virgin would conceive and give birth, but He also predicted the

19

baby's name. He will be called, "Immanuel," which means "GOD WITH US."

Isaiah reveals four more titles in chapter 9:

> For to us a child is born, to us a son is given, and the government will be on his shoulders. And he will be called Wonderful Counselor, Mighty God, Everlasting Father, Prince of Peace (Isa. 9:6).

Let's move on to the New Testament. Nearly 800 years later, God fulfills His earlier prediction.

> This is how the birth of Jesus Christ came about. His mother Mary was pledged to be married to Joseph, but before they came together, (That is, before they were married, before they engaged in intercourse – while she was still a virgin, just as Isaiah said . . .) she was found to be with child through the Holy Spirit (Matt. 1:18).

Can you imagine what Joseph must have thought? He knew HE wasn't the father; she claimed God was the Father! He wanted to believe her, but that had never happened before! (Nor since.) So he decided to quietly call off the wedding.

> But after he had considered this, an angel of the Lord appeared to him in a dream and said, "Joseph, son of David, do not be afraid to take Mary home as your wife, because what is conceived in her is from the Holy Spirit. She will give birth to a son, and you are to give him the name Jesus, because he will save his people from their sins" (Matt. 1:20,21).

Matthew goes on to say:

> All this took place to fulfill what the Lord had said through the prophet: "The virgin will be with child and will give birth

20

to a son, and they will call him Immanuel" – which means, "God with us" (Matt. 1:22,23).

Already, in three brief passages, we've been introduced to six of Jesus' names: Immanuel, Wonderful Counselor, Mighty God, Everlasting Father, Prince of Peace and Jesus. Now those six are a mouthful, but there are many more than these. I won't take time to give all 700, but let me list a few. He is called: The Son of God. The Son of Man. Messiah. The Servant of God. The Good Shepherd. The Divine Physician. Savior. Prophet. King. The Cornerstone. The Bridegroom. The Bread of Life. The Light of the World. The Gate. The Vine. The Way. The Truth. The Life. The Resurrection. The Lamb of God. The Mediator. The Alpha and Omega. The Advocate. The Hope of Glory. The Holy One. The Great I Am. The Lord.

Why so many names? I think it's because one name could never fully capture Him. You see, a name, although descriptive, is also restrictive! To only call Jesus "The Lamb of God" restricts our view of him, because the Lamb is also "The Lion of Judah!" The Servant of God was also the Ruler of Man! In a very real sense, Jesus is UNNAMEABLE! His glory and His dominion defy description!

I came across a piece written by John Godfried Sax, entitled, "The Blind Men and the Elephant."

It was 6 men of Industan, to learning much inclined, who went to see the Elephant, though all of them were blind. That each by observation might satisfy his mind.

The first approached the elephant and happened to fall against his broad and sturdy side; and at once began to bawl, "God bless me! The elephant is very like a wall!"

The second, feeling of the tusk, cried, "Oh, what have we here? So very round and smooth and sharp. To me it's mighty

clear! This wonder of an elephant is very like a spear."
The third approached the animal and happened to take the squirming trunk within his hands. Thus boldly up and spake, "I see," quoth he, "the elephant is very like a snake!"
The fourth reached out an eager hand, felt about the knee, "What most this wondrous beast is like is mighty plain," quoth he. "'Tis clear enough the elephant is very like a tree!"
The fifth, who chanced to touch the ear, said, "Even the blindest man can tell what this resembles most. Deny the fact, who can? This marvel of an elephant is very like a fan!"
The sixth no sooner had begun about the beast to grope, than seizing on the swinging tail that fell within his scope. "I see," quoth he, "The elephant is very like a rope!"
And so these men of Industan disputed loud and long, each in his own opinion, exceeding stiff and strong, tho each was partly right, and all were in the wrong.

Get the point? If your mental portrait of Jesus includes only a few of your favorite names; if you only allow those brush strokes which speak of His love and mercy and grace; and if you fail to include the truth of His judgment and His wrath, then your portrait of Him will be entirely inaccurate. All of Jesus' names are required if your portrait of Him is to be an accurate one.

Another reason for so many names is that Jesus' function was constantly changing. The focus of His ministry was always being adapted to the pressing need of the moment. When it was time for instruction, He was "Rabbi." When it was time for something to drink, He became "living water."

I've noticed that my names have also changed through the years. When I first became a parent, I was called "Da-da." Then it evolved into "Daddy." Now I find that my twelve year old is starting to prefer "Dad." When I was in youth ministry, the kids used to call me "Stevie Wonder." Now they call me "Mr. Wyatt." Gag! That's my Dad, not me! There was a time when I was known as Tom Wyatt's son. I longed to be known for being "Steve." Now? I'm "Andrea Wyatt's Daddy."

That same shift happened in Jesus' ministry. In the Gospels, He is most often called, "Jesus." In Acts, He is most often referred to as "Jesus Christ," as the Apostles sought to emphasize His Messiahship. Then, by the time you get to the Epistles, rare is the passage that refers to Him only as Jesus. In fact, only 17 times in all of the epistles is that name used alone. The term that comes to the fore is "Lord." In fact, although "Lord" is used less than 40 times in the Gospels, Paul uses it nearly 240 times in his letters, 14 times in one chapter alone!

I discovered also that at times, the more a person was with Jesus, the more His name changed. For example, In John 4, Jesus meets the Woman at the Well. She greets Him by calling Him "Sir." At that moment He was nothing more to her than just another man. But when He told her about her five husbands and that she wasn't even married to the man she was then living with, she said, "I perceive that you are a Prophet." No kidding! But when Jesus explained to her about the coming Messiah, she dropped her water jar, ran to the city and said to her friends, "Come, see a man who told me everything I ever did. Could this man be Messiah?" (John 4:29). What a change! From "Sir" to "Prophet" to "Messiah" in less than 30 verses!

In John 9, Jesus heals a man who had been born blind. Later, his neighbors asked about the man who had healed him. He said, "The man they call Jesus healed me" (John 9:11a). Then, because the Pharisees were out to get Jesus and because he had healed on the Sabbath, they called the man into court and said, "What do you have to say about this man who healed you?" Now he's had some time to think about it.

Nobody else, including the Pharisees, could heal him. Only
the man they called Jesus. So, having thought it through, He
now says, "He's a prophet!" (John 9:17b). "There's no way
around it, guys! He's different than the rest of us!"
Then the Pharisees were furious! They said,

"He's not a prophet! He's a sinner!" The man replied,
"Whether he's a sinner or not, I don't know. One thing I do
know. I was blind but now I see! (John 9:24b,25).

Well, they threw him out of the courtroom, and when Jesus
heard what had happened, He found the man and said,

"Do you believe in the Son of Man?" The man said, "Who is
he, sir? Tell me so that I may believe in him." Jesus said,
"You have now seen him; in fact, he is the one speaking with
you." Then the man said, "Lord, I believe!" (John 9:35b-38).

Talk about a change in perspective! We're talking about a
"man" who became a "prophet" and then, finally, in one short
afternoon, was called "LORD!"
LORD. That's what *we* call Him, too. We call Him Lord.
Without question, the most common title used to address
Jesus after His resurrection is LORD. Consider, for example,
Philippians 2. This magnificent passage of Scripture is so precious. I love it! Paul wrote a section of doctrine that takes us,
with great economy of words, all the way from heaven to the
manger to the cross and, ultimately, to the throne! The verses
are so poetic that I can't help but think this was a praise chorus in the worship of the early church. And the primary thrust
of the passage centers around what Paul calls, "the name that
is above every name." Look:

Your attitude should be the same as that of Christ Jesus: Who,

being in very nature God, did not consider equality with God
something to he grasped,

Though while he was literally, "exactly equal" with God,
He did not cling to that lofty position. Instead, He willingly
surrendered it.

but made himself nothing,

Literally, "He emptied Himself." Now understand, He did
not empty Himself of His deity; only the voluntary display of
His deity. That's what He gave up. He didn't STOP being
God! It's just that while He was on earth, for 33 1/2 years,
Jesus practiced His deity at the discretion and will of the
Father. In John 5:25, Jesus said, "I do nothing on my own, but
only what the Father has taught me."

taking the very nature of a servant, being made in human likeness

When Jesus was born, He was born just like you and me.
He ate, talked, walked, felt, hurt, spoke just like any other
man. He was different from all other men, in that though He
was very much human, He was still fully divine. Now there
was no halo on Jesus' head; no aura surrounded Him. He
didn't walk around with an angelic look carved into His features. Paul assures us of that.

And being found in appearance as a man, he humbled himself
and became obedient to death – even death on a cross!

The One Who was equal with God willingly died the worst
death man has ever devised. But He didn't stay dead, did He?
No! Three days later He burst out of that tomb defeating sin,

death and the grave in one fell, swoop!

Therefore God exalted him to the highest place

Literally, "He has super-exalted Him." *Huperupsosen.* Super-exalted!

and gave him the name

Look at that – again with the names! But this name is different . . .

that is above every name, that at the name of Jesus every knee should bow, in heaven and on earth and under the earth,

Paul wasn't about to let anyone slide by. A day will come when all beings – the angels, the departed saints, all those still living, those tortured residents of hell, even the demons and yes, Satan himself – will bow the knee . . .

and every tongue confess that Jesus Christ is Lord,

There's the name. One day the pre-eminent name of Jesus will be formed by the lips of every one who has ever walked this planet. And in unison chorus we will declare, "HE IS LORD! HE IS LORD! HE IS LORD!"

That's what Thomas said when He saw the scars in Jesus' hands. He fell to his face and cried, "My Lord and My God!" (John 20:28).

Mary Magdalene raced from the open tomb to the upper room and shouted, "I've seen Him! I have seen the Lord!" (John 20:18a).

Peter stood boldly before the masses gathered at Pentecost

26

and announced, "Let all Israel be assured of this: God has made this Jesus, whom you crucified, both Lord and Christ!" (Acts 2:36).

And it was Paul who announced to the Romans, "If you confess with your mouth, 'Jesus is Lord,' and believe in your heart God raised Him from the dead, you will be saved" (Rom. 10:9).

But on this grand and glorious Day – the day which Paul describes in Philippians 2 – on that day this confession will be for many (no, most) a confession of regret. Imagine the torment of realizing the truth of Jesus' identity only to return to the Abyss of eternal torture. Imagine knowing and never being able to escape the truth. "He really was Lord. He really was."

But for the believer, oh what a day that will be! All injustice will be vindicated as the Suffering Servant will be ultimately and eternally crowned King of kings and Lord of all!

WHAT DO WE MEAN
WHEN WE CALL HIM LORD?

The Greek word translated "Lord" is *kurios*. It wasn't coined by Christians to be used in reference to Jesus. It was a term which had enjoyed wide usage prior to its adoption by believers. According to Arndt and Gingrich (widely acknowledged Greek scholars), there were three major usages of the word.

KURIOS DENOTED OWNERSHIP

A man who owned a vineyard was called the *"lord of the*

vineyard." If he owned a business, he was "*lord of the business.*" Now Jesus, as Lord of all, functions also as OWNER
OF ALL. Scripture says He owns "the cattle on a thousand
hills" (Psa. 50:10). And that all silver and gold belongs to
Him (Haggai 2:8). Think of it: The infinite expanse of the
universe is His playroom. This pygmy planet is but His foot-
stool. In fact, He holds my life in the palm of His Hand.
INDEED, HE IS LORD!

KURIOS ALSO SPOKE OF AUTHORITY

It was a term acknowledging a person's lofty position. For
example, a father was called "Lord" by his children. A master
was called "Lord" by his slaves. Certainly Jesus claimed All
authority" (Matt. 28:18) And when Jesus spoke, He spoke as
One Who had authority! Talk about authority! He didn't swim
in water, He walked *on* water! He didn't just feel compassion
toward the sick, He healed them! He didn't just weep with the
blind, He restored their sight! He didn't cower before the
winds and the waves, He silenced them! He didn't just grieve
at the grave of Lazarus, He raised Him! No one else has ever
or could ever do that. That's why we can Him Lord! He has
"all authority!"

KURIOS WAS ALSO USED
TO ADDRESS DEIFIED RULERS

It was this very point which brought the Church into direct
conflict with Rome. You see, the later Roman emperors began
to view themselves as gods! So that ultimately, every Roman
citizen was required to come before the emperor, burn some

incense, bow the knee and say, "*Caesar is KURIOS.*" But that was something the Christians just could not do. They could not take the highest name of Jesus and speak it of anyone else – not even Caesar. To those early Christians, Jesus was Lord; and no one and no thing would ever make them say otherwise. So thousands of Christians died – some by the cross, others by the flames, still others in the arena. They died because that name above every name belongs to Jesus, and to Jesus alone, because He alone is the Ruler.

With those three concepts of *kurios* in mind, allow me to close this chapter with three simple words of application:

#1 – WHEN WE CALL JESUS "LORD," WE FREELY ADMIT THAT HE ALONE IS RULER.

We acknowledge His power and His alone can span beyond the confines of the grave. That only He can save. That only He can forgive. Not Caesar, not Gorbachev, not Khaddafi. Only Jesus. Scripture clearly declares it:

> Salvation is found in no one else, there is no other name under heaven given to men by which we must be saved (Acts 4:12).

#2 – WHEN WE CALL JESUS "LORD," WE WILLINGLY BOW TO HIS OWNERSHIP.

If He's Lord, He's Lord! Right? He owns me! He bought me with a price!

Think it through: Not only did He create me, He has redeemed me! Not only do I owe Him my very existence, but also my hope for eternity! I wouldn't be alive if it weren't for Jesus, and I won't know eternal life apart from Him either. So when I call Him Lord, I'm acknowledging His right to be in complete charge of my life.

A. W. Tozer writes:

> How can we live lives acceptable to God? The answer is near thee, even in thy mouth. Vacate the throne room of your heart and enthrone Jesus there. Set Him in the focus of your heart's attention and stop wanting to be a hero. Make Him your all in all and try yourself to become less and less. Dedicate your entire life to HIS honor alone and shift the motives of your life from self to God. Let the reason back of your daily conduct be Christ and His glory, not yourself, not your family, nor your country, nor your church. In all things let Him have the pre-eminence.

Did you get that? As Lord, He demands pre-eminence. Not prominence. A lot of people are willing to let Jesus be prominent in their lives. But that won't cut it. He won't settle for being just a priority either. He demands pre-eminence. And considering Who He is and What He has done; and considering who we are and what we have done – the only imaginable relationship between us is full ownership on His part and complete submission on our part. We owe Him every honor we can muster. To give Him anything less is utter blasphemy.

#3 – WHEN WE CALL JESUS "LORD," WE OPENLY AFFIRM HIS ULTIMATE AUTHORITY.

What does that mean, practically speaking? It means that there is nothing in this world that He, in His awesome power, cannot handle. Nothing. Isn't that wonderful? Because He spoke the world into existence, because He bridged the gap between man and God and because He conquered death itself – there is nothing else that could ever trip Him up. He possesses ALL AUTHORITY!

There's no temptation He can't handle. No disappointment, no past failure, no pain, no worry, no sin, no disease that will ever prove too much for Him. After all, HE IS LORD. And He can bring peace in the midst of conflict. Joy in the midst of heartache. Stability in the midst of temptation. He can bring hope to those who are in despair. Meaning to those who are empty. Companionship to those who are alone. Pardon for those trapped in sin. He is Lord!

Truly He is from everlasting to everlasting. He has no match in heaven or on earth. He entertains no fear, He has no ignorance, He has no needs. There is nothing that can limit Him. He never makes a mistake. He always does that which is right. He possesses the power to bring everything to His perfect conclusion and according to His ultimate goal. He is invincible . . . immutable . . . infinite and self-sufficient. His judgments are unsearchable and His ways unfathomable! He guides, He does not guess. He controls, He does not hope. He directs, He does not wish.

HE IS LORD! And He alone deserves our highest praise, our constant devotion, our daily obedience, our willing hearts.

The Ruler Without Rival

2

Imagine that you are *Gabriel*, the archangel. And imagine that you are responsible not only to *prepare* for God's arrival on earth, but you are also to *plan* how He will come. If you could design the entire scene, how would you write the script? Now think before you answer: You've never read the Christmas story, OK? You know nothing of Bethlehem. The trappings of Messiah's entrance are yours to unfold. You have been handed a clean sheet of paper and are assigned the task of orchestrating God's entrance to planet earth.

I wonder, how would you do it? Would you have him born out of wedlock to a little peasant girl not yet 16 years old? Would his first bed be a feeding trough? Would his father be a lowly carpenter in a dusty, little, no-name village? No! That's no way to usher in royalty! If you're like me, you'd want God to come to earth on the back of a beautiful, white-winged stallion. And He probably wouldn't arrive as a defenseless little baby, either. No way! He'd burst onto the scene as a full-grown, fully-matured Prince! His blood would bleed royal blue, and his headquarters would be the palace of Rome. That would be *my* plan. How else will the people know that He is from God? No lesser plan could adequately communicate His royalty. Right?

An anonymous author, considering the lofty role Jesus enjoyed in heaven and sensing the irony of His lowly entrance to planet earth, wrote these words:

> He was born in an obscure village, the child of a peasant woman. He worked in a carpenter shop until he was thirty, and then for three years he was an itinerant preacher. He never wrote a book, He never owned a home, He never went to college. He never had a family. He never traveled more than two hundred miles from the place where He was born. He never did any of the things that usually accompanies greatness.
>
> While still a young man the tide of popular opinion turned against Him. His friends ran away. One of them denied Him. Another betrayed Him. He went through the mockery of a trial and was nailed to a cross between two thieves. His executioners gambled for the only piece of property He had on earth, and that was His cloak. When He was dead, He was taken down and placed in a borrowed grave, through the pity of a friend.
>
> Nineteen wide centuries have come and gone, and today He is the centerpiece of the human race. I'm far within the mark when I say that all the armies that have ever marched and all the navies that have ever set sail, all the parliaments that ever sat and all the kings that ever reigned – *put together* – have not affected the life of man on this earth as powerfully as that ONE SOLITARY LIFE!

How true. Isn't it amazing that a man of such humble beginnings has impacted our world as dramatically as He?

I'm talking, of course, about Jesus. And in these pages, you and I have shouldered the rather awesome task of painting what I have called, *"A Portrait of Jesus."* But we're not using paints and brushes and canvas to prepare our portrait – we're using the many names revealed to us in Scripture, names designed by God to introduce us to Jesus and to help us know Him intimately that we might live as He lived. For example, in Chapter One we saw that this one solitary life is *"THE LORD."* The BOSS. But now, I want take that title one step further, because Scripture augments Christ's Lordship by calling Him not only "Lord" but in fact, *"KING OF KINGS and LORD OF LORDS."*

Let me show you just a few places where Scripture undeniably and unapologetically declares that Jesus is indeed the *RULER WITHOUT RIVAL.*

Let's travel back to Deuteronomy 10. Let's start with the very first reference of this title and trace its usage from Deuteronomy all the way to the final pages of Revelation.

> And now, O Israel, what does the Lord your God ask of you but to fear the Lord your God, to walk in all his ways, to love him, to serve the Lord your God with all your heart and with all your soul, and to observe the Lord's commands and decrees that I am giving you today for your own good?
> To the Lord your God belong the heavens, even the highest heavens, the earth and everything in it. Yet the Lord set his affection on your forefathers and loved them, and he chose you, their descendants, above all the nations, as it is today. Circumcise your hearts, therefore, and do not be stiff-necked any longer. FOR THE LORD YOUR GOD IS GOD OF GODS AND LORD OF LORDS," (*That is the earliest reference to this title in all of Scripture.*) the great God, mighty and awesome, who shows no partiality and accepts no bribes. He defends the cause of the fatherless and the widow, and loves the alien, giving him food and clothing. Fear the Lord your God and serve him. Hold fast to him and take your oaths in

his name. He is your praise; he is your God (Deut. 10:12-18, 20-21a).

Truly the Lord God is God of gods and Lord of lords.

Now let's go to Psalm 136, a beautiful Psalm, evidently designed by David to be sung antiphonally. Perhaps a soloist would sing the first phrase of each verse – then the congregation would sing in reply the phrase that's repeated throughout the Psalm: "His love endures forever." By the way, the word translated *"love"* literally means *"loyal love."* It's a love that never gives up. Never.

> Give thanks to the Lord, for he is good.
> *His love endures forever.*
> Give thanks to the God of gods.
> *His love endures forever.*
> Give thanks to the Lord of lords.
> *His love endures forever.*

There's that title again. David is saying, "When you prepare to worship, make certain that the One you worship is the God who reigns above all other gods. Make certain He is the Lord who rules over all other authorities. Make certain when you worship, you worship the top banana. *THE RULER WITHOUT RIVAL.*"

Perhaps you're struggling with the concept that God has no equal. If so, I want to introduce you to a man who also struggled and learned the hard way that our God really is God of gods. That He does, in fact, rule as Lord of lords. Daniel 4 revolves around a dream of King Nebuchadnezzar. Now Nebuchadnezzar was a proud man. But this dream troubled him. He broke out in a cold sweat; he was gripped by fear. But he couldn't find any of his wise men who could interpret the dream for him.

Finally, he heard about a prophet of God named Daniel.

Daniel was ushered into the throne room, and not only did he interpret the dream, but he also exhorted the dreamer. Daniel courageously looked Nebuchadnezzar right in the eye and told him the cold, hard facts. But don't take my word for it – read it for yourself:

> This is the interpretation, O king, and this is the decree the Most High has issued against my lord the king: You will be driven away from people and will live with the wild animals; you will eat grass like cattle and be drenched with the dew of heaven. Seven times will pass by for you until you acknowledge that the Most High is sovereign over the kingdoms of men and gives them to anyone he wishes (Dan. 4:24,25).

By the way, there are still people today who must face similar periods of instruction before they are willing to admit that Jesus is King of kings and Lord of lords. Maybe not as severe, but still a time of breaking. A time when God puts you in a *place* of distress, when He levels you to a *position* where the only way to look is up, as He reduces you to a *posture* of weakness and dependency until you, like Nebuchadnezzar, are willing to acknowledge that "the Most High is sovereign over the kingdoms of men."

You see, Nebuchadnezzar thought HE was sovereign! But Daniel said, "Think again, King. God is. There is only One who rules without rival. And if you don't figure that out real quick, you're going to be reduced to living like an animal. And you will remain as an animal until you acknowledge that the only sovereign ruler is the Most High God Himself."

Nebuchadnezzar had lived his whole life thinking He was King. Can you imagine what he felt about Daniel's little speech? *And do you know how he responded?*

Twelve months later, (*God has patiently allowed Nebuchadnezzar plenty of time to think it through. A year later, he draws his conclusion.*) as the king was walking on the roof of the royal palace of Babylon, he said, "Is not this the great Babylon I have built as the royal residence, by my mighty power and for the glory of my majesty?" *(Unbelievably, he rejects Daniel's exhortation. But look what happens . . .)* The words were still on his lips when a voice came from heaven, 'This is what is decreed for you, King Nebuchadnezzar: Your royal authority has been taken from you. You will be driven away from people and will live with the wild animals; you will eat grass like cattle. Seven times will pass by for you until you acknowledge that the Most High is sovereign over the kingdoms of men and gives them to anyone he wishes' (Dan. 4:29-33).

Nebuchadnezzar went mad! His mental train de-railed! He lived, literally, in the field. He lost all conventional restraint and wisdom and logic. He was totally unable to do the work of Sovereign. He lived like a beast. A wild, untamed, unkempt beast. Nebuchadnezzar was absolutely and utterly broken!

I think of David when I read that. The King of Israel. A mighty warrior who had never known defeat. His people stood at the city gates and sang his praises. The problem began when David started humming along. He started thinking that maybe he was so great and so powerful that he was above God's law. That's when he murdered Uriah and took Bathsheba as his wife. He lived in rebellion for nearly a year, until finally a prophet named Nathan confronted David with his sin. And David, with heart-felt repentance, openly acknowledged God's sovereignty, pleads for God's forgiveness – and confessed,

When I kept silent, my bones wasted away through my groaning all day long. Day and night Your hand was heavy on me; my strength was sapped as in the heat of summer (Psa. 32:3,4).

In other words, David had been broken. He thought HE

was in charge. He learned the hard way that the Most High was still on the Throne. And when he finally recognized that, he was restored.

I wonder, where are you at in all this? Perhaps you have already fully acknowledged that God is your ruler. For you, it's a settled issue. But then again, perhaps you are still strutting your stuff. Like Nebuchadnezzar, God has granted you a temporary reprieve, but you have no intention of acknowledging His lordship. You like calling the shots. Perhaps you are right now in the process of being broken. God is obviously trying to break you so that He can use you. It's likely that your battle isn't as dramatic as Nebuchadnezzar's, but it's a battle nonetheless. The problem is, you're not ready to surrender! You're still not convinced that He's the one Who is to be in ultimate control of your life! If that's where you are, let me assure you, friend, *God will get your attention.* A day will come, and I hope the day is soon, when you will acknowledge that, indeed, He is King of kings and Lord of lords. And when you do, that inner peace you long for will return.

Back to Daniel. Imagine Daniel handing the pen to Nebuchadnezzar and saying, "Here, you write the rest of the chapter." And here are the King's own words:

At the end of that time, I, Nebuchadnezzar, raised my eyes toward heaven, and my sanity was restored. Then I praised the Most High; I honored and glorified him who lives forever.
His dominion is an eternal dominion;
his kingdom endures from generation to generation.
All the peoples of the earth are regarded as nothing.
He does as he pleases with the powers of heaven
and the peoples of the earth.
No one can hold back his hand or say to him: "What have you done?" (*Note that. We'll come back to that.*)
At the same time that my sanity was restored, my honor and splendor were returned to me for the glory of my kingdom.

My advisers and nobles sought me out, and I was restored to my throne and became even greater than before. Now I, Nebuchadnezzar, praise and exalt and glorify the King of heaven, because everything he does is right and all his ways are just. And those who walk in pride he is able to humble (Dan. 4:34-37).

My heart beats fast when I consider the enormity of that truth. I struggle with it, yes. But there is no doubt that our God is God of gods. He has no peer.

We leap ahead in our Scripture survey to the New Testament book of I Timothy. The Apostle is writing to his protege, Timothy, and in his charge to Timothy, he writes one of the most magnificent descriptions of God in all Scripture.

In the sight of God, who gives life to everything, and of Christ Jesus, who while testifying before Pontius Pilate made the good confession, I charge you to keep this commandment without spot or blame until the appearing of our Lord Jesus Christ, which God will bring about in his own time – God, the blessed and only Ruler, (*The King James Version reads*, "*absolute potentate.*") The King of kings and Lord of lords, who alone is immortal and who lives in unapproachable light, whom no one has seen or can see. To him be honor and might forever. Amen (I Tim. 6:13-16).

We end our Scripture search in the seventeenth and nineteenth chapters of the book of Revelation. So far this title has been generically applied to entire Godhead. *But now, it is undeniably assigned to Jesus.*

They will make war against the Lamb, but the Lamb will overcome them because he is Lord of lords and King of kings (Rev. 17:14a).

Jesus' first trip to our planet was an ironic contrast: A King born in a modest stable. Born in an unfamiliar village because a pompous king named Augustus Caesar wanted to know how many people were under his rule. So Jesus' mother was forced to ride on the back of a donkey at term, and, as a result, Jesus was born among cattle. But my, how the story has changed! Because today, that mighty emperor, Caesar, is nothing more than a piece of lint on the page of history, a footnote in the chronicles of prophecy, question #37 on someone's world history exam.

Meanwhile, Jesus stands tall and immortal! And long after all the so-called heavyweights of this world are laid to rest and their mighty conquests are all but forgotten – *JESUS WILL MAKE ANOTHER TRIP TO THIS PLANET*. Let me tell you about his arrival this time:

> I saw heaven standing open and there before me was a white horse, whose rider is called Faithful and True. With justice he judges and makes war. His eyes are like blazing fire, and on his head are many crowns. He has a name written on him that no one but he himself knows. He is dressed in a robe dipped in blood, and his name is the Word of God. The armies of heaven were following him, riding on white horses and dressed in fine linen, white and clean. Out of his mouth comes a sharp sword with which to strike down the nations. He will rule them with an iron scepter. He treads the winepress of the fury of the wrath of God Almighty. On his robe and on his thigh he has this name written:

> *KING OF KINGS AND LORD OF LORDS!* (Rev. 19:11-16).

Hallelujah! Even so, come Lord Jesus! Come! Christian, if that doesn't light your fire – your wood's wet!

KING OF KINGS AND LORD OF LORDS. There is no way you can mistake the meaning, is there? The obvious inference is, "He is King over all who reign as king and Lord of those who rule as lord." He is, by His own declaration

THE HIGHEST OF ALL KINGS and THE GREATEST OF ALL LORDS!

Now, so there's no misunderstanding, let me give you THREE IMPLICATIONS of that truth:

1. AS KING OF KINGS AND LORD OF LORDS ... JESUS RULES WITHOUT RIVAL.

He has no equal. He is the Supreme One. Nothing exists above Him, nothing is beyond Him – HE IS THE HIGHEST AND THE GREATEST. There is none greater.

2. BECAUSE HE IS KING OF KINGS AND LORD OF LORDS ... HIS POWER KNOWS NO LIMIT.

The story is told of a man in South Africa who had ordered a Rolls Royce. He went to the Rolls dealer and asked him about some of the car's features. He asked about the interior and his question was answered. He asked about color combinations and was answered to his satisfaction. Then he asked about the horsepower. The salesman said, "You know, nobody has ever asked me that. I don't know. But since you're spending so much money on this car, I'll find out!" He sent a telegram to the headquarters in London and asked how much horsepower there was in a Rolls Royce. The next day he got the telegram back and it had one word on it: It said, "ADEQUATE."

When I first heard that story, I thought: "That's the way God is! He is thoroughly adequate for any need – because His power knows no limit!" Think about that. When you turn to the King of kings, you turn to One who has never been frightened, worried or even frustrated. He has never sighed, nor has He ever lifted His hands in despair. He has never come up faced a barrier He cannot overcome. He has never confronted a need that He could not meet. He has never seen a problem that He cannot solve.

3. BECAUSE HE IS KING OF KINGS AND LORD OF LORDS . . . HE IS ABSOLUTELY INVINCIBLE.

He not only *won't* be conquered, He *can't* be conquered! That's why Abraham went to the mall and bought a crib! God said he would have a son, and not even Abraham's old age would stop the plan God had put into motion! That's why Noah built an ark in the middle of the desert. For, when the Most High says it's going to rain – even if it's never rained before in all of history – IT'S GOING TO RAIN! That's why David grabbed his trusty slingshot and headed toward Goliath! The whole Israelite army said, "Look how much bigger Goliath is than David!" But David said, "Look how much bigger God is than Goliath." They said, "He's too big to hit." David said, "He's too big to miss." He had God on his side. And when God is on your side, NOTHING CAN DEFEAT YOU. Because He is invincible!

I could go on – so I will! That's why Gideon whittled down his army. That's why Rahab hid the spies. That's why Nathan confronted David. That's why Elijah climbed Mt. Carmel. That's why Daniel stayed on his knees. That's why Joseph married Mary. That's why Peter preached at Pentecost. That's why Stephen accused the Sanhedrin. That's why Paul went to Rome.

WHY? Because THE GOD THESE SERVED, AND THE GOD WE SERVE, is the Ruler without Rival. His power knows no limit, and He is absolutely invincible!

So what? What difference does that make in my life? I conclude with *FIVE UNAVOIDABLE APPLICATIONS.*

#1 – AS KING OF KINGS AND LORD OF LORDS, JESUS IS UTTERLY HOLY. THEREFORE, I APPROACH HIM IN REVERENCE.

Do you know what struck me as I prepared for this chapter? We are living in a time when man, in some attempt to "make" God relevant, has cheapened God. In order to make Christ palatable to our sophisticated friends, we have all but stripped Him of His awesome grandeur and majestic nobility. Yet when I read Scripture, I find God so elevated, so exalted in His eminence, that there is an awesome wall of separation actually protecting man from the blast of God's blazing holiness.

When Isaiah had his vision of heaven, he "saw the Lord, seated on a throne, high and exalted, and the train of his robe filled the temple!" (Isa. 6:1b).

When Joshua was ushered into the presence of God, he "fell face down to the ground" as though he were dead. (See Joshua 7:6-10).

When God occupied Mt. Sinai, He told Moses, "Don't let the people touch the mountain. For "whoever touches the mountain shall surely be put to death" (Exod. 19:12b).

And when Ezekiel saw the Lord, he couldn't begin to describe Him. He just pictured Him in the clouds as a series of spinning wheels, spinning to the glory of heaven. (See Ezek. 1).

Folks, we're talking about the King of kings and Lord of lords. He is Holy. He is exalted. He is Creator. He is ruler! And He demands our reverence!

If I'm ever invited to 1600 Pennsylvania Avenue, I guarantee you, I won't greet the head of the house by saying, "Hey, Willie!" No. It'll be "Good morning, Mr. President." And if I ever tour Buckingham Palace, it won't be "Big Chuck and Little Di." It'll be "Prince Charles and Lady Diana." And if I ever visit 10 Downing Street, I won't say, "Hi Johnny," I'll say, "Hello Mr. Prime Minister."

Now if I can muster proper dignity and respect for my temporal rulers and leaders, why would I ever think I could approach the throne of God as though He was my buddy, my pal or my chum? Now certainly God loves us, and He wants to enjoy a dynamic relationship with us – and there's plenty of room for laughter and joy in His presence. But not frivolity. Not cheapness. Christian, approach your King with awe. Suck in your breath, lower your gaze and meet Him in silence.

#2 – AS KING OF KINGS AND LORD OF LORDS, WHAT JESUS ALLOWS I DARE NOT QUESTION.

Remember Nebuchadnezzar's words? He said, "God does as He pleases. And no one can hold back his hand or say to him: 'What have you done?'"

Do you know why that is? Paul tells us:

Oh the depth of the riches of the wisdom and knowledge of God! How unsearchable his judgments, and his paths beyond tracing out! Who has known the mind of the Lord? Or who has been his counselor? Who has ever given to God that God should repay him? For from him and through him and to him are all things! (Rom. 11:33-36a).

The Lord exists far beyond man's comprehension. In fact, if the brightest minds of mankind could gather for inspection and just a tiny speck of God's glory be revealed, it would leave the whole crowd flabbergasted! Paul says, "Who has known the mind of the Lord?" Who has ever informed God or taught God about anything? Have you ever successfully given God advice? No way. Yet we continue to try, don't we? We still try to advise Him. We do our best to try to clue Him in, to give Him the scoop.

I did that recently. I was struggling with a problem that just wouldn't go away, so I told God what I thought was the best way to handle it. Wasn't that nice of me? And I'm sure He was thrilled to get my input. There I was, with my thimble full of knowledge, strutting into the Throne room of heaven, supposing that my little thimble would make even the tiniest of splashes in God's vast ocean. I said, "Look God, here's the way I think it ought to happen!"

Tinkle. Pause. ROAR! The waves of God's inscrutable wisdom crashed around me and I heard Him say: "Steve, who counsels God?"

You might not understand all that is happening to you right now. I certainly don't understand what's happening to me. Give it up! You'll die not understanding. Chances are good if you allow the King of kings to rule in your life – if you give Him full operating power in all that you do – you will still understand very little about your life. But then, you are being directed by the unfathomable, unsearchable, un-rivaled God!

You see, our perspective is severely limited. We see what's happening right now. God sees past, present and future in the same instant. Our focus is microscopic, but God's focus is telescopic. And herein lies the struggle. Because what we see as pain, He sees as progress. What we consider adversity, He understands as advance. What we think will make us miserable, He *knows* will bring ultimate meaning!

Problem is, because our focus is so limited, our first response is to tell God to take the problem away! To our way of thinking, that's the only solution that has merit! We don't want to hurt! But God doesn't always "take it away," does He? Often we pray for a loved one to get well, but he dies. We pray for a new job offer, but it falls through. We pray for our children, but they rebel. Then, when God doesn't do as we wish, we decide, "God is not listening! He doesn't care!" When the truth is, He cares a lot. It's just that He sees the big picture. He knows that behind the struggle is an even greater reward.

That's the beauty of God's panoramic perspective. He

views what we cannot see. He understands what we will never comprehend. So that even in those difficult, abrasive times when it seems that the rug has been pulled out from beneath us and those things we think we need are held back, God is accomplishing an eternal plan which is for our ultimate and eternal good. But in the process of accomplishing that plan, He doesn't owe me an explanation. As if I could understand it if He gave me one.

He is King of kings and Lord of lords. The Only One who has sufficient understanding. The Only One who knows the true purpose behind your pain. The Only One Who possesses all-encompassing knowledge. What He allows, we dare not question.

I agree with Martin Luther. He sat around the dinner table one evening with a group of his students and listened as they struggled with deep, thoughtful questions, like: "Why does God allow suffering?" "Why does God choose some and not others?" "Why doesn't God do it this way? Or that way?" Luther leaned back in his chair, paused and said, "MEN, LET GOD BE GOD."

#3 – AS KING OF KINGS AND LORD OF LORDS, WHAT JESUS PROMISES, I KNOW HE WILL PROVIDE.

These two fit together, don't they? It's only as I learn to trust Jesus that I develop the deep, settled confidence that He is in control, and that nothing will happen to me that He and I together cannot handle.

Whenever I think of this truth, I'm reminded of Tim Hansel, a man who has endured more than his share of painful setbacks. In one of his books, Tim talks about a plaque which he displays in his home. It reads:
"Tim,

Trust Me.
I have everything under control!
Jesus."

Ironically, the glass that covered the message was broken during shipping. He writes, "I have never replaced the glass because, to me, the message is even stronger behind the shattered glass. We can know a joy that transcends circumstances and is of a substance and faith that is beyond situations. If we are to have this kind of joy in our lives, we must first discover what it looks like. It is not a feeling; it is a choice. It is not based upon circumstances; it is based upon attitude. It is free, but it is not cheap. It is the by-product of a growing relationship with Jesus Christ. It is a promise, not a deal. It is available to us when we make ourselves available to him. It is something that we can receive by invitation and by choice. It requires commitment, courage and endurance."

And may I add – it is based upon our conviction that He Who promises is able to provide!

Listen, when you sink your head in your pillow tonight and sigh over the problem which you are now facing – if you call upon the Lord, you are calling on one who is absolutely reliable. And you will never hear Him say, "You know, Steve, I don't know what to do about that either! That's a toughie!" He will never answer you like that. Never. What will He say?

Do not fear, for I am with you. Don't be dismayed, for I am your God. I will strengthen you and help you. I will uphold you with my righteous right hand (Isa. 41:10).
I will never leave you nor forsake you (Heb. 13:5).
Don't let your hearts be troubled. Trust in God, trust also in Me (John 14:1).

Why Jesus? Why trust You? "Because I am the King over all who call themselves king, and I am Lord over all who say they are lord. And whatever I promise, I am faithful to provide."

#4 – AS KING OF KINGS AND LORD OF LORDS, HE MUST INCREASE. I MUST DECREASE.

After all, if He is the King, then I must be His subject. Which means He's on the throne, and I am not. You see, when I acknowledge Jesus Christ as Lord of all, I commit to Him all that I am, all that I have and all that I will ever be. That means I am to be diminished and He is to be exalted. It makes sense, doesn't it? As Paul said,

> You are not your own, you have been bought with a price. Therefore glorify God with your body (I Cor. 6:19b, 20).

And when is God most glorified? When we cut away everything that would keep us from Him.

The story is told of a forester who met with a terrible accident one day. Long wooden shoots had been built in the forest to slide tree trunks down the slope to the valley and into the river. They were hundreds of yards long, smooth and polished inside, and the foresters used them when the logs weren't being shipped. They'd sit on the floor of the shoot or an axe-handle and go tobogganing down to save themselves the trouble of walking. Well, this man caught his foot in a hole in the shoot and couldn't get it free. And at that moment he heard a shout of warning up above, which meant that a tree trunk was on its way down the shoot! He saw the thing coming and he still couldn't free his foot. So he hacked it off with an axe and jumped clear just in time. He was crippled for life, but at least he was alive.

After recording that story, Robert Raines reflected this prayer:

O God, Give me the courage to cut out of my life that liaison which is threatening my family's happiness. That indulgence which is sapping my strength of purpose. That doubt which is leading me to disobey you. That disobedience which is causing me to doubt you. O God, heal my faithlessness and restore me to health!"

Have you ever prayed that kind of prayer? Have you ever said:

God, you can have all that I am! You want my foot? You've got it! Lord, root from my heart all those things that I have cherished, so that You can reign without rival. Lord, diminish me, that You alone might be exalted. Lord, I am willing to receive what you give. To lack what you withhold. To relinquish what you take. To suffer what you allow. To be what you require.

As King of kings and Lord of lords, He deserves nothing less.

#5 – AS KING OF KINGS AND LORD OF LORDS, HE IS THE LORD WHO REIGNS. I FREELY BOW TO HIS AUTHORITY.

That's what's so powerful about this NAME. It demands that I make a decision about Jesus. Either I am here on this earth by design or I'm here by accident. If my presence is the result of some freak of nature, then I'm my own boss. But if I'm here by the plan and design of the living Lord of the Universe – then He's the boss. And I must bow before His authority.

And it's exactly at that point where many people say, "Jane! Stop this crazy thing! I want off!" Do you realize that the primary reason many people claim to not believe in God is that they want to be autonomous? Most assert that they don't believe, when the truth is, they believe, but they'd rather be in charge. There is an instinctive understanding that if you claim to believe in a God who claims to be King of kings and Lord of lords – then you're going to have to submit to Him. And many don't want to do that. So they claim disbelief, which is a cover-up. In truth, they simply refuse to submit.

Many faces in my past fit that description, but two seem to bubble to the top of my memory.

The first was Gary (not his real name). Gary was a sharp-thinking, intelligent young professional who began asking some very significant questions about his existence and the presence of personal God. So we spent several hours together, often over lunch – combing the Scriptures, examining the evidence which so clearly points to an ultimate deity. Finally I said,

"Gary, do you have any more questions?"
"No."
"Then you believe that what I've been telling you is true?"
"Yes."
"Great! Then you're ready to accept Christ as your Lord, right?"
"No. Steve, I know that what you are telling me is true. But if I accept the Lord, I'm going to have to change my life, and I don't want to do that."

And just like the Rich Young Ruler, Gary "went away sorrowful." And there was not another word I could say.

The second face belonged to a man I never knew. I had been asked to conduct his funeral service, even though I had never met him. I was asked, because someone in the family had attended another funeral I had conducted and felt I would do an adequate job. I learned during family visitation that he had committed suicide. He had fallen into bad money troubles, had just separated from his wife, and his children despised him. I also learned that his troubles were primarily due to a life-long involvement with the mob. Just before the service, his brother told me to not "get too religious," because it just wasn't his style. Only slightly offended, I hate to admit that when the last song was played just prior to the service, I had to choke back a smile, being thoroughly amused at the irony of the final musical selection. Here laid a man who evidently thought he was something pretty special – but his kingdom crumbled, and, in utter hopelessness, he took his own life. The final song played at his funeral?

"I DID IT MY WAY."

BIG DEAL! Listen, friend: God being Who He is, and I being who I am, there is only one goal that to me really matters. When I die, I want those who knew me to say, "HE DID IT GOD'S WAY." Being King of kings and Lord of lords – that's what He demands, and that's what He deserves.

We Call Him Messiah

3

When you hear the word, "MESSIAH," what is your first thought? Invariably my mind is drawn to a journal of music written nearly 250 years ago.

Back in the 18th century, there lived a man named George Frederick Handel. But Handel had a tough way to go. He endured what seemed to be constant failure. He hit bottom in 1737, when he was so much in debt that he actually faced the possibility of being sent to debtor's prison. In an attempt to raise the much needed funds, his friends encouraged him to try a totally new concept in the field of music. They suggested that he play a musical benefit concert – and charge money for it! Can you imagine? They hoped that the financial bonanza would cover his debts and keep him out of prison. The only problem was, the Church was adamantly opposed to the idea! As a result, Handel was heavily criticized by church leaders for taking God's music to the secular theater, the people were forbidden to attend the concert and, predictably, the benefit was a total flop. Handel lost so many friends through that fiasco that eventually, by his own admission, he felt as though he had lost his last friend.

By 1741, Handel was regarded by the music community to be a has-been. His character had been tarnished. His career was at a standstill. As a result, Handel slipped into the dark, foreboding pit of depression.

Then, amazingly, Handel was commissioned, in the summer of 1741, to write an oratorio based an the message of the Redeemer. The lyrics were to be written entirely from Scripture. The focus was to be exclusively on Jesus. Thrilled with this inexplicable opportunity, Handel sketched out his plan, originally estimating that such a task would require at least one, perhaps even two years to complete.

Little did he know Who had planned to collaborate on the project. Here are the facts: On August 22, he began the project. Six days later he had completed Part I; in nine days he had written Part II; and in another six, he completed Part III. He took an additional three days to fill out the orchestration. In 24 days, he had managed to fill 260 pages of manuscript!

Sir Newman Flower writes:

> Considering the immensity of the work and the short time involved, it will remain, perhaps forever, the greatest feat in the whole history of musical composition.

Having done a little composition myself, I can't imagine composing the "MESSIAH" in 24 days. I can't even write one song in 24 days. But Handel didn't do it alone, did He?

The Messiah came to his aid in much the same manner in which He came to the aid of this planet nearly 2,000 years ago – bringing peace and comfort, ministering grace and mercy, extending His strong hand of support. Handel first experienced that glory for himself; then, for the benefit of Christians of every succeeding generation, he scribbled notes and words onto a score which never fail, whenever I hear them, to take me to the very throne room of God.

And I'm not alone. When "Messiah" debuted in Dublin on April 13, 1742, the congregation became so enraptured with praise that it spontaneously rose to its feet as the choir proclaimed:

Hallelujah! Hallelujah! Hallelujah! For the Lord God omnipotent reigneth! Hallelujah! Hallelujah! Hallelujah! The kingdom of this world is become the kingdom of our Lord and of His Christ! And He shall reign forever and ever. King of Kings! Forever and ever and ever! Hallelujah! Hallelujah! And Lord of Lords! Forever and ever and ever! Hallelujah! Hallelujah! King of Kings and Lord of Lords. And He shall reign forever and ever! Hallelujah!

What interests me is that many Christians, who have enjoyed Handel's music and who have read from our Lord's Book for years, still have no idea what "Messiah" means. I think perhaps the average church-going Christian would say, "Well, it's one of the names Jesus was called a lot." Well, that's true, yet it's not true. Jesus was called *"Messiah,"* but not a lot. In fact, only four times in Scripture does the name actually appear. It's found twice in the Old Testament, both times in the book of Daniel; then twice in the New Testament, again both times in the book of John. We won't take the time to look at those passages now, but we will before we're through.

The name "MESSIAH" is an interesting word. It comes from a Hebrew word which means, *"To anoint; to smear or spread a liquid."* However, by New Testament times the church grew beyond the region of Palestine, and Greek became the official language of Scripture. As a result, Messiah came to be referred to as *Christos*, a Greek word, which, when transliterated reads, "CHRIST." But the meaning remains the same. Both "Messiah" and "Christ," in the verb form, mean *"to anoint."*

That may be news to you. Perhaps you thought Christ was just Jesus' last name. You know, Jesus CHRIST. Just like Fred Smith. No, it's not a proper name. It's a statement of Jesus' divine office.

You might want to remember it like this: *Jesus was His name, Lord was His title, Christ was His office.* Does that help? Whenever you call Him, "The Lord Jesus Christ," you are identifying His personness, His exclusive title and His divine role. And it is just as accurate to call Him, "Lord Jesus, The Messiah." It means the same thing. The words "Christ" and "Messiah" are interchangeable.

Now in the Old Testament, THREE DIFFERENT KINDS OF PEOPLE WERE ANOINTED. Three differing functions required that a liquid be used to set them apart for their divine assignment.

The PROPHET was anointed. He was set apart for the task of bringing God's message to man. The PRIEST was also anointed. His task was to bring man's need to God – to intercede for man, in the offering of sacrifices and the indulgence for sin. And then finally, the KING was also anointed. In Israel's governmental system, the King functioned as God's human authority – to lead, guide and protect the nation.

I find it interesting that in the New Testament, Jesus is revealed as all three – PROPHET, PRIEST and KING. He was PROPHET in that He revealed to us the glory and mind of God. He unveiled God's plan of redemption for all the ages.

He was PRIEST in that He came to intercede for man. He laid down His life for our sins. What's interesting about the anointing of the Old Testament priest is that before a priest could serve, he had to be dipped in water, and then anointed. This normally was done at age 30. Do you know what happened when Jesus was 30? He was baptized. And when He was baptized, the Spirit descended upon Him like a dove – anointing Him for the task that lay before Him.

He was also KING, and, in fact, He was presented to Israel on Palm Sunday as the King. His triumphal ride into Jerusalem (as we will see later) was a declaration of His sovereign rulership. This is why Handel quoted Revelation 11:15 in his oratorio, "The kingdom of the world has become the kingdom of our Lord and of His Christ. And He will reign forever and ever."

Ultimately, among the writers of the Old Testament, the word for anointing became the official title for the Promised One of God. The One Who would, indeed, function as Prophet, Priest and King. He would be called, "The Anointed One" (Messiah), and He was prophesied in the Old Testament as the One through Whom God would restore Israel. So Israel waited for Messiah to come. And waited. And waited.

It's doubtful that we Gentiles will ever fully appreciate what that must have been like, but try to imagine. This One Who was to come was the HOPE OF ISRAEL! There were literally hundreds of references to this Coming One in Scripture as well as other rabbinical literature. In fact, from the very beginning, from Genesis all the way through Malachi, one theme is constantly struck – "MESSIAH IS COMING! MESSIAH IS COMING! MESSIAH IS COMING!" They were told that He would bring freedom to those in captivity. He would put an end to the bloody sacrifices. He would end oppression. He would restore the glory to Israel. So they looked for Him. And waited.

Because the coming of Messiah was the universal focus of Israel, I want to take a careful look at the CHRONOLOGY OF HIS COMING. Not the prophecies that told of His birth in Bethlehem or being born of a virgin – but the prophecies which deal with the timing of His coming.

Let's go first to Daniel 9. If you've ever wondered why Jesus came when He came, Daniel 9 will answer that question. I mean, why didn't Jesus come 1000 years earlier? Or 3000 years later? Daniel reminds us that the specific time of His coming had been determined before creation and that He came, as Paul puts it, "at just the right time" (Rom. 5:6).

Daniel is one of my all-time favorite Old Testament books, primarily because of the great stories that are found here.

What parent hasn't told their kids about how Daniel refused to eat the rich, tasty goodies from the King's table? Remember? Daniel, at age 15, said, "Give (me) nothing but vegetables to eat and water to drink" (Dan. 1:12b). Can you imagine your teenager making such a request? My kids would say, "Give me nothing but pizza and Coke!" Yet after 10 days, he looked healthier and better nourished than those who ate the fried chicken and mashed potatoes and pecan pies.

Then there were Shadrach, Meshach and Abednego. These young fellows refused to bow before the image of the king, so they were tossed into the fiery furnace. But as our youth minister, Todd Bussey, told our congregation sometime ago, those

boys wouldn't budge, they wouldn't bend, – and they didn't
burn either! Great stuff!

Then, of course, there was Daniel in the lion's den. Now
we tend to lose touch with the chronology. Do you realize that
Daniel was in his 80's when he spent the night with those
hungry felines? He wasn't some crazy teenager! He was a
man who had walked with God all of his life, and he wasn't
about to start compromising now.

Now those are great stories! However, the stories aren't the
point. They help *illustrate* Daniel's point, but they're not the
point. Daniel wrote this book of prophecy somewhere around
535-540 B.C. And at this time in Israel's history, things were
bad. Israel was in captivity.

She no longer lived in her homeland, she was no longer
governed by her own king; she was imprisoned at Babylon.

As a result, the people were disillusioned. Politically, they
were losing their rights. Socially, they were in moral decline.
It was bad, folks. Public orgies were commonplace. Homo-
sexuality ran rampant. Pornography was blatant and explicit.
And because there was no religious underpinning to hold
them together, the very heart and soul of Israel was crum-
bling. So God speaks to His people through the prophet
Daniel. And His theme was a message of hope.

THERE ARE, IN FACT, TWO MESSAGES OF HOPE IN
DANIEL.

The first was "THIS CAPTIVITY WILL NOT LAST
FOREVER. IT WILL COME TO AN END."

Sometimes that's all you need, isn't it, to hang on? To
know that what you're going through won't last forever?
However, it wouldn't end soon, either. God, through the pen
of Daniel, revealed the unfolding of Israel's captivity. Here's
a thumbnail sketch of His message:

The people were saying, "Lord, will this ever end?" God said, "Yes it will. Here's how it will happen. Right now you are under captivity to the Babylonians. But I'm going to destroy the Babylonians." "Great! That's wonderful, God!" "Hold on! I'm going to replace the Babylonians with the Medo-Persians. They will come in and rule over you just as the Babylonians have."

"Lord, that's not what we were hoping for."

"Oh, but then we'll get rid of the Medo-Persians."

"Great."

"Yeh, I'll bring the Greeks in to destroy them."

"And the Greeks?"

"Yes, they will rule over you too. But then Rome will destroy the Greeks –"

"That's means Rome will be our master, right?" "Right. But here's the good part. A day is coming when all the kingdoms of man, all the great empires that have ruled over you and held you captive will be destroyed!"

Now God does the same thing with us. We pray, "Oh, God, get me out of this mess!" But He comes through with a little more mess. I want out of this problem by Tuesday, but He dumps yet another load on Monday night! And I think, "God, don't you care? Can't you help me?" Of course He cares. Of course He's able. But He has a greater plan in your life, just as He had a plan for Israel.

That's where message #2 comes into the storyline. Daniel tells the people that not only will man's kingdoms be destroyed, but someday "MESSIAH (the Anointed One) WILL COME TO EARTH AND HE WILL DELIVER HIS PEOPLE FROM ALL BONDAGE."

Are you with me? Man's kingdoms will one day be destroyed. That's message #1. In their place, a messianic kingdom will be established, and the Messiah will personally travel to our planet and deliver us from bondage. That's message #2. And do you know what the people did when they heard that? They hung onto it! They bought into Daniel's prophecy hook, line and sinker! They waited and they looked and they searched for any sign that Messiah was on His way.

Let's read the prophecy together so we can appreciate just how significant DANIEL'S CHRONOLOGY OF EVENTS really was.

"Seventy 'sevens' are decreed for your people and your holy city" (Dan. 9:24a).

Who were the people? Israel! And the holy city? Jerusalem. And Daniel says that "seventy 'sevens' are decreed." What does that mean? The thought is seventy sevens of years. So what is 70 X 7? Sure, 490. Four hundred ninety years are decreed for Israel and her city. These years are decreed to accomplish several things:

To finish transgression, to put an end to sin, to atone for wickedness, to bring in everlasting righteousness, to seal up vision and prophecy and to anoint the most holy. Know and understand this: From the issuing of the decree to restore and rebuild Jerusalem until the Anointed One, the ruler, comes, there will be seven sevens, and sixty-two sevens (Dan. 9:24b-25a).

Let's do some more math: How much is 7 + 62? Right. 69. But we're talking 69 sevens, right? So what's 69 X 7? Just subtract 7 from 490. Right. 483. So we're talking 483 years. The prophecy is this: There will be a passage of 483 years between the time that the decree to rebuild Jerusalem is issued and the ruler, Messiah, comes to present Himself as the Anointed One. Got that? 483 years.

Now hold on, because this is fascinating. Because of a

handful of wonderful discoveries in archaeology, we can pinpoint this prophecy to the very day. We know, for example, that the decree to rebuild Jerusalem took place on March 4, 444 B.C. in the 20th year of Artaxerxes Longimanus. Now the prophecy says, "483 years after the decree, MESSIAH WILL PRESENT HIMSELF AS KING!"

By the way, Zechariah 9:9 describes what that presentation will be like. Listen to this: "Rejoice greatly, O Daughter of Zion! Shout, Daughter of Jerusalem! Your King comes to you, righteous and having salvation, gentle and riding on a donkey." Now that event will happen 483 years after the decree to re-rebuild Jerusalem.

Here's how it unfolds. The prophetic year followed the Jewish Calendar, which has 360 days per year. 483 X 360=173,880 days. If you translate the dates to our Gregorian calendar, add in 116 leap years, and add the 24 days between March 4 and March 29, again you arrive at 173,880 days. Now you count 173,880 days from the time of the decree forward, and you will arrive at March 29, 33 A.D. Do you know what we call that day today? PALM SUNDAY! The very day Jesus rode triumphantly into Jerusalem on the back of a donkey. It was the first time in all of His ministry when He allowed the people to praise Him and bow to Him and lay down their palm leaves and laud Him as the Messiah come to free them and restore them! The very day!

There was no mistaking this prophecy. And it's import certainly was not lost on the people. They could count, just like us. As a result, by the time we come to first century Palestine, the excitement and anticipation in Jerusalem was electric! They knew that Messiah would arrive very soon. They were literally counting on it!

That's why Aristobulus was murdered. He was Israel's

High Priest. But because he proclaimed the soon advent of the Messiah, Herod the Great had him killed. Herod refused to tolerate a rival king.

In fact, Herod killed his own wife and family, because he feared that perhaps his oldest son was Messiah. That his own flesh and blood would undercut his authority and displace him as king. So he killed them!

That's why, when the Wise Men arrived in Jerusalem looking for the King of the Jews, Herod lost it. He thought he had sufficiently trounced this idea of a Messiah. He was so troubled by this turn of events that he issued a death sentence for every boy under the age of two living in Bethlehem. But no human monarch possesses the sufficient power to frustrate the plan of God. So Jesus, the Messiah, was born.

And when it came time for Jesus to be presented in the Temple, Joseph and Mary (providentially) bumped into two very anxious believers, Simeon and Anna. Now Simeon had been promised that he would not die until he saw Messiah. And Anna worshiped God day and night, fasting and praying for the redemption of Israel. And when they saw Mary's baby, they praised God! Simeon cried out, "My eyes have seen your salvation!" (Luke 2:30). And folks, these were just two of untold thousands of people who also were anticipating the imminent arrival of Messiah.

That's why, when John the Baptizer hit the scene, there was so much confusion about his identity. He did so many wonderful things and spoke with such thunderous authority that many said, "This is Him! John is Messiah!" But John made it clear that he was not. It was terribly important to John that the people realize he was not Messiah; he was simply paving the way for Messiah.

He looked like Messiah. He sounded like Messiah. He

came when Messiah was supposed to come. That's why the people thought he was Messiah. But He wasn't. He was merely the forerunner.

His chance to clear up the confusion came during the time when he was baptizing at the Jordan near Bethany. Jesus happened along, and John, when he saw Him, said to his men, "Behold the Lamb of God!" (John 1:29b,36b).

Andrew heard what John said. And he understood the implications fully. That's why he ran to find his brother. And when he had found Simon Peter, he said, "We have found the Messiah!" (John 1:41b).

Do you see the implication? He said, "We have FOUND Him!" That must mean they were looking for Him, right? If you're looking for a certain dress to wear to some special occasion, and finally find the one you're looking for, what do you tell your friends? "I FOUND IT!" That means you don't have to look anymore. You've been looking, but now the search is over. Andrew's comment was no off-cuff announcement. "Oh, by the way, Pete, I bumped into Messiah today." No! He said, "Peter! I've seen Him! He's come! Just as it was prophesied!"

The knowledge of this prophecy was so universal that even the WOMAN AT THE WELL, a Samaritan – a non-Jew – was informed enough to say,

I know that Messiah is coming (John 4:25a).

The Jews had been promised that Messiah would come. Daniel's prophetic chronology pinpointed the very time of His arrival. And the hopes and dreams of all first century Israel were focused on His imminent arrival!

What would happen when He came? I find in Daniel 9:24-

28, six specific events which would accompany the coming of Messiah.

First, He will "finish transgression and put an end to sin." (Dan. 9:24a). Now please understand – Messiah would not eliminate the PRESENCE of sin, but He would put an end to the POWER of sin. Paul tells us of the fulfillment of that prophecy in Romans 8, when he declares,

> We know that our old self was crucified with Him so that the body of sin might be rendered powerless, that we should no longer be slaves to sin. Therefore, do not offer the parts of your body to sin, but rather offer ourselves to God (Rom. 6:6a, 13a).

Do you see what Paul is saying? "Because Messiah has come, you are no longer in bondage to sin. You don't have to sin anymore!" Now let me assure you, you *will* sin. You *will* blow it. Expect it. It will happen. But, because Messiah has come, sin no longer can control you. Certainly Jesus "put an end to sin."

Second, Messiah will "atone for wickedness" (Dan. 9:24b). Now as Gentiles, we can't appreciate the full impact of that prophecy. But the Jew understood. By law, if a sinful Jew wanted to atone for his sin, there had to be bloodshed. An innocent animal had to be slaughtered and burnt on an altar. So that by the time Daniel had written this prophecy, literally hundreds of thousands of animals were slaughtered. But the problem is, even with all that bloodshed, sin still was not permanently atoned! It was just rolled back. Even on the Day of Atonement (Yom Kippur), when the scapegoat was sprinkled with blood and sent into the wilderness, symbolically removing the sins of the entire nation, even then, this blood did not permanently atone for sin. And the people knew that. They knew it was merely a symbol of The GREAT LAMB OF GOD who would one day come and take away all sin forever.

Daniel is saying, "Wait 173,880 more days and when Messiah is nailed to a tree, sin will be atoned, and you'll never have to perform another sacrifice." And that's exactly what happened: In Hebrews 10, the author writes:

> We have been made holy through the sacrifices of the body of Jesus Christ once for all.
> When He offered for all time one sacrifice for sins, he sat down at the right hand of God.
> There is no longer any sacrifice for sin" (Heb. 10:10,12,18).

Third, Messiah will "bring everlasting righteousness" (Dan. 9:24c). Through Messiah, all men – by faith, not by the observance of the law – will be declared, through the power of Jesus Christ, righteous. That's why Paul said, "I am not ashamed of the Gospel of Christ" (Rom. 1:16) Why? Because it brings "everlasting righteousness."

Fourth, He will "seal up vision and prophecy" (Dan. 9:24d). Now there can be no doubt Jesus fulfilled the Old Testament prophecies and visions which foretold of Messiah's first coming. He fulfilled prophecies which spoke of how and where He would be born and how and why He would die. Certainly he "sealed up" prophecy.

Fifth, He will be "anointed as the most holy" (Dan. 9:24e). Now that happened (at least in part) when the temple veil was torn from top to bottom at the moment of His death. Jesus, in that moment, became the new Holy of Holies – so that there is no longer a dividing wall which separates man from God. But it will happen in completion when He returns and is anointed and reigns forever as King of kings and Lord of lords!

Sixth, Daniel tells us that the Anointed One "will be cut off and will have nothing" (Dan. 9:26a). What's interesting about the construction of that phrase is that it's written in the active, not passive voice. What's so interesting about that? It's interesting because it tells us that this "cutting off" was not something that was done TO Christ, but it was done BY Christ. And that relates to Philippians 2, which tells us that Jesus "emptied himself." No one made Him do that. He did it by His own will. Jesus said,

> I lay my life down *of My own accord*. No one takes it from Me (John 10:18).

And sure enough, just as Daniel prophesied, five days after Jesus was presented as King, He was crucified as a criminal. He laid down His life, accomplishing forever what had been the hope of Israel for generations.

But Jesus didn't stay dead, did He? Three days later He burst out of that tomb gloriously alive! And when He did, He promised that He would come again! And so we wait. And hope. We now are the ones who long for His appearing.

You see, our situation is not that far removed from Israel, is it? We're not in captivity to another nation, but we are held hostage by a growing national debt, the enormous heartache of drugs, the disintegration of the family and the threat of horrible diseases such as cancer and AIDS. We talk about peace, but we can't seem to do anything about it. Our superpower nation is powerless to do anything about a handful of terrorists in Beirut. And neither a strong economy, nor sex education, nor an overhauled Social Security program will change the storyline. Man's condition is desperate.

H.L. Makien said, *"Man is a sick fly on a dizzy wheel."*

And the only hope for lasting peace, the only plan for ultimate harmony, the only promise of permanent healing IS THE PROMISE THAT ONE DAY MESSIAH WILL RETURN. When the time is right, when history has been completed, the ultimate plan of God will come to fulfillment. That's our hope, Christian! And there's no other message that brings such hope. All the way through the Bible, the focus is on Jesus. When He comes, He will deliver. When He comes, He will make all wrongs right. "Even so, come Lord Jesus" (Rev. 22:20b).

Allow me to close with three implications of Messiah. Two relate to His first coming, the third to His second.

First, BECAUSE JESUS CLEARLY ASSUMED THE ROLE OF MESSIAH, WE PROCLAIM HIM AS THE ANOINTED ONE OF GOD.

Consider Luke 4. Jesus has returned to His hometown and, as was His custom, on the Sabbath He went to the synagogue. Someone evidently recognized him as a prophet and handed Him a scroll. So He stood to read.

> The scroll of the prophet Isaiah was handed to him.
> Unrolling it, he found the place where it is written:
> "The Spirit of the Lord is on me,
> because he has anointed me
> to preach good news to the poor.
> He has sent me to proclaim freedom for the prisoners
> and recovery of sight for the blind,
> to relieve the oppressed, to proclaim the year of the Lord's favor."
> Then he rolled up the scroll, gave it back to the attendant and sat down. The eyes of everyone in the synagogue were fastened on him, and he said to them, "Today this Scripture is fulfilled in your hearing" (Luke 4:17-21).

Oh, what a moment! Most of them thought, "Wow! It really IS Him!" Others thought "The son of a carpenter? No way!" Still others accused Him of blasphemy. So they laid plans to crucify Him.

I mentioned earlier that the Samaritan woman at the well said, "I know that Messiah is coming. When He comes, He will explain everything to us" (John 4:25). What I didn't tell you is Jesus' response. He replied, "I who speak to you am He" (John 4:26b). Don't let anyone kid you: Jesus clearly assumed the office. The paper trail left by the prophets leads us directly to the foot of Jesus' cross. There will be no other Messiah. He has already come. And all that is left for us is to fall at His feet and worship Him.

But there's another implication of His first coming. BECAUSE MESSIAH HAS COME, OUR SEARCH FOR GOD IS OVER.

Peter put it best. Remember when Jesus started losing followers? Many had followed only to get the free meals, so Jesus thinned the ranks by talking about death and taking up crosses. As the crowds left, Jesus looked at His men and said, ' "You do not want to leave too, do you?' Simon Peter answered, 'Lord, to Whom would we go? You have the Words of eternal life!' " (John 6:67,68). Isn't that gripping? "Even with all the bad that's happening, Jesus, I still believe that You are Messiah! That there is no other!"

And there isn't. And there won't be. Search all you care to search, and you'll not find another plan. I used to say that Christianity was the best game in town. I don't say that anymore. Truth is, it's the *only* game in town. There is not one other strategy out there upon which you can build your life. There is no other plan which can, without fail, direct your existence. So stop looking for a cheap imitation of the real thing. Don't look for another Redeemer. There is no other.

Jesus alone is Messiah.

But let me close with perhaps the most exciting truth of all: BECAUSE SCRIPTURE LOOKS TO ANOTHER COMING, WE BELIEVE THAT HE WHO CAME WILL COME AGAIN.

If He came the first time on time, then He's going to come back this time on time, too! If what was said about Him was true in the first century, then what was said about Him is still-true today. He is the HOPE OF THE AGES. He is Messiah. He is the only hope that we can hold to. And He's coming again.

DO YOU KNOW HIM? Have you appropriated His payment into your life? Have you given Him everything that you are so that He might give to you everthing that He is?

A man was going to board his plane at the airport. As he was walking to the gate, he saw some people standing in a line. Curious, he went over to see what they were waiting for. He watched as they stood one at a time at a big scale that told their weight and fortune. The man thought it was dumb, but he decided to give it a try. He stepped onto the machine, put in his quarter and out came a little slip of paper that read, "You are 37 years old, weigh 175 pounds and are on your way to Chicago." The guy was shocked! He WAS 37, he DID weigh 175 pounds, and he WAS on his way to Chicago! But then he thought, Well, a lot of people are on their way to Chicago from this airport." So he got back on the machine, put in another quarter, and sure enough, it said, "You are 37 years old, weigh 175 pounds and are on your way to Chicago." "That proves it," he said. "It says the same thing every time. I'll just get somebody else to do it and that will prove I'm right." But he couldn't find anyone else, so he said, "OK, I'll try it one more time." He found a quarter and stepped onto the machine, and out came the little paper. "You are 37 years old, weigh 175 pounds and are on your way to Chicago. However, you've messed around so long with this machine you just missed your plane."

Now I don't know your age, weight or destination, but I *do* know that if you mess around with Messiah, you're going to miss the plane.

Jesus is Messiah. He wants your worship. There is no other Who is worthy. His plan will never be thwarted. He Who came will come again.

DO YOU KNOW HIM?

There was a time in my life when I wasn't sure I believed it. I thought I could live my own life, chart my own course and do my own thing. But I was wrong. That's why I stopped messing around with Messiah and I accepted Him as my eternal Redeemer. And now? I take my cues from Him. And He has never failed me yet. Just thinking about it makes me want to sing! Care to join me?

KING OF KINGS!
AND LORD OF LORDS!
AND HE SHALL REIGN FOREVER AND EVER
AND EVER AND EVER! HALLELUJAH!
HAL-LE-LU-JAH!

I Am ... The Bread of Life

4

The Apostle John records in his Gospel six so-called "I am" claims of Jesus. Those claims are as follows:

I am the bread of life.
I am the light of the world.
I am the gate.
I am the good shepherd.
I am the way, the truth, and the life.
I am the true vine.

We'll examine four of those claims in this book, but the one that captures our attention in this chapter is recorded in John 6. "I am the bread of life."

As I wrote this chapter, I found myself mentally listing the many occasions when food was used as a vital part of Jesus' ministry. Let me give you just a partial listing of those that came to my mind.

We all know that Jesus was born in Bethlehem. What you may not know is that Bethlehem was widely known in the first century as *"The House of Bread."*

When Jesus turned 30, He left his career as a carpenter and was baptized. He immediately was led by the Spirit into the wilderness and fasted for 40 days. After that, Satan came to him and said,

> "If you are the Son of God, tell these stones to become bread." But Jesus said, "Man does not live by bread alone." (Luke 4:3,4).

Where did Jesus perform His very first public miracle? Sure, it was a feast, wasn't it? A marriage feast in Cana!

And who can forget the time He fed 5,000 men PLUS women and children using only five loaves of bread and two small fish. That story seems to overshadow the fact that He did it again sometime later, this time feeding 4,000 people with seven loaves and just a few fish.

When he met a diminutive social outcast named Zacchaeus, He stopped in mid-parade and invited himself to Zacchaeus' home. To do what? To have dinner, of course!

And even on the night Jesus was betrayed, do you know how He spent those final hours with His men? They shared a meal together, alone, in an upper room. In fact, it was at that meal that Jesus instituted a ceremony of remembrance. He cared very much that His act of sacrifice would never be forgotten. The emblems He used were simple and ready available foodstuffs: bread and wine.

After his resurrection, knowing that Peter was devastated by his denial, Jesus sought to reinstate him. So He went to the seashore one morning to find him. And do you know what He did when He waited for Peter to come ashore? He fried some fish and prepared some bread. And after they had eaten the food, Jesus turned to Peter and said, "Peter, feed my sheep" (John 21:17b).

Then finally, in John 8, when Jesus made His first claim as to His identity, He said, "I am the Bread of Life." He used a common, well known reality, BREAD, to illustrate a deeper, spiritual meaning. The only trouble was, because Palestine was largely a wilderness region, bread often came at a premium. The people Jesus ministered to knew what it was to go hungry. So when Jesus started talking about "Bread," they thought, "Food! He's going to make us some more food!" They didn't understand that the food Jesus really came to provide was not food for the stomach, but rather, food for the soul.

Before we examine this claim, we need to ask two questions that will help us build an historical framework which will help to augment our understanding.

The first question is this: WHAT WAS THE CHRONOLOGY OF THE MESSAGE?

The next day . . . (John 6:22a).

The next day after what? After He had fed them. The first 13 verses of this chapter record the feeding of the 5,000. All He had to work with was a few loaves of bread and a couple of fish. Yet when the disciples cleaned up afterward, John assures us that everyone had "as much as they wanted" (John 6:11). Their stomachs had been filled. For all we know, perhaps for the first time in their lives they actually ate until they didn't want to eat anymore. They were full! But you know what happens after you've had a big meal, don't you? Sure! A few hours later, you're famished! So they go looking for their new-found meal ticket:

> The next day the crowd that had stayed on the opposite shore of the lake realized that only one boat had been there, and that Jesus had not entered it with his disciples, but that they had gone away alone. Then some boats from Tiberias landed near the place where the people had eaten the bread after the Lord had given thanks. Once the crowd realized that neither Jesus nor his disciples were there, they got into the boats and went to Capernaum in search of Jesus (John 6:22-24).

They are determined to find Him! Why? Because He fed them! *"And if He did it yesterday, certainly He'll do it again today!"*

Which brings us to the second question: WHAT WAS THEIR MOTIVE IN SEARCHING FOR JESUS? That's obvious. They wanted another free meal! But they weren't stupid. When they finally locate Jesus, that's not what they say. They try to hide their true agenda.

> When they found him on the other side of the lake, they asked him "Rabbi, when did you get here?" (John 6:25).

That appears on the surface to be a rather innocent question, but Jesus, with that laser-like vision of His, looked beyond the question and saw their real motive:

> Jesus answered, "I tell you the truth, you are looking for me, not became you saw miraculous signs but because you ate the loaves and had your fill. Do not work for food that spoils, but for food that endures to eternal life, which the Son of Man will give you. On him God the Father has placed his seal of approval" (John 6:26,27).

I find it intriguing that it mattered to Jesus WHY they were there! They didn't come to see Him, did they? No! They came to eat dinner.

I wonder if perhaps we are guilty of the same thing. We come to the place where spiritual food is served, but we seek instead food that perishes. Let's face it, some people go to church because they want to feel good about themselves. (And a few come because mom makes them!) Some do acts of servanthood in order to receive public acclaim. Some are involved in the spiritual disciplines in order to alleviate guilt. Others feign a commitment in order to appear devout and respectable in the eyes of their peers.

How many of us, I wonder, do our religious thing – but we do it with ulterior motives? Jesus knew what these people wanted, but He also knew that it was time to lift their focus from the temporal to the eternal, from the material to the spiritual. And His attempt to do so resulted in a dramatic and hostile confrontation.

Verse 27 is the pivotal verse in Jesus' message. If you get this, you'll get the whole deal. Jesus makes TWO SIGNIFICANT POINTS IN VERSE 27.

First, please note two phrases: "food that spoils" and "food that endures." There is within each of us TWO APPETITES.

One is an appetite for PHYSICAL FOOD. But physical food perishes. If you don't eat it, it spoils. If you do eat it, it turns to waste (or, perhaps more accurately, it turns to waist). Physical food, although essential for life, ultimately perishes.

This reminds me of what Jesus said in His Sermon on the Mount:

Do not store up for yourselves treasures on earth, where moth and rust destroy, and where thieves break in and steal. But store up for yourselves treasures in heaven, where moth and rust do not destroy, and where thieves do not break in and steal. For where your treasure is, there your heart will be also (Matt. 6:19-21).

Now the "treasure" of Matthew 6 faces the same problem which plagues the "food" of John 6. They both perish. Neither food nor money can ultimately and finally satisfy. Maybe you've already learned that. Good for you if you have. Perhaps you've achieved a certain level of financial security. But do you remember what you thought *before* the money came along? You know, the promises of instant happiness and fulfillment? I wonder, did money deliver on its promise? No! Because it can't. It's "food that perishes."

It was Solomon who said:

Cast but a glance at riches, and they are gone, for they will surely sprout wings and fly off to the sky like an eagle (Prov. 23:5).

Have you experienced that in your life? Perhaps you once enjoyed the security of a fat bank account – but now it's gone. For whatever reason, your money did the eagle routine and left you reeling. So you understand when Jesus says, "*Listen, what you're going after won't satisfy. Because money and the things money can buy are temporary at best. Seek instead that which is eternal!*"

Maybe you haven't learned this lesson yet. Perhaps your driving ambition in life is to accumulate tall piles of food that spoils. Do you know what Jesus said about that ambition? He said,

Watch out! Be on your guard against all kinds of greed!

Why, Jesus?

"For a man's life does not consist in the abundance of his possessions" (Luke 12:15).

In other words, that's not what life is all about! True fulfillment and happiness cannot be bought with American Express. Think about it: Money can buy a hospital, but it can't buy health. Money can buy a bed, but it can't buy sleep. Money can buy a house, but it can't make that house a home. Money can buy sex, but it can't buy love. Money can buy pleasure, but it can't buy happiness.

That truth was brought home to me sometime ago when one of the men in our church pulled me aside and showed me a post card he had received from his sister. On the front was a captivating photograph of St. Thomas at dusk. The description read, "Raindrops glisten along the waterfront in the glow of a tropical sunset." Sounds enticing, doesn't it? She wrote only six words on the card.

"Been there . . .
   Done that . . .
      What's next?"

I wanted to cry. He did. She was spending a week on an island paradise, and all she could muster was "Been there . . . done that . . . what's next?" That's what I call "food that spoils." And all of us have an appetite for that kind of food. But hear me now: IT WILL NOT SATISFY! Period.

Now there's another kind of appetite; and it also is necessary. However, sadly, it's not nearly as well developed. It's certainly not as universally expressed. *It's an appetite for SPIRITUAL FOOD.* The "food" which, Jesus says, "endures." And although most of your friends have tasted the satisfying

79

nourishment of Jesus Christ, most of our world has not. Although our spiritual appetites have been satisfied and continue to be satisfied, there are others, in fact, most, who have yet to know what it is to be filled.

Do you ever wonder how they cope? Do you ever wonder how the unbeliever handles it when the bottom drops out of his life? When the "physical food" perishes and the "treasures on earth" corrode?

Well, the tragic fact is, most aren't coping. They erect what they believe to be an iron wall of security, but it turns out to be nothing more than aluminum foil. They build high piles of possessions, then watch helplessly as the moths invade and destroy.

But the good news about the "food that endures" is that it is eternal. No matter what happens, no matter what may be stripped from your grasp, you will always have at your disposal the necessary strength to stand firm. The food Jesus offers can carry you through financial disaster. It can help you endure the loss of a loved one. It can keep your heart strong when your last friend fails you and it seems that nobody cares.

"Food that endures" and "food that spoils" are what biblical commentators call a "contrastive parallel." But that's not the only contrastive parallel in this passage. Verse 27 contains another. It is built upon Jesus' use of two monosyllabic words, "work" and "give."

> Do not *work* for food that spoils, but for food that endures to eternal life, which the Son of Man will *give* you (John 6:27a).

Now when Jesus says, "Do not work," He is not building a case for laziness. He is simply contrasting our logical and necessary efforts to earn physical food in order to survive, with our completely illogical efforts to earn spiritual food in order to be saved.

Be assured, Jesus understood and affirmed the value of hard work. Jesus was Himself a carpenter, a hard-working businessman! And after Joseph died, Jesus became the bread-winner for His family. He knew what it was to work for a living. He knew what it was to put food on the table. So Jesus is not espousing some anti-work ethic. Not at all.

In fact, nowhere in Scripture can you find such a doctrine. Just the opposite. The Apostle Paul said quite bluntly, "If a man doesn't work, he shouldn't eat" (II Thess. 3:10). That was the work ethic in first century Palestine. And it was deeply entrenched in their value system, much more so than in our welfare-minded generation.

But even in our day, because of the free enterprise system which we enjoy, hard work still pays rich dividends. There are exceptions, but generally, the harder we work, the better we eat. The more diligent our efforts, the more rewards we enjoy. And that's as it should be.

The problem is, we tend to carry that work ethic with us into the spiritual realm. We think, "If I'm to be satisfied spiritually, I need to work for that, too! I need to give up this and release that. I need to be moral and honest. I need to pay my bills and go to church and love my wife and hug my kids. Then, when I've jumped through enough religious hoops, God will smile on me and all of the gunk of my life will just ooze away and God will welcome me into His family!"

But that's a sham! Trusting in your ability to earn spiritual food is like jumping out of an airplane with a sack of cement strapped to your back. You can yank all the cords you like, you can yell "Geronimo" until you're blue in the face; but you're going to end up busted. Your personal goodness, your long list of achievements, your religious progress sheet will not get you one step closer to heaven. Because you cannot, note that, **CANNOT** EARN SPIRITUAL FOOD.

I'm reminded of the story of the man who died and went to heaven. When he got there, he met the gatekeeper who said,

"Hold on, buddy. It takes 1000 points to get in here."

He said, "What do you mean, 1000 points? I never heard that in Sunday School."

"Well, that's the way it is. It takes 1000 points, that's the deal! So why don't you tell me what you've done, and I've got my computer here, and I can get you a readout on your tally."

The guy said, "Well, I went to church – every week."

"OK, that's three points."

"Three points?! But I went for ten years!"

"Alright, four points."

"I gave money, too. Yep, I tossed some in the plate. I even sacrificed *big* for the building program!"

"That's good, we're up to seven points now."

"7 points? That's all?"

"Yes, I'm afraid you need a few more to get to 1000."

"Well, I've been basically a good guy. I tried to be good to my family, I was faithful to my wife, I helped poor people – I even taught Sunday School once!"

"Alright, we're up to 10 points. Can you think of anything else?"

"Listen, buddy, I'm just about bankrupt. I've done all I could do."

AND THAT'S EXACTLY THE POINT!

Then he remembers. "Oh, by the way, when I was younger, I accepted Jesus as my personal Savior."

The gatekeeper said, "Why didn't you say so? That's worth 1000 points. NEXT!"

You see, that's the problem with trying to earn spiritual food. After you've done all that you can do, you discover that all you can do still isn't enough.

Jesus is saying to us, *"Don't get hung up on trying to provide food that will spoil. Instead, receive My free gift to you, the gift of food that endures. You don't have to work for it. In fact, you can't. You must either accept it or reject it. You can't pay for it, because it has already been paid for, in full, at Calvary."*

Now you and I understand what Jesus is saying, primarily because we're standing on the back-side of Calvary. We have the benefit of perfect 20-20 hindsight vision. But these people were so locked into filling their hungry stomachs and working real hard to earn God's favor, that they just couldn't understand what Jesus was trying to tell them.

Because of the crowd's confusion, Jesus' message turns into sort of a public debate. In verses 25-58, we find a series of SIX QUESTIONS from the crowd and Jesus' corresponding answers. They bring up an objection, and Jesus responds to it. Yet, sadly, even though He answered every question, most of the crowd left in angry disagreement rather than enlightened acceptance.

We've already examined the first question. They said in verse 25, "Rabbi, when did You get here?" Which translated reads, "Jesus, we're hungry! Feed us again! Just like You did yesterday!" So Jesus said,

I tell you the truth, you are looking for me, not because you

saw miraculous signs but because you ate the loaves and had
your fill. Do not work for food that spoils . . . (John 6:26,27a).

*"Don't make physical food your primary ambition. After
all, that's why you're back again today. It's because you've
eaten physical food, but physical food perishes. Instead, look
for . . ."*

Food that endures to eternal life, which the Son of Man will
give you (John 6:27b).

*"There's the food you really need. In fact, I offer it to you
as a gift. You don't even have to work for it! And it's a food
that will forever satisfy that deep, internal craving which
you've never been able, on your own, to satisfy."*

And even though Jesus had just told them that He wanted
to GIVE it to them, they were so caught up in the Pharisaical
mindset of the day, the legalistic mindset which taught that
you *could* work for God's acceptance – and earn it by somehow being good enough – they said to Him:

What must we do to do the works God requires? (John 6:28).

Now let's not jump too quickly in criticism of these people.
They wanted the spiritual food! And they were willing to DO
anything to get it. But Jesus told them that it's not a matter of
DOING anything!

Jesus answered, "The work of God is this: to believe in the
one he has sent (John 6:29).

That's it. That's all you can do. That's all you need to do.
The only work which cuts any mustard before God is when

you by obedient faith, put your trust wholly and completely in the One Whom the Father sent.

Now these people weren't dummies. They knew that by those words, Jesus was claiming to be the MESSIAH. So they said,

> What miraculous signs then will you give that we may see it and believe you? What will you do? (John 6:30).

"Jesus, if you want us to believe that you are the One Who is mightier than Moses, then do one better than Moses. He brought manna from Heaven. Let's see what you can do, Jesus!"

Isn't that incredible? They had watched Jesus still the storm, they watched Him heal the sick, they watched Him restore sight to the blind! What more proof could they want? Why, just the day before He had fed 5,000 people from one little sack lunch! I don't know about you, but I get the sense that they were just needling Jesus in order to get another hand-out. They weren't interested in identifying the Messiah, they wanted another meal.

"Show us a sign, Jesus. Show us what you can do!" The night before they'd gone to bed with full stomachs. But now, that is all but forgotten. How could they forget such a wonderful miracle? And yet, just like the Jews, you and I tend also to forget what the Lord has already done. We approach His throne with a, sort of "What have you done for me *lately*?" attitude.

God proves Himself wonderfully faithful. He helps me conquer some unconquerable problem. But then tomorrow I face a brand new set of problems and I go to Him and say, "God, if You're really there, HELP!" And I sense Him screaming from heaven, "What do you mean, 'IF I'M HERE!' What about yesterday? What about last week? What about last year?" It's amazing, but when it comes to the divine assistance of God, it's unbelievable how forgetful we become.

But do you know why David was able to kill Goliath? Do you know what it was that gave him the confidence to march out into that valley with no greater arsenal than a slingshot? It was because burned deeply into David's memory was the vivid reality of victories past. He remembered how he was able, through the power of God, to take a lion and kill him with his bare hands; and how he did the same with the bear. And when his friends tried to hold him back, he said, "Look, the same God that took care of the lion will handle this overgrown Philistine." David had power because he hadn't forgotten. He remembered what God had done.

But not these people. "You say You're the Messiah, Jesus? Prove it! Moses gave us manna. Do him one better, Jesus, and maybe we'll believe You!"

To which Jesus replied:

I tell you the truth, it is not Moses who has given you the bread from heaven, but it is my Father who gives you the true bread from heaven. For the bread of God is he who comes down from heaven and gives life to the world (John 6:32,33).

"Moses didn't give you that bread, God did. And that same God has now delivered to you the genuine article – the true bread Himself in human form." They replied, "Sir, from now on give us this bread" (John 6:34). "We want that bread, Jesus! You've convinced us. Give us some of that stuff." You see, it still hadn't clicked! They were still thinking about their

stomachs. "Jesus, feed us some of that bread today."

Then Jesus declared, "I am the bread of life. He who comes to me will never go hungry, and he who believes in me will never be thirsty." (John 6:35).

There. He said it. There was no mistaking His meaning now. *"I am that bread. And if you come to Me you will never again go hungry. You will find satisfaction like the world cannot provide. Because when you partake of me, you will NEVER again know what it is to be spiritually hungry."*

Look at the word "never." That's a big word, isn't it? It struck me, as I studied that verse, just how big that little word is. We're talking NEVER, folks! And the bigness of the word is enlarged when you consider Who it is making the promise.

Suppose someone walked up to you and promised to give you a million dollars. How would you respond to that? "Well, it depends." Depends on what? "Well, it depends on who made the promise." What do you mean? "Well, for one, does he even have a million dollars? For another, is he telling the truth? And beyond that, is he a fruitcake?" Now if I were the one making the promise, you'd probably smile kindly, pat me on the shoulder and say, "Steve, I think you need some time off." Why would you say that? Because there is no way that I could make good on that promise! I don't have the capacity to pull it off!

But here is God in the flesh. He says, *"You come to Me and you will never be hungry again."* Then when you remember that God has never forgotten a promise, that there never has been a time when He has failed to make good on His word, that a promise from God is as good as already done, then it really means something when He says, "never." When Jesus said, "never," that's exactly what He meant.

By the way, I found some other "NEVER(S)" IN SCRIP-TURE:

David, looking back on his life, writes, "I was young and now I am old, yet I have NEVER seen the righteous forsaken or their children begging bread" (Psa. 37:25).

Sometime later he said, "Cast your cares on the Lord and he will sustain you; He will NEVER let the righteous fall" (Psa. 55:22).

In Mark 9, Jesus used the word, except this time it was not a promise of blessing, but a warning of future danger. He said, "If your hand causes you to sin, cut it off. It is better for you to enter life maimed than with two hands to go into hell, where the fire NEVER goes out" (Mark 9:43).

To the woman at the well He said, "Whoever drinks the water I give him will NEVER thirst" (John 4:14).

The Apostle Paul wrote, "Love NEVER fails" (I Cor. 13:8).

And in Hebrews 13:5, we read that wonderfully reassuring promise, "never will I leave you; NEVER will I forsake you."

Then finally, Peter offers us ultimate assurance when he writes, "Therefore, my brothers, be all the more eager to make your calling and election sure. For if you do these things, you will NEVER fall" (II Pet. 1:10).

Back to John 6. There was no doubt now. Jesus was claiming to be the Promised One of God. He clearly asserted that He was the spiritual food which would endure.

At this the Jews began to grumble about him because he said, "I am the bread that came down from heaven." They said, Is this not Jesus, the Son of Joseph, whose father and mother we know? How can he now say, 'I came down from heaven'? (John 6:41,42).

"We were in Sabbath School together! We remember Him in shop class. We remember Him building cabinetry for our kitchen. And now He has the audacity to claim to be Messiah? No way!"

> "Stop grumbling among yourselves," Jesus answered. "No one can come to me unless the Father who sent me draws him and I will raise him up at the last day."
> I tell you the truth, he who believes has everlasting life. I am the bread of life. Your forefathers ate the manna in the desert, yet they died. But here is the bread that comes down from heaven, which a man may eat and not die. I am the living bread that came down from heaven. If a man eats of his bread, he will live forever. This bread is my flesh, which I will give for the life of the world." To which they replied, How can this man give us his flesh to eat?" (John 6:43, 47-52).

Meaning? "We're not cannibals!" You see, they were still taking Jesus' words literally. They were so hooked into the material realm that all they could think was, "You mean we have to *eat* Him to be saved?" (Oooo!)

Have you ever talked to a non-believer about spiritual things, only to have him look at you like you're talking in a foreign language? You talk about man's soul, not just his body. You refer to man's deepest spiritual needs, not just his physical needs – and the poor guy looks at you with a blank stare that says, "What in the world are you talking about?" It just doesn't make any sense to him. He's so preoccupied with the world that all he can understand is the material, certainly not the spiritual.

That's what happened here. So Jesus tried to clarify:

> I tell you the truth, unless you eat the flesh of the Son of Man and drink his blood, you have no life in you (John 6:53).

Now some commentators tell us that Jesus was referring

here to the Lord's Supper. And certainly the imagery is strikingly parallel to our observance of that sacrament. But Jesus hadn't even instituted the Lord's Supper yet. That wouldn't happen for another year. No, what Jesus is saying here is that we must fully appropriate Him into our lives. We are to symbolically eat Him. To allow Him absolute entrance into the very core of our lives. And He promises that when we do that – when we eat Him and drink His blood – that He will save us and He will sustain us. That He will supply us with all the necessary strength we need to endure. That's what Jesus is saying. "If you will allow Me to fully enter your life, I will nourish you and empower you for all that life will bring your way. If you *don't* eat of me, however . . . "

> You have no life in you.
> Whoever eats my flesh and drinks my blood has eternal life, and I will raise him up at the last day. For my flesh is real food and my blood is real drink. Whoever eats my flesh and drinks my blood remains in me, and I in him. Just as the living Father sent me and I live because of the Father, so the one who feeds on me will live because of me. This is the bread that came down from heaven. Your forefathers ate manna and died, but he who feeds on this bread will live forever (John 6:53b-58).

What striking imagery! We are not called to simply dabble in Jesus things, we are to ingest Him. He comes to us not desiring to be a mere priority; He demands pre-eminence.

I'm afraid that much of modern day Christendom has reduced the call to come to Christ into much less than that. We've taken the call to fully "eat" Christ into some easily followed formula: (1) a ritualistic prayer; (2) a ceremonial dip; or (3) a carefully worded confession. We stand in our pulpits and ask people to consider "accepting Christ." And the picture we paint suggests that Jesus is beckoning, even pleading for the sinner to respond. But when Jesus offered an invitation, that's not how He handled it. He said, "Repent and follow Me" "Deny yourself." "Take up a cross!"

Jesus said, "YOU MUST EAT ME! You must allow Me absolute entrance into your very self. You must wholly and completely surrender to Me. Only then will you possess eternal life. Only then will you possess the food that endures. Only then will you ingest the bread which alone can fully satisfy."

There were TWO RESPONSES to Jesus' message that day. And those same two responses happen every time His message of salvation is repeated.

The first response? DEFIANT REJECTION. Up until this time, Jesus had built quite a following. Huge crowds thronged after Him, longing to watch His miracles, not to mention the free meals. So much did they enjoy His side-show that they graciously tolerated His preaching, until He started talking about "eating His flesh" and accepting His control and allowing Him ultimate Lordship. That's when they said,

This is a hard teaching. Who can accept it? (John 6:60).

"Jesus, if you want to heal people, if you want to help the poor, if you want to talk about world peace and justice for all men, we're with You! But Jesus, don't ask me to limit my life according to Your plan. Don't expect me to plan my future according to Your perspective. Keep this talk up, Jesus, and I'm out of here." And in fact . . . .

From this time many of his disciples turned back and no longer followed him (John 6:66).

91

There's something about the claims of Jesus that forces people to draw conclusions about their convictions. Many people claim faith in God. They claim to appreciate and follow the teachings of Scripture but when push comes to shove, when you try to nail down what it is they believe about Jesus, people start stuttering and stammering like crazy! You see, this Book is filled with wonderful, encouraging promises. Statements of hope and affirmation. People love that about the Bible. That's what attracts them to these pages. But this Book also clearly and fundamentally identifies Jesus Christ as Lord of all. He's the only gate through which man can find salvation. He's the Author and Sustainer of all life. And it's at that point that people start dropping like flies!

But if that's the way it has to be, that's the way it has to be. Jesus is not a namby-pamby, lily-livered, shallow, lovey-huggy, rubbery backboned Messiah. He's not some deity you can take out to play, have a good time with and then when you're through, put back in His box.

HE IS THE BREAD OF LIFE,
YOUR ONLY SOURCE FOR ETERNAL LIFE.

HE IS THE SPIRITUAL FOOD.
THE ONLY FOOD THAT TRULY SATISFIES.

And if you refuse to ingest Him into your life, you have no life in you. You will *NEVER* know what it is to really live. All you'll do is continue to exist.

But thank God, there was a second response that day. I call it CONFIDENT ACCEPTANCE. As the crowds were leaving in droves, Jesus said to the Twelve,

You do not want to leave too, do you?

Don't tell me Jesus doesn't care what you do with Him. He cares plenty.

Simon Peter answered him, "Lord, to whom shall we go? You have the words of eternal life. We believe and know that you are the Holy One of God." (John 6:67-69).

Do you see the order? It always happens that way. First must come faith. Then and only then does God prove Himself to be true. But we want it to work the other way. "God, I'll believe, IF!" God says, "You believe, THEN!" He says, "*I offer you eternal life through Jesus Christ. You can accept it or you can reject it. But it's all by faith. The proof won't come until you believe.*"

Peter said, "Lord, ever since the first day I believed, You have continually proven yourself over and over and over again. I'm not about to go anywhere but wherever you go."

Pascal said,

There is a God-shaped vacuum in all of us and nothing fits but God.

Augustine said,

Thou has created us for Thyself and our hearts are restless until they find their rest in Thee.

Have you filled your God-shaped vacuum? Has your heart found rest in the Lord? Let me put it this way: If the very foundation of your life was torn from your grasp, what would hold you together? To Whom would you turn? Where would you go to find peace and comfort and strength to carry on? If you don't know Jesus, you have nothing to hold onto. No one to turn to. No place to hide. But Jesus offers Himself to you as a gift. He says, *I am the bread of life. He who believes in me will have everlasting life. He who comes to me will never again go hungry. He who receives me will never again be alone.*

The Sovereign Servant

5

One of the intriguing realities about the Lord Jesus Christ is our absolute inability to capture Him. We feed information about Him into our cranial computers, but no all-inclusive composite emerges. We sit in our Bible Study groups and attempt to label His parts so that we can define Him, but His character transcends all attempts at definition. That's one of the reasons I continue to be attracted to Him. That's why, in fact, my pursuit of Him is more intense today than even the first day I called Him my Savior. You see, you just can't put Jesus under the microscope, analyze Him fully and then put him in a box and file Him away. No, just about the time you think you have a handle on His reality, He throws you a curve. For example,

One minute He's claiming "All authority in heaven and on

earth" (Matt. 28:18). The next minute He's cooking fish for his disciples.

In one scene He's stilling the storm and quieting the waves; in the next He's holding seven snotty-nosed kids on His lap – laughing and tickling and teasing them.

On one page, we see Him restoring sight to a man born blind; on another we see Him weeping at the grave of a close friend.

One day He denigrates the Pharisees, calling them "a brood of vipers" (Luke 3:7). The next day He mercifully defends a woman caught in the very act of adultery.

CAN'T YOU JUST SENSE
THE PARADOX OF HIS LIFE?

So far in our study, we have seen Jesus presented to us as LORD. And not just any lord, but LORD of Lords. The KING of Kings. We examined Jesus as MESSIAH – the Promised One of God, the King of the Jews, the Coming One Who would restore to Israel her glory! And in the last chapter, we listened as Jesus claimed to be the only source of eternal nourishment. The Bread of Life! Pretty heady stuff, wouldn't you say? It's safe to say that, so far, our portrait of Jesus smacks of royalty and dignity and authority!

Yet when we go to Jesus personally and ask Him why He came here, when we interrogate Jesus, hoping to discover His reasons for visiting our planet, what He says forces us to make a dramatic shift in the way we paint His portrait.

Do you remember His words?

For the Son of Man did not come to BE served, but to serve, and to give His life a ransom for many (Mark 10:45).

There it is! When asked the purpose of His incarnation,

Jesus spoke straight from the heart. No heavy-duty word studies are required. No need to go back to the original language. Jesus said, "I came to SERVE. Not to BE served." Not to attract attention. Not to be inducted into the Rabbinical Hall of Fame. No! He came, simply, *TO SERVE.*

And didn't He prove that by the way He carried out His ministry? Jesus didn't measure His effectiveness by the size of His congregation or the power of His preaching. No, He was most concerned with helping people. He was moved with compassion to assist those who were hurting.

That's why the crowds thronged to follow Him. Not because He was charismatic in personality, but because when they came for healing, He healed them; when they were hungry, He fed them; when they were broken-hearted, He comforted them! Often neglecting His own needs – on numerous occasions going without proper nourishment and adequate rest – Jesus continually gave Himself in SERVICE to others.

One of the Twelve, Matthew, having seen Jesus' servant heart "up front and personal," quotes from the prophetic writings which portrayed Messiah as a servant. Quoting from Isaiah 42, he wrote, "Here is my servant whom I have chosen, the one I love, in whom I delight; I will put my Spirit on Him" (Matt. 12:18). Matthew penned that prophecy in order to advocate its fulfillment in Jesus.

Paul further documents Jesus' identity when, in Philippians 2, he reminds us that Jesus "took on the very nature of a servant" (Phil. 2:7). Those two passages are necessary to document His identity, but by far the most powerful statement is Jesus' own words, "I did not come to BE served, but to serve."

NOW HERE'S THE CLINCHER: Remember what I said at the beginning of this book? I said that our goal was to come to know Jesus more intimately so that we might imitate Him more perfectly. Remember? Now, if Jesus personally described Himself as a servant, if His contemporaries lauded Him as a servant and if His constant involvement with people was marked by humble gestures of servitude – THEN IS IT FAR-FETCHED TO ASSUME THAT GOD DESIRES THE SAME FROM US? And would it be inaccurate to say that we are most like Jesus when we do as Jesus did? When we serve as He served?

Now those are hard words to choke down, especially in a world that seems totally obsessed with personal pleasure, piles of possessions and plenty of perks. Let's face it: Whether we are teachers, accountants, laborers, attorneys, homemakers, merchants or preachers, we're caught up in the fast lane of life in the '90's. We dash through airports, sit through meetings, dial our cellular phones, make heavy-duty decisions, bark out orders and change dirty diapers – barely taking time to even acknowledge the people with whom we are interfacing. Their needs, their heartaches, their burdens are all but ignored. It's so easy, isn't it, to lose sight of our call to be a servant?

But then contrast our conflicting priorities with the example of Jesus. He came with a pretty heady agenda as well. He came to purchase redemption for all of mankind. The sins of the whole world – past, present and future – were His sole responsibility. Yet He still found time in His brief 33 years to stoop low and to serve. If Jesus could do that, my friends, then no matter how important we think we may be, we *must* do that.

In this chapter, I want you to see with me *THE SOVEREIGN SERVANT*, the Lord Jesus Christ, modeling servanthood in perfect humility and compassion.

John 13 provides for us a very familiar glimpse into the servant's heart of our Lord. But before we go to the verses, let me remind you that in first century Palestine, they didn't have asphalt streets and concrete expressways. All of the main thoroughfares were good old-fashioned dirt roads. The people didn't have shoes either! Not even sandals, at least as we know sandals. Their version of the "sandal" was merely a slab of leather held to the foot by a single leather strap. Now add to the dirt roads and the sorry sandals the fact that Palestine was a land of open sewage! Beasts of burden roamed freely through even the busiest of thoroughfares. In such an environment, it's not difficult to imagine the sort of filth that could be accumulated on one's feet! The prevailing weather conditions didn't help. It seemed that in Palestine it was either extremely dry or unbelievably wet. If it was dry, the roads would become quite dusty, and the pedestrian's feet would become caked with dust. If it was a wet day, the roads were muddy and the feet would become caked with mud. Either way, whenever you went anywhere, your feet got dirty!

As a result, a custom developed. In every home, at the entrance to that home was a basin, a towel and a pitcher. Here's how it worked: If someone were planning to visit in your home, you would fill the pitcher with water, and, as your guest entered your home, you would wash his feet! He would then leave his sandals at the door and enjoy the evening with clean, albeit bare, feet. If a large group was expected, one of the guests would often volunteer to care for the others' feet. Such a gesture was as common in Jesus' day as offering to remove your guest's coat is in our day.

But, amazingly, in John 13, although a large group had assembled, nobody volunteered to take care of all those dirty feet! And this was no stuffy crowd, either. These men were

Jesus' handpicked disciples. Men who had spent the better part of four years following the One who had called Himself a servant.

Neither was it just an unfortunate oversight! These men knowingly shuffled past that pitcher and basin with absolutely no interest in being anyone's servant! The truth is, they were more interested in power and clout than humility and servanthood! In fact, Luke 22 tells us that during the evening meal, the disciples were arguing over who would be the greatest in Christ's Kingdom. They were still expecting Jesus to lead a political coup against Rome, and because they sensed that the time was near, they had already begun positioning themselves for the top governmental positions.

Now if that weren't so tragic, it would be comical! Peasants from a tiny sea-village in a remote region of Galilee, following a penniless, itinerant preacher – and they're concerned about pecking order? Who would care who among that motley crew was the greatest? But that's the scene. Frankly, I'm convinced that the motivation was not merely that all twelve of them wanted to be "the greatest," but that none of them wanted to be "the least."

That's why nobody wanted to play "servant-for-a-night." Servanthood wasn't high on their agenda at the moment. They weren't in the mood to bow before anyone. They wanted someone to have to bow before them!

Let's go now to the verses:

> It was just before the Passover Feast. Jesus knew that the time had come for him to leave this world and go to the Father.

In other words, the time for Jesus' death was at hand. Each tick of the clock was yet another reminder that before another

THE SOVEREIGN SERVANT

day passed, His life would come to an end. Yet . . . .

> Having loved his own who were in the world, he now showed
> them the full extent of his love (John 13:1).

By the way, one reason many give for not being involved
in servanthood is because, "Well, things are tough right now."
"I'm really under the gun, and I need to just back off and handle my own problems." Maybe you're dealing with that very
issue.

HOW CAN I HELP SOMEONE ELSE WHEN I FEEL LIKE I NEED SOMEONE TO HELP ME?

I want to suggest that's the best time for you to help. That's
what Jesus did. He was a matter of hours removed from the
cross, yet . . . "He showed them the full extent of His love"
(John 13:1).

> The evening meal was being served, and the devil had already
> prompted Judas Iscariot, son of Simon, to betray Jesus. Jesus
> knew that the Father had put all things under his power, and
> that he had come from God and was returning to God; so he
> got up from the meal, took off his outer clothing and wrapped
> a towel around his waist. After that, he poured water into a
> basin and began to wash his disciples' feet, drying them with
> the towel that was wrapped around him (John 13:2-5).

Can you picture that? The argument is getting intense.
Jesus, no doubt disappointed, perhaps even disgusted, draws
some water and kneels before His men one by one and does
the very deed one of them should have already done. In so
doing, He illustrated for them, and through Scripture for us,
FIVE PRINCIPLES OF SERVANTHOOD. Five attitudes and
actions that we who serve the Sovereign Servant are expected

to reflect in our lives. Let me share them with you.

FIRST, THE SOVEREIGN
SERVANT'S SERVANT SHUNS PUBLIC FANFARE.

Isn't that just like Jesus? He didn't say a word; He just does the deed. He didn't make some dramatic announcement; He just modeled the attitude.

Maybe you never stopped to think about it, but Jesus' feet were dirty too! After all, He didn't walk on air while He was among us. He was human. He had walked to the Upper Room, just like the Twelve. And the dust He kicked up no doubt aggravated his allergies and certainly soiled his sandals. At the end of a yet another intense day of ministry and conflict, Jesus' body was aching, and His spirit was exhausted. He didn't feel like washing feet either! Add to His exhaustion the tremendous burden of knowing that in less than 24 hours, His body would be lying in a tomb! Yet there He is, with dirty feet, listening to men who should have known better, argue over who was going to be His right hand man! It made Him sick!

I'm certain there were wild feelings and emotions swimming through His mind. He probably thought,*"Men, after three years with Me, you still don't understand! Don't you know what I'm going to do for you tomorrow? The least you could do is wash My feet! I wonder how in the world you blockheads are going to carry on this message after I leave!"* Yet without a word, Jesus grabbed the towel, drew the water and quietly began to wash feet. He refused to draw attention to Himself. He simply did the deed.

I have a preacher friend who loves to say, "I've got a

tremendous sermon on humility and as soon as enough people show up, I'll preach it!" You see, that's the problem with humility. Humility cannot be showcased: the moment it goes on display is the moment it ceases to be.

The word "humility" comes from a compound Greek word which, when put together, means: "to think with lowliness, to be lowly in mind." It is the antithesis of arrogance and boastfulness. The implication of humility is unmistakable: if you are consciously aware (and in fact, quite impressed) with the impressive humility undergirding your actions, then you're not being humble.

I love the story I heard about the flamboyant boxing promoter, Don King. He was being interviewed some time ago and was asked about his many notable accomplishments. And he said, "Sometimes I amaze myself! And I say that with all humility." No he didn't. Nothing can be "said" in humility. It must be done. Quietly. Without announcement.

That's the way Jesus handled it. He didn't make a big deal, He didn't call the press to cover the story, He didn't tell His men what He was about to do, and He didn't expect them to fall all over themselves just because He did it, either. He just did it.

> He came to Simon Peter, who said to him, "Lord are you going to wash my feet?" Jesus replied, "You do not realize now what I am doing, but later you will understand." "No," said Peter, "you shall never wash my feet." (John 13:6-8).

The emphasis seems to be, "No! Never! Not even until eternity will you wash my feet!" Now that *sounds* humble, doesn't it? It sounds like he's saying, "You know, Lord, I really ought to be washing your feet!" But that's not the thought.

What Peter is expressing is not humility, but rather, pride. The kind of self-sufficient pride that refuses to admit that there might just be a need someone else can fill. I picture him, mildly miffed, hiding his feet, and saying, "Hey, I can take care of my own feet, Jesus."

This brings us to the second principle:

THE SOVEREIGN SERVANT'S SERVANT SCORNS FALSE CLAIMS TO SELF-SUFFICIENCY.

Just as Peter tried to cover his dirty feet, we often do the same, attempting to hide the truth of our lives under a facade of sufficiency; adamantly refusing to admit our need. Hey, it's tough to admit you have dirty feet, isn't it? Especially if you are a Peter.

Several months ago I was going through an especially difficult time, although being a Peter, I didn't realize it. Or if I did, I was in that mode that assumes that preachers aren't supposed to have down times. I mean, I'm supposed to always have the right answers, isn't that true? Isn't that what "Chilton's Guide to Pastoral Leadership" says? And I'm always supposed to know just the right Scripture to use. And I'm always supposed to be on top of the program. But I wasn't. Vanessa, my wife, pulled me aside and said, "What's wrong, honey? I know something's bothering you, and I want to help." I pulled my feet under my robe and said, "No problems! Thing's are going great!" The next day, one of my associates pulled me aside and said, "What's wrong, Steve? I know something's bothering you, and I'd like to help." Again with the feet! "Hey, I got it wired, brother! No problem!" A few days later, another close friend caught me in the hallway at church and said, "Steve, tell me what's wrong." "Wrong? Nothing's wrong! What are you talking about?" Does that sound like anybody you know? Competent, strong, capable, hard-working, independent and, God forbid!, never vulnerable.

But I was always told that if one person calls you a horse, ignore him. If two people call you a horse, look in the mirror. If three people call you a horse, buy a saddle. So I bought a saddle. I got alone, sat down and listed all the pressures that I was facing – and the list filled an entire page. I showed the list to Vanessa and perhaps for the first time in our marriage, I said, "I need you, honey. I need you to help me with my feet."

Are you a Peter-type? Do you find it difficult to unmask your life and admit that you might just have a need? Your friends reach out to try to help, you family tries to assist, but you continue to play the game – pretending to yourself – and fooling only yourself into thinking that you can somehow handle it. Part of being a servant is a willingness to lose that tough-guy image. It's being able to say, "You know, my feet are dirty, and I really could use the help."

Now I'm sure Peter thought his little tirade would end this uncomfortable confrontation, and he would be left alone to contemplate his dusty toes. But Jesus had no intention of backing off. He snapped back,

Unless I wash you, you have no part with me (John 13:8).

That's the third principle:

THE SOVEREIGN SERVANT'S
SERVANT STANDS FIRM UNDER PRESSURE.

Jesus was certainly no wimp, was He? One of His men was

out of line, and Jesus was determined to make His point and make it stick. He didn't say, *"Fine, Peter. You want dirty feet? It's OK by Me!"* No. He said, *"Look: as long as you're playing on My team, you're going play by My rules. If that's not acceptable to you – there's the door!"*

Being a servant doesn't mean that you have to clone Don Knotts! No way! Certainly, a servant *is* called to bend low in order to help others, but when truth is threatened or the character of Christ is challenged, the true servant of God refuses to bend!

The plot thickens:

When he had finished washing their feet . . . (John 13:12).

Look at the word, "their." Now think with me: Do you know who the "their" includes? JUDAS! Jesus washed Judas' feet, too! Can you imagine stooping before your betrayer, loosening the clasp of his dusty sandals, pouring the water over his feet and massaging each toe dry with His towel? What grace! What humility! To serve without prejudice. To serve with no thought as to who it is you are serving.

That's the fourth lesson:

THE SOVEREIGN SERVANT'S SERVANT SERVES WITHOUT PARTIALITY.

May I share with you a story that illustrates this principle more powerfully than I ever could?

Many doctors withdraw from the practice of medicine every Wednesday afternoon. Some spend the time on the golf course, others go fishing. I go to the library, where I join elderly men and women who gather in the main reading room to read and sleep beneath the world's newspapers and periodicals. How brave and how reliable these people are! They plow through (you name what kind of inclemencies) to get to the library shortly after it opens. So unbroken is their attendance that were one of them missing, it would arouse the suspicion of others and, really, of me! For I furtively at first, but with reckless abandonment, have begun to love these dear people.

The tribe consists of a corps of six regulars, somewhat less constant pool of eight others, of whom two or three can be counted on to appear at any given moment. On very cold days, all eight of them may show up, which causes a bit of a jam at the newspaper rack.

Either out of loyalty to certain beloved articles of clothing or from scantiness of wardrobe, they tend to wear the same thing everyday. For the first year or two, I identified them as "Old Stovepipe," "Mrs. Fringe," "Neckerchief," and "Old Galoshes" just by what they wore. By the time I arrive, they have long since settled into their customary places. One or two, likely "Galoshes" and "Stovepipe," are sleeping. They seem to need all the rest they can get. "Mrs. Fringe," on the other hand, her hunger for information unappeasable, will be well into the *Journal of Abnormal Psychology*, whose case histories will keep her riveted until the library closes.

As time went by, I came to think of them as my colleagues. Fellow readers, who were engaged with me in the pursuit of language. I noticed they didn't waste much time talking to one another; reading was serious business.

Only in the basement on a break by the vending machine would animated conversation break out. Upstairs in the reading room, this vow of silence was sacred.

I do not know by what criteria these selections are made, but "Old Neckerchief" is my favorite. He is a man in his 80's with a kind of pink face that always looks like it just came out of the cold, a single drop of watery discharge, like a little bead, hangs at the tip of his nose; his gait is very stiff-legged with tiny quick-shuffling steps accompanied by wild-arm swinging in what seems to be either an effort to gain momentum or to maintain balance.

For a long time I could not decide whether this manner of walking was due to arthritis of the knees, or to the fact that he usually wore at least two or three pairs of pants. But then one day as I held the door to the men's room for him, he pointed to his knees and announced by way of explanation – "The old hinges is really rusty." The fact was stated with a wry smile and not the least bit of self-pity. "No hurry," I said. And once again I paid homage to Sir William Osler, who instructed all of his medical students to listen to the patient – he will always try to tell you what's wrong with him. From that day on, "Neckerchief" and I were friends. I learned that he was a widower, living in a roominghouse six blocks away. He had no children, no family, and the Boston Globe was the best newspaper in the library. He learned approximately the same number of facts about me.

One day I watched "Neckerchief" as he journeyed back to his seat from the magazine rack. One flapping hand rattled the "Saturday Review." As he passed, I saw that his usually flaccid expression was replaced by a look of sheer pain. His lower lip was caught between his teeth. His forehead was stitched in lines of endurance and he was hissing. I waited for him to take his seat, which he did with a gasp of relief, then I slipped up behind him and whispered, "The hinges?" "Nope," he said, "it's my toes." I said, "What's wrong with your toes?" He said, "My old arthritis won't let me get down there anymore, and my toenails is too long! They've grown down over the end of my toes and they're underneath and they're cutting my feet. And it hurts when I walk."

I left the library and went back to my office. "What are you doing here?" asked my nurse. "It's Wednesday afternoon." "I know," I said. "I need my toe-nail cutters. I'll bring 'em back tomorrow." "Neckerchief" was right where I had left him; however a brief survey showed me that he had made one more trip to the magazine rack. I could only guess what the exchange cost him.

Go on down to the men's room," I said, "I want to cut your toenails." And I showed him my clippers. Big, heavy-duty kind you grip with both hands, with jaws that can bite through bones. One of the handles was a rasp. I gave him a head start, and then followed him to the men's room. There was no one else in there. "Sit here," I said, pointing to one of the booths. He sat on the toilet. I knelt and began to take off his shoes. "Please don't untie 'em," he said. "I can't get to 'em anymore.

I just kind of slide 'em on and off." Two pairs of socks were another story. I had to peel them off. The under-pair snagged on a toe nail, and "Neckerchief" winced. "How do you get these things on?" I asked. "I'm sorry," he said, "They're a terrible mess, ain't they?"

The nail of each big toe was the horn of a goat, thick as his thumb. It curved and projected down over the tip of the toe to the underside. And with every step the nail cut painfully into the flesh. There was dried blood all over both of his feet and all over his socks.

"How do you walk?" I said. And I thought of the eight blocks that he covered twice a day just to be with his friends.

It took me an hour to do each big toe. The nails were far too big for my cutters. They had to be chewed away, little bits at a time, then flattened with a rasp - occasionally pieces flew up and hit me in the face. The eight other toes were easy. Now and then someone came and went at the row of urinals. Twice somebody occupied the booth next to ours. I never once looked up. I just thought, "They're just going to have to wonder."

"Neckerchief" said, "Hey Doc, it don't look decent, you know."

"Never mind," I told him.

Then I wet some paper, and with warm water and soap I washed his feet. I dried his toes. I put his shoes back on, along with his outer socks. He stood up and took a few steps like someone testing the fit of a new pair of shoes.

Wow," he said. "Doc, that's a cadillac of a toe job! How much do I owe ya?" "It's on the house," I said. "How is it?" "Oh man!" he said. "It don't hurt!" And he gave me a smile that I will keep in my safety deposit box at the bank until the day I die.

The next week I did "Stovepipe" and then "Mrs. Fringe," who was a special problem. I had to do her in the Ladies' Room, and we tied the place up for almost an hour.

But I want to tell you something – since that experience, I never go to the library on Wednesday afternoon, or anywhere, without my nail clippers in my briefcase. Because I've learned something: YOU NEVER KNOW WHO WILL NEED YOU IN A WAY THAT YOU'VE NEVER

DREAMED OF IN ALL OF YOUR LIFE. (Condensed from "Letters to a Young Doctor" by Richard Seizer, *Wednesday Afternoon in the Reading Room*.)

That's the point Jesus made when He had completed His task.

> When he had finished washing their feet, he put on his clothes and returned to his place. "Do you understand what I have done for you?" he asked them. "You call me 'Teacher' and 'Lord,' and rightly so, for that is what I am. Now that I, your Lord and Teacher, have washed your feet, you also should wash one another's feet." (John 13:12-14).

Now you might have expected Him to say, "*Look, I washed your feet, now you wash Mine!*" But He didn't. Not once in this entire scene did Jesus attract any attention to His own dusty toes. That's something a true servant doesn't do. He wasn't interested in employing heavy-handed guilt tactics or manipulative mind-games. He was simply making a point.

The point was: "*You need to be doing that for each other. You need to be looking at your fellow man with servant's eyes, not merely looking for what others can do to help you, but what you can do to help others.*" And as if to drive the point home, He said,

> I have set you an example that you should do as I have done for you (John 13:15).

Now cultures change. We no longer get dusty feet when we go to a dinner party. So Jesus is not suggesting that the actual process of foot washing was to become a lasting sacrament of the church. But behind the dusty feet is a divine principle: THE ONE WHO SERVES THE SOVEREIGN SERVANT

SERVES WITHOUT PARTIALITY. Period. It may be finances, it may be your time, it may be something as simple as a pair of nail clippers. But if your Teacher and Lord washed dirty feet, you also must wash dirty feet.

And the point is: DO IT!

> I tell you the truth, no servant is greater than his master, nor is a messenger greater than the one who sent him. Now that you know these things, you will be blessed if you do them (John 13:16,17).

Lesson #5 teaches us that:

THE SOVEREIGN SERVANT'S SERVANT SMILES MOST WHEN HE IS SERVING.

The word "blessed" means "happy." Jesus is telling us that true happiness results from a servant lifestyle. And you know, it's true! By the far, the happiest, most enthusiastic people I know are people who have forgotten themselves – not those who are constantly trying to find themselves! The most fundamentally content people I know are those who freely give themselves to meet the needs of others.

Dr. Karl Menninger, a famous Christian psychiatrist, once gave a lecture on mental health. After the lecture, he answered questions from the audience. One attendee asked, "What would you advise a person to do if that person felt a nervous breakdown coming on?" Most expected him to say, "Consult your psychiatrist . . . go on a vacation . . . take a leave of absence." But to their astonishment, he replied, "Lock up your house, go across the railroad tracks, find someone in need and do something to help him." There you have it: not from a preacher, but from a psychiatrist. Sound mental health is rooted in selfless service.

You know, maybe that's why you're not happy! Your own feet are sparkling clean – but when's the last time you lifted a finger to help someone else? In your home, when was the last time you did something . . . for them? When was the last time you did something for your mate without worrying about what you'd get in return? When's the last time you volunteered for a thankless, behind-the-scenes assignment? When's the last time your prayers were more focused on another's need than your own? That's why you're so miserable! That's why you're so unhappy!

> Servanthood is giving when you feel like keeping,
>   praying for others when you need to be prayed for,
>   feeding others when your own soul is hungry,
>   living truth before people even when you can't see
>   results,
>   hurting with other people even when your own
>   hurt can't be spoken,
>   keeping your word even when it is not convenient,
>   it is being faithful when your flesh wants to run
>   away."

Happy are you when you do that. Don't ask me to explain why, I just know that it's true.

Jesus said, "*I left you an example. Do as I have done to you.*" So how about it? Don't tell me you're too busy. Don't assume someone else will take care of the need. Don't think you're too important, because you are not. There are children who need your time. Kids who don't know the songs of Jesus. Babies who need to be held and loved by people who know the Lord. There are third graders who are hungering for answers. Teenagers who are struggling with decisions. There are single parent homes who could really use your attention. There's an older gentleman who really wants to learn to read, a pregnant teenager who needs a place to live, an addict who needs a friend to care.

And you know what? You can meet those needs. At least some of them. Perhaps only one. But you've got what it takes to do that. You know you can teach, but you're not teaching. You have a beautiful home, but you won't make it available. You could be a prayer warrior, but you're a critic instead. You have been blessed of God financially – and you could make a significant investment in Kingdom business, but you've never gone beyond convenience giving. Perhaps you are waiting for the big ego job to open up before you volunteer.

I agree with Dietrich Bonhoeffer:

> The Church does not need brilliant personalities, but faithful servants of Jesus and the brethren. The Church will place its confidence only in the simple servant of the Word of Jesus Christ because it knows that then it will be guided, not according to human wisdom and human conceit, but by the Word of the Good Shepherd. The question of trust, which is so closely related to that of authority, is determined by the faithfulness with which a man serves Jesus Christ, never by the extraordinary talents which he possesses.

Listen, if our goal is to know Christ more intimately in order to imitate Him more perfectly – I guess that means the ball is in your court. We know now that Jesus was called to earth to model servanthood. We have seen Him in action, selflessly stooping low to serve His men.

So how about you? Is "servant" a word people would use to describe you? Listen, if you really want to be blessed of God, if you really want to know fulfillment and satisfaction – then grab a pitcher, roll up your sleeves, find some dirty feet and get to work.

I Am... The True Vine

6

It's Passion Week. And what a week it has been. On Sunday, Jesus was the object of adoration as crowds lined the roadside leading to Jerusalem, waving palm branches and crying, "Lord save us!" Within hours, He becomes the object of derision, as in righteous anger He chases the thieves and robbers out of the Temple. Later, He's the object of scorn, as the Pharisees question His right to teach in the Temple courts. After such a fast, roller-coaster ride to the bottom, Jesus, physically tired and emotionally spent, chose to spend his final hours before the cross with his men, the Twelve, who had been with Him from the beginning. They meet together in a tiny Upper Room and share a meal together.

Following the meal, a number of amazing things occurred. Jesus graciously modeled humility and mercy by washing the disciples' dirty feet. Then He again predicted His crucifixion, this time by instituting a ceremony which we call "The Lord's Supper." But then, unbelievably, Satan entered the heart of Judas, who stormed out of the room, hell-bent on betrayal. And if that weren't enough, Peter is informed that he will deny Jesus. Then, Jesus informs these men, who had left all to follow Him, that He will be leaving them, that He must go and prepare a place for them. But He said, "Do not let your hearts be troubled" (John 14:1a).

Their hearts were troubled nonetheless. They were confused, shocked, frightened by this terrifying turn of events. It's finally sinking in – their Leader is not going to be around much longer! And all of their plans for conquest and power and freedom were laid bare. Their spirits were crushed. Their hopes dashed.

So Jesus, sensing their need, revealed to His men one of the most significant truths of the Gospel. He unveiled for them, and through Scripture for us, what is the TRUE SOURCE OF ALL SPIRITUAL POWER.

Here's how it happened: When the meal was completed, Jesus said, "Come now; let us leave" (John 14:31b). So they gathered their belongings, slipped on their sandals and headed out into the darkness in a somber parade toward Gethsemane. And it was either at Gethsemane itself or at some point along the way that Jesus revealed this secret to His men.

Who knows what prompted Jesus to use the analogy He employed. Perhaps it was the cup at the table, which contained wine drawn from the vine. Perhaps it was the jingling of coins in Judas' money bag as he fled from Jesus' presence, causing Jesus to remember that on those coins was depicted the vine. Perhaps they passed the Temple on the way to the Garden and He noticed the golden display of the vine poised at the Temple entrance. Maybe as they entered the Garden itself, Jesus saw a clump of grapes, and, taking them in hand, He taught His men.

Whatever the prompting, Jesus once again used the physical to illustrate the spiritual, the familiar to unveil the hidden. I picture Him taking those grapes in hand and saying, *"Men, I want to give you the secret of victorious Christian living. Here it is: I am the TRUE VINE."*

That's the dramatic scene of John 15. But before we roll up our sleeves and get into that, let me briefly introduce to you the CAST OF CHARACTERS which Jesus employs in this lesson. Let me first identify them; then we'll go back and examine each more closely.

I find four main characters in verses 1-11:

• In verse 1, Jesus mentions the TRUE VINE.
• Also in verse 1, THE GARDENER.
• In verse 5, we learn about THE BRANCHES.
• Then finally, THE FRUIT. It's mentioned seven times in verses 1-11. And the emphasis surrounding the fruit has to do with "bearing fruit." In fact, He mentions "bearing fruit" in verse 2; but by the end of the verse He is extolling the virtues of being "even more fruitful;" and in verse 5, He speaks of bearing *"much* fruit."

The obvious point of the passage is: VINES ARE INTENDED TO BEAR FRUIT! You've got to understand that if the passage is to have meaning! You don't plant a garden just to enjoy the thrill of tilling soil, fertilizing and spraying for bugs and pulling weeds. No! The purpose of a garden or vineyard is to produce a crop. To enjoy the FRUIT of your labor.

We'll come back to that, but before we do, let's talk about the first character introduced in Jesus' analogy. Verse 1 reveals to us the TRUE VINE. The identity of the TRUE VINE is unmistakable. Jesus said, "*I* AM THE TRUE VINE." Now you need to understand that to make such a claim was no small assertion. Notice, Jesus is claiming to be the TRUE vine. True as opposed to false. Genuine as opposed to artificial. The real thing as opposed to just a copy.

So who or what was the *false* vine? Listen to the words of Isaiah:

I will sing to the one I love. (*That's God. The prophet is singing a love song to His Redeemer.*) A song about his vineyard: My loved one had a vineyard on a fertile hillside. He dug it up and cleared it of stones and planted it with the choicest vines. He built a watchtower in it and cut out a winepress as well. Then he looked for a crop of good grapes, BUT IT YIELDED ONLY BAD FRUIT (Isa. 5:1,2, emphasis mine.)

God, the Vinedresser, carefully cultivated and protected His chosen Vine. And all He wanted from the Vine was good fruit. But all He received was rotten, sour, tasteless produce.

Now you dwellers in Jerusalem and men of Judah, judge between me and my vineyard.
What more could have been done for my vineyard than I have done for it? When I looked for good grapes, why did it yield only bad?
Now I will tell you what I am going to do to my vineyard: I will take away its hedge, and it will be destroyed; I will break down its wall, and it will be trampled.
I will make it a wasteland, neither pruned nor cultivated, and briers and thorns will grow there. I will command the clouds not to rain on it (Isa. 5:3-6).

Then the song ends and the Prophet tells us who the Vine

I AM THE TRUE VINE

is – "The vineyard of the Lord Almighty is the house of
Israel" (Isa. 5:7a). That's why the coins were engraved with
vinery. That's why the entrance to the synagogues and the
Temple were adorned with vines. Israel was God's chosen
Vine. Dozens of times in the Old Testament she is called just
that. Therefore, the people took up the symbol as sort of a
national flag!

Oh, how God poured Himself into those people! He chose
them from among all the nations to be uniquely blessed.
Psalm 80 tells us that He brought her up out of Egypt and
planted her in a fertile land. He provided her with every pro-
vision necessary to bear good fruit. He sent her prophets and
judges and kings; He protected her from invaders; He
endowed her with great riches and enormous military might
and notoriety throughout the world. Yet when He went to her
branches seeking good fruit, He found none. Hosea said he
found the branches "empty." Isaiah said the fruit He did find
was "bad." So God said, *"What more could I have done?
Therefore, Israel, I will cut you down. I will remove you from
My vineyard."*

That's why Jesus, on the night He was betrayed, said to His
men, *"I am the TRUE VINE. Israel failed to produce good
fruit, so in her place I have been planted."*

Let's move on: WHO IS THE GARDENER? "My Father
is the gardener" (John 15:1b). That's not too hard to figure
out, is it? Now before we look at the work of the Gardener,
please note that this is symbolic, poetic language. There is no
literal vine and there are no literal branches. This is merely an
analogy derived from nature designed to help these men grasp
a deep, significant, spiritual truth.

And here's the message behind the metaphor: *Jesus is the
True Vine.* He is the source of spiritual life. From Him all

spiritual power flows. Now as we'll see shortly, we (those who are believers) are the BRANCHES. And as branches, we are intended by God to bear fruit.

So the Father, as Gardener, in order to produce fruit-bearing branches, carries out a two-fold task:

> He cuts off every branch in me that bears no fruit (John 15:2a).

This makes sense. Certainly a branch that bears no fruit is a dead and useless branch. So He cuts it off. If He leaves it on the vine, it can cause disease and decay. So He removes it. His second job?

> While every branch that does bear fruit he trims clean so that it will be even more fruitful (John 15:2b).

Now I am certainly no expert on gardening. I can't even get crab grass to grow! My green thumb is actually a rather drab brown. So, in an effort to understand the "why" behind the pruning process, I went to the library. In my search I came across an article published by *Horticulturist Magazine*. In the article, Roger Swain described the important place pruning assumes in viticulture (that is, the science of caring for vines). He described the surprise of his neighbor whose grapevine he had pruned. He said she was astonished to see that he had cut away 90% of its growth! Its once long, luxuriant branches and tendrils had been ruthlessly cut back, until there was hardly more than a stump remaining. Now although to the lay-gardener such extensive pruning might seem drastic, Swain says it's necessary if the vine is to bear good fruit. Now understand, an unpruned vine *will* bear fruit, but it will bear MORE fruit and BETTER-TASTING fruit if it is cut back. Otherwise, the life of the vine goes into the growing of wood, rather than the production of fruit. Swain concludes: "You have to get used to the fact that something so drastic can also be so beneficial."

The same is true in the spiritual realm. Our heavenly Father, the Gardener of our souls, wields a pruning knife. His job is to slice through the dead branches and toss them aside. But He also cuts back the live branches, those that are bearing fruit, and although on the surface His actions may seem cruel, it is from the pruned branches that greater fruitfulness is found.

Have you ever experienced the pruning knife of God? If you're a believer and bearing any fruit at all, you have. The Father carefully examines each branch – and when He finds a branch that is beginning to bear fruit – He takes out the knife and cuts it back. If He didn't, spiritual wood would begin to steal away the nutrients designed to produce fruit. Pride might set in, or complacency, or a sense of self-sufficiency.

You see, Satan is just as committed to your branches as the Gardener, except that He wants them to produce sour grapes – resentment, selfishness, greed. So in order to keep the branches clean, the Gardener lovingly trims us back.

But He also prunes us so that we can bear even more fruit. I make a point of that because many Christians assume that suffering is always a result of one of two reasons. Either:

(1) God is punishing me for some sin in my life; or
(2) Satan is attacking me.

Either way, it's bad news. But Jesus offers a third reason:

(3) Suffering can also be the Father's reward for faithfulness

(See Phil. 1:29, 30; I Pet. 4:12f; Heb. 12:4f). He takes the faithful branch, and He cuts it back, knowing that the pruning process, although at the moment painful, will result in even greater fruitfulness!

Sometimes we suffer – not because we are in sin, nor because we are under Satanic attack – BUT RATHER, BECAUSE WE ARE FAITHFUL! This is one of the forgotten truths of the Gospel, isn't it? We think that if we love God and commit our lives to Him and diligently serve Him, then He will see to it that life for us will run smoothly and we won't have any more problems. But it doesn't work that way. Problems are often God's reward for our faithfulness and His preparation for our even greater fruitfulness.

F.B. Meyer said,

The more dear we are to God, the more care He will expend on us. The more fruit-bearing qualities we possess, the more thoroughly shall we be pruned.

Margaret Clarkson wrote:

Perhaps the greatest good that suffering can work for a believer is to increase the capacity of his soul for God. The greater our need, the greater will be our capacity; the greater our capacity, the greater our experience of God. Can any price be too much for such eternal good?

A. W. Tozer put it best:

It is doubtful that God can use any person greatly until He has hurt him deeply.

And I believe that. In fact, I believe the deeper the hurt, the greater the use. The more extensive the pruning, the more luxuriant the produce. Without exception, I've found that to be true.

Let me switch analogies on you. Let's move from branches to birds. I'm told that there is a breed of eagle which every seven years goes through a very strange ritual. The eagle flies to a high, desolate place on the side of a mountain; there he begins to pull out the strong wing feathers which are the very source of his flying and, therefore, his survival. When the wing feathers are pulled out, the eagle begins to break off the claws that have served him to grasp food or to hold him secure on some lofty perch. Bedraggled and defenseless, the eagle is a mockery of his once proud self; but he's still not through! The beak is next. On a jagged rock, the eagle grinds and grinds his great beak until only a nubbin is left.

After a few weeks, a strange transformation takes place. New and stronger wing feathers grow to replace the frazzled and worn old feathers; new and more powerful talons have grown to replace the split and broken old claws; a sharp, new beak has formed, replacing the chipped and nicked old beak. The eagle has been renewed! With greater strength now, he leaps from the mountain to soar again; up, up into the sky he goes – higher than ever. Stronger than ever.

Are you going through that process of renewal right now? Has your beak been ground down to a nubbin? Have your feathers been plucked?

Back to our branch metaphor: Is God using the sharp knife of painful circumstances to cut away from you anything that would keep you from producing His harvest?

I'm not asking you to like the process. No one likes it. All of us would prefer to avoid it. All I'm saying is, SUBMIT TO IT. Don't resist it. He's the Gardener, and He knows what He's doing. His ultimate goal for you is a bountiful crop of luscious fruit. So stop wrestling; submit to GOD'S KNIFE.

Jesus said, "I am the vine; you are the branches" (John 15:5a). That's why we must submit. The source of all life is God! It's only as we're connected to Him that we have life! Because we're just branches, He's the vine! He alone is the life-giving supply!

You know, that's the toughest topic I have to communicate. I can talk about hell and eternal judgment without much trouble. I can talk about money issues and not sweat it. I can deal with sexual issues and feel relatively competent. But the great challenge of my life is trying to convince people (even Christian people) that true life is found only in the Vine. And since I only have life because I am connected to Him, He, therefore, has the right to do to me and through me whatever He chooses.

Paul put it like this:

I consider my life worth nothing to me. I simply want to complete the task the Lord Jesus has given me (Acts 20:24).

In Philippians 3, he wrote,

I consider everything a loss compared to the surpassing greatness of knowing Christ. It's all rubbish; all I want is to gain Christ (Phil. 3:8-10).

To the Galatians, he wrote,

I am crucified with Christ and I no longer live but Christ lives in me (Gal. 2:20).

Now those are great verses, but when I talk about them, most people's eyes glaze over. It's like I'm from another planet, speaking arcane, fanciful gibberish. But Jesus makes it

clear that the source of true life is in the vine. And whether
we like it or not – whether we understand it or not – the Gardener has the right to do to us and through us whatever He
chooses.

Now, as branches we are to bear fruit, right? BUT WHAT
IS THIS FRUIT THAT WE ARE TO BEAR? Go back to Isaiah to find the answer. I'm amazed at how many Christians
assume that this is a reference to winning souls. And certainly
it is a wonderful joy to introduce someone to Christ, but that's
not the fruit Jesus has in mind. Isaiah tells us what the fruit is:

> The vineyard of the Lord Almighty is the house of Israel . . .
> and He looked for justice, but saw bloodshed; for righteous-
> ness, but heard cries of distress (Isa. 5:7).

God came to His vine looking for justice and righteousness; instead he found oppression, cruelty and exploitation.

The word righteousness can be defined as "walking consis-
tently with God's standard." I want to suggest that the fruit
God is looking for among His branches is just that. The fruit
He desires is the character and lifestyle of godliness, which
was modeled to perfection by Jesus when He was here.

Romans 8:29 tells us that's what God wants from us. It
says that "He predestined us to be conformed to the likeness
of His Son." God's great goal for His branches is that we
might become like He is. That we might be like Christ.

Paul uses the same terminology in Galatians 5:

> But the fruit of the Spirit is love, joy, peace, patience, kind-
> ness, goodness, faithfulness, gentleness and self-control
> (Gal. 5:22,23).

When Jesus says, "Remain in me, so that you can bear

fruit," He's saying, *"Remain in me so you can produce character traits of godliness. Of Christlikeness."* That's the thought.

Let's look now at the COMMAND OF CHRIST. Although the goal of the branch is to bear fruit, I find it interesting that that's not the command.

> Remain in me, and I will remain in you. No branch can bear fruit by itself; it must remain in the vine. Neither can you bear fruit unless you remain in me (John 15:4).

Imagine! The command is not, "BE FRUITFUL!" That's the job of the vine. That's the responsibility of the Gardener. The COMMAND is not that we agonize and worry and fret about producing these wonderful characteristics we just read about. That's not our responsibility. Our responsibility is to REMAIN IN CHRIST.

WHAT DOES THAT MEAN? Well, it means that you live a connected, dependent life. It means that you willingly exchange your dreams for His design. You give the Lord free and complete operating power in your life. If He wants to prune you, He can prune you. He wants to fertilize you, He can fertilize you. He has *Carte Blanche* in your life. Your trust is in Him. Your hope is in Him. Your motivation, your direction, your meaning, your purpose in life is in Him. Now don't let your eyes glaze over. I know that's foreign to our culture – but that's the command: GLUE YOURSELF TO JESUS.

In fact, He goes on to say,

> If a man remains in me and I in him, he will bear much fruit; apart from me you can do nothing (John 15:5b).

But we don't really believe that, do we? No, we think we

CAN do it. We think we OUGHT to do it! So we operate under huge loads of guilt. We respond to heavy-handed manipulation as we struggle and strain to become like Christ. We want to make fruit! But that's not our job. Yet when we try, the fruit we do produce is a phony, tasteless, plastic imitation of the real thing.

Let me ask you, have you ever seen a grape pump iron? Have you ever seen an apple eat vitamins? Or a banana groan? NEVER. All fruit can do is hang on the vine, and the vine shoots the necessary nutrients into the fruit to make it into a plump, juicy, tasty treat.

And that's all you can do, too. The command is – "REMAIN IN ME." If you do that, Jesus said, *"I'LL* PRO-DUCE THE FRUIT."

What a strange cow," said the man from the city to his farmer cousin. "Why doesn't that cow have any horns?" "Well, you see," explained the country boy, "Some cows are born without horns and never had any, and others shed theirs. Some we de-horn, and some breeds aren't supposed to have horns at all. There are lots of reasons some cows ain't got horns. But the reason that cow ain't got horns is that it ain't a cow – it's a horse.

A lot of Christians are stretching and straining, striving hard to become like Christ – and all they're becoming is weary and tired. They're like horses pretending to be cows. It may be a cliche, but it's true: THE CHRISTIAN LIFE ISN'T DIFFICULT – IT'S IMPOSSIBLE. It has only been lived in perfection by one person – Jesus. And if it is to be lived successfully by you, it will only happen as you are intimately connected to Him.

Yet how many believers, when they feel the loss of spiritual power, go to a conference? When they're not experiencing

what they think they need to experience, they decide, "Well, I
need to read the Bible more." "I need to pray more." "I need
to go to church more! Then everything will be fine."
NO IT WON'T! Because that's not the way it works. We
are to remain in Christ! IF YOU WANT TO BEAR FRUIT –
REMAIN IN CHRIST! Don't go on a pilgrimage to the Holy
Land; don't do something religious like get baptized in water
shipped directly from the Jordan; don't start wearing religious
trinkets; don't read a religious book; don't buy another sermon tape. *IF YOU WANT TO BEAR FRUIT – GET CLOSE
TO JESUS!* Stop doing things and start being with the Lord.

If you do that, something wonderful will happen in your
life. If you don't? Well, that's another story. What happens is
what I call THE CALAMITY OF COMPROMISE.

So what **is** the Calamity of Compromise? What will happen to me if I *don't* remain in Christ?

If anyone does not remain in me, he is like a branch that is
thrown away and withers (John 15:6a).

Now think with me: *"If a branch, by an act of his own free
will, determines to go it alone; if, having professed faith in
Me, he then refuses to allow Me to live in Him and work
through Him – even if he remains EXTERNALLY connected to
Me, he will be cut off."* When a branch no longer feeds or
draws nourishment from the vine, not only does the branch
cease to bear fruit, it withers and dies. So what do you do
with dead branches?

Such branches are picked up, thrown into the fire and
burned (John 15:6b). ("Fire" is a reference to eternal hell.)

Now I don't want to unduly frighten anyone, but even

more, I can't, in good conscience before God, try in any way to soften the blows of Jesus' words. I cannot take the bite out of this, because I believe Jesus said exactly what He meant to say. He said that withered, dead branches, which seem externally connected but are not, will be gathered up, thrown in the fire and burned. And that's what He meant.

Now this isn't a sin issue. He's not saying that a time will come, when, if you commit 5,473 sins in row, God's going to kick you out of the Kingdom! Neither is He saying that one of these days God's going to get tired of having you around, and He's just going to give you your walking papers.

What He is saying is: *"If you habitually and knowingly and defiantly live in separation from Me, even if you once claimed to be in Me; if you continue to live apart from Me – you exist in the unspeakable danger of the fires of Hell!"*

We don't hear that much these days, do we? No, on a disturbing number of fronts, the message we proclaim is not Jesus' message. Today's Gospel appeal smacks of Madison Avenue, doesn't it? "Come to Jesus," we say, "and see what Jesus can do for you." Yet we fail to mention the necessary repentance, surrender and obedience required on our part. We hear only of the blessings, only the benefits that Jesus is longing to lavish upon you!

"All you have to do is say a prayer or submit to baptism and you're saved! Then you're headed for heaven – no matter what happens!" The thought seems to be: "Do whatever you want to do and God will still save you. I mean, after all, you fulfilled the ceremonial rites of entrance!"

As a result, we have an entire generation of professing believers, who, on the whole, live not that much differently than their heathen counterparts. Approximately 1.6 billion people in the world consider themselves Christian. Nearly one-third of all Americans claim to be born again. But the testimony of their lives betrays the testimony of their lips. And the world doesn't know what to think!

We've been snookered into believing that the only criterion for salvation is a ritualistic invitation, a ceremonial dip or a carefully-worded confession. And that's it! You're in! Do as you please!

But that's not the Gospel of Jesus Christ. When He called people to follow, He called them to a rigorous obedience, to a demanding self-sacrifice. He put sinners on notice, "If you want to walk with me, walk in holiness."

Remember what He said in His very first sermon?

> Not everyone who says to Me, "Lord, Lord," will enter the kingdom of heaven; but he who does the will of My Father who is in heaven. Many will say to Me on that day, "Lord, Lord, did we not prophesy in your name, and in your name cast out demons and in your name perform many miracles?" Then I will declare to them, "I never knew you; depart from Me, you WHO PRACTICE LAWLESSNESS!" (Matt. 7:21-23, emphasis mine).

Friend, there is no past experience in your life – not prophesy, nor even the casting out of demons – which will serve as the guarantor of your salvation apart from a continued life of faithful obedience.

Judas is an example of that. He'd been with the Lord. He ate, walked and prayed with the Lord. He heard Jesus' sermons. He witnessed Jesus' miracles. He even performed a few miracles himself. He preached on a number of occasions. But He didn't REMAIN. At one time He was connected, but not now. He cut himself off. He turned his back on all he had seen and done. And as a result, he withered up. He betrayed the Lord for a pittance of a ransom and, within hours, he had committed suicide. Judas, one of the Twelve, yet ushered into eternity with NO HOPE!

How about you? Are you remaining in Christ? Now I'm not asking, "Do you attend church?" "Do you tithe?" "Are you serving?" I'm asking: Are you intimately connected to the Vine? Is the God of the universe living and moving in your frame so that you are growing in love? In joy? In forgiveness? In grace? Are you moved with compassion when others are hurting? Do you find that your heart is broken by the things which break God's heart? Is it your deepest desire to please Him? Or are you on some rebellious bent toward pleasing only yourself? Friend, it's quite possible to do all the right stuff and say all the right words – and yet never be connected to the only One who can bring to you TRUE LIFE. I ask again, "Are you IN Christ?" Be thoughtful; be wise as you consider your response. Your eternal destiny hangs in the balance.

Enough calamity. Let's flip the coin. What if I DO remain in Him? What if I choose to comply with His command? What then?

I want to give you FIVE RESULTS (or benefits) that come from a life intimately connected with Jesus.

The first result? *I HAVE SPIRITUAL POWER.*

Jesus said, "If a man remains in me and I in him, he will bear much fruit." (John 15:5a). This is exciting, because verse 4 says that you can't bear any fruit without Him. And not only that, but "apart from me (Christ) you can do nothing."

Now many would read that and say, *"You know, He's right. Without God, I can't do very much."* But that's not what He said. He said, "Apart from Me, you can do NOTHING!" Apart from Christ, you are spiritually powerless. But as Scripture says, "With God, all things are possible!" (Matt. 19:26).

131

"I can do ALL THINGS through Christ Who gives me strength!" (Phil. 4:13).
The second benefit I enjoy is: *EFFECTIVE PRAYER.*

If you remain in me and my words remain in you, ask whatever you wish, and it will be given you (John 15:7).

Now don't snatch this verse out of context and run wild with it! This is not a promise forcing Jesus to grant favorably every chance whim of your heart. But it is a promise that as long as you are vitally connected to Him, your "whatevers" will never be a problem. You will not truly desire any "whatever" that He would not want you to have. But His point is, when you are connected to Jesus, your telephone lines to heaven are always in place, a line is always available and the Lord Himself is standing by to receive your call. When you remain in Christ, the prayers and desires of your heart are readily heard and answered by God.

The third benefit? *I HAVE THE ASSURANCE OF SALVATION.*

This is to my Father's glory, that you bear much fruit, showing yourselves to be my disciples (John 15:8).

Isn't that amazing? Assurance of salvation does not come from performing good works; it's not a result of feverish activity – it is a state of being. If you are connected to Christ, the manifestation of the life and character of Christ (the fact that you are growing in love, joy, peace, long-suffering, etc.) not only brings glory to God, but it is also a proof that the central hypothesis for your faith is correct. That life with Christ is the only way to live. And it is in the obvious display of fruit that there is assurance. Assurance that behind everything, even the veil of death, there exists for you eternal rest.

The fourth result is: *ABIDING LOVE.*

> If you obey my commands, you will remain in my love, just
> as I have obeyed my Father's commands and remain in his
> love (John 15:10).

Sounds a lot like Romans 8, doesn't it?

> For I am convinced that neither death nor life, neither angels
> nor demons, neither the present nor the future, nor any pow-
> ers, neither height nor depth, nor anything else in all cre-
> ation, will be able to separate us from the love of God that is
> in Christ Jesus our Lord (Rom. 8:38,39).

You obey the commands of Jesus, you remain in connection with Him – and fear is gone! Because you know that
there is nothing that you could ever do – and nothing that
could be done to you – that would ever make Jesus stop loving you. There's nothing Satan or any other power can throw
your way to drive a wedge between you and Jesus. Nothing.

Ruth Harms Calkin writes:

> God, I may fall flat on my face; I may fail until I feel old
> and beaten and done in. Yet Your love for me is changeless.
> All the music may go out of my life, my private world may
> shatter to dust. Even so, You will hold me in the palm of
> Your steady hand. No turn in the affairs of my fractured life
> can baffle You. Satan with all his braggadocio cannot dis-
> tract You. Nothing can separate me from Your measureless
> love – pain can't, disappointment can't, anguish can't. Yes-
> terday, today, tomorrow can't. The loss of my dearest love
> can't. Death can't. Life can't. Riots, war, insanity, unidenti-
> ty, hunger, neurosis, disease – none of these things nor all of
> them heaped together can budge the fact that I am dearly
> loved, completely forgiven, and forever free through Jesus
> Christ Your beloved Son." AMEN.

There's a fifth blessing: *FULL JOY*.

I have told you this so that my joy may be in you and that your joy may be complete (John 15:11).

Full and running over. That's the thought. It's impossible to describe joy, isn't it? It defies description! I can't define joy, but I know it when I see it. You give me enough time with someone and I'll tell you if there's joy in his or her life. And it has nothing to do with laughter or a bubbly personality. It's something that just wells up from within. Joy shines through even the most difficult heartache. It's a spirit of harmony and peace and hopefulness and quiet confidence in God.

And it's a gift. Jesus says, *"It's MY joy, IN YOU!" I want to give it to you. And the only condition is that you remain in Me."*

Tim Hansel tells the story of an elderly gentleman, having been a pastor for 52 years, who was struggling with skin cancer. He had endured 15 operations. Besides the pain, he was so embarrassed by his appearance that he refused to leave his home. But one day he read John 15:11, and he realized that Jesus wanted to give him joy. That it was a GIFT! He didn't know what to do, so he got on his knees. Then he didn't know what to say, so he said, "Well, Lord, give it to me!" And suddenly, as he described it, this incredible hunk of joy came from heaven and landed on him. "I was overwhelmed," he wrote. "It was like the joy talked about in Peter, a 'joy unspeakable and full of glory.' I didn't know what to say, so I said, 'Turn it on, Lord, turn it on!'" And before he knew it, he was dancing around the house. He felt so joyful that he actually felt born again – again. He had to get out of the house, he couldn't keep all that joy to himself. So he went to a restaurant. A lady saw how happy he was, and asked, "How are you doing?" He said, "Oh, I'm wonderful!" "Is it your birthday?" she asked. "No, honey, it's better than that!" "Your anniversary?" "Better than that!" "Well, what is it?" she asked excitedly. "It's the joy of Jesus. Do you know what I'm talking about?" She shrugged and answered, "No, I have to work on Sundays!"

Here's the bottom line, folks. Everything works best when it's plugged in. Whether it's a curling iron or a microwave, it works best when the plug is in the socket. The same thing is true with life:

**LIFE IS BEST WHEN IT'S PLUGGED
INTO THE POWER SOURCE.**

When you are vitally connected to the TRUE VINE, it is only then that you will know spiritual power, effective prayer, assurance of salvation, abiding love and full, maximum joy.

The choice is yours. You can choose to live in barren fruitlessness – or you can choose to be connected to the life-giving vine. You can choose to go it alone – or you can choose to abide in Jesus. If you go it alone, you will face a life of stark emptiness and aloneness. If you choose to abide, your life will know peace, hope, joy and eternal assurance.

Now I don't have a fancy ribbon to tie around this chapter to make it sparkle and glisten. Just two very tough-minded questions. So take a look at your life. Remove all other thoughts from your mind. Nothing else could possibly matter but these two questions:

ARE YOU IN CHRIST?

If not, that's the place of beginning. You need to come to

Him by obedient faith. If you *are* in Christ, you need to ask this question:

AM I REMAINING IN CHRIST?

The test of your answer is in the fruit. If your answer to either question is "No," then you have some homework to do. Why not do it right now?

A Lesson In Shepherd-ology
7

As times change, so do the words which describe those
changing times. This is why the meaning of some words is
much different today than it once was. For example:

There was a time when the word "cruise" described a
trip on a boat, not a log-jam of teenage dare-devils on
Friday night.
There was a time when "time-share" meant being
together, not buying a condo.
And there was a time when to say that something was
"bad," meant you thought it was bad.
There was a time when "safe sex" referred to
monogamy, not condoms.
There was a time when "interface" meant a nice way to

137

end a date, not the way you work with a computer.
And speaking of computers, there was a time when a
"chip" was something you ate; when "hardware"
meant hammers and screwdrivers; and "software"
wasn't even a word. There was a time when "Give me
the Fax" had to do with Dragnet, not electronic mail.
And there was a time when "closets" were for clothes,
not for coming out of. There was a time when "bun-
nies" were small rabbits, not half-dressed waitresses.
When "Grass" was mowed, not smoked; "Coke" was
something you drank, and "Pot" was something you
cooked in.
There was a time when "Made in Japan" meant junk,
and "Heavy Metal" was lead.

I thought about that as I studied yet another of the names
of Jesus. I turned to a number of Old Testament and New Testament passages which describe Jesus as "THE SHEPHERD"
and those who follow Him as "THE SHEEP." And it occurred
to me that, although such vernacular was quite familiar to
Jesus' audience, the implications of a shepherd and His sheep
are at best obscured, if not, in fact, totally lost on us. I say that
for a couple of reasons.

First, the implications are obscured because we see sheep
so rarely, especially those of us who live in urban areas. But
not in Jesus' day. Dotting every hillside and traversing
through every hectic marketplace would be a shepherd leading his sheep. At sunrise, the shepherd would be at his post,
watching his flock lazily graze along the rocky terrain. At
dusk, he could be found herding his flock into the safety of
the fold. A shepherd caring for his sheep was as familiar a
sight in Palestine as fleas on a dog. But for us, it's an

unknown factor. The picture of a shepherd doesn't click.

The second reason this analogy is difficult for us is because we see sheep so rarely, we tend to view sheep romantically. When we think about sheep, we think about cuddly, wooly, little playthings. We make stuffed animals to look like lambs. We sing songs about lambs and recite poetry which extols the virtues of lamb-dom. The pre-school in our church is called, "Little Lambs Preschool" primarily because little lambs are sweet and soft and loveable. Right? WRONG! Lambs may look adorable, folks, but they are the most difficult, smelly, stubborn and stupid animals you could imagine. And cuddly? Forget it! You've not lived until you've cleaned up after a bunch of sheep. Shew! They smell horrible! And they're not good for manual labor, either. The sheep has a big, fat body which is supported by a set of scrawny, little legs. Sheep are cumbersome, awkward, ugly, dirty, rebellious, stupid animals.

Now Jesus, being quite familiar with the obvious and undeniable shortcomings of sheep, called His followers "sheep." (So much for your pride problem.) But, thank God, He also called Himself our "shepherd." Isn't it good to know that, although we are stubborn and dirty and rebellious and confused and foolish, at least we have a faithful shepherd to watch out for us and protect us?

In this chapter I want to examine three New Testament passages which present Jesus as SHEPHERD from three different vantage points.

First, in John 10, Jesus identifies Himself as "THE *GOOD* SHEPHERD."
Then in Hebrews 13, the author calls Jesus, "THE *GREAT* SHEPHERD."
Then finally, in I Peter 5, the apostle calls Him, "THE

CHIEF SHEPHERD."

Let's go first to John 10. Now in Palestine, sheep were not raised for their meat, but rather for their fleece. The wool which grew around them would be shorn and taken to the market to sell, but the sheep would live on. As a result, it was not uncommon for a shepherd to be with the same sheep for several years, even decades. Because of that, the shepherd would develop names for his sheep. Verse 3 tells us that he "calls his sheep by name." I don't know if "name" is a reference to some pet-name like "Bubba" or "Tiny;" or whether it was a particular cluck of the tongue or whine in the voice. Whatever, the shepherd and his sheep became friends – inseparable companions. He knew each of his flock by name.

> When he has brought out all his own, he goes on ahead of them, and his sheep follow him because they know his voice (John 10:4).

You see, at night, the shepherd would bring his flock to a large, communal pen. A night watchman was hired by several shepherds to watch their sheep through the night, so that a number of flocks would be corralled in the same pen. Then in the morning, the shepherd would come and call to his sheep and the sheep would immediately recognize his voice. And no matter what they were doing or where they were, even though they were in a pen intermingled with dozens of other flocks, they would stop whatever they were doing and come to the shepherd. The would even leapup and dance around the shepherd, because he was their beloved caretaker and after a long night of separation, they finally had heard his familiar voice.

Then through the day, the shepherd would lead his sheep.

He would "go on ahead of his sheep," verse 4 says, leading
them from pasture to pasture for the purpose of finding food.
And because he loved his sheep, the shepherd would never
intentionally lead his sheep into peril. He would lovingly lead
them away from sharp cliffs or heavy thickets. He would protect them with his rod from wolves and other treacherous animals.

Remember David talking about his experience as a shepherd? He told Saul,

> When a lion or a bear came and carried off a sheep from the
> flock, I went after it, struck it and rescued the sheep from its
> mouth. When it turned on me, I seized it by it hair, struck it
> and killed it (I Sam. 17:34b,35).

Such was the job of the shepherd. It was second nature to
the shepherd to think of his sheep even before he thought of
himself.

Now that's what Jesus was talking about in John 10:1-10.
He is simply rehearsing the well-known facts about the role
of a shepherd. And I picture His audience squirming in their
seats and rolling their eyes thinking, "What are you getting at,
Jesus? We know what a shepherd does! What's your point?
What does that have to do with you?"

> I am the *good* shepherd (John 10:11a, emphasis is mine).

The emphasis is on "good." And it means "good" as in
"ideal, fit for the assignment, the model shepherd." Jesus is
saying, "*I am the PROTOTYPE SHEPHERD. I am qualified
for the assignment. Because I know my sheep and they know
me. I care for my sheep, I protect my sheep.*" Not only that,
but,

The good shepherd lays down his life for the sheep (John 10:11b).

Look at that phrase: He "lays down his life." What amazes me is that five times in these eight verses Jesus repeats the thought.

Verse 11: "Lays down his life."

Verse 15: "Lay down my life."

Verse 17: "Lay down my life."

Verse 17: "Lay it down."

Verse 18: "Lay it down."

Do you know why Jesus is emphasizing that? Because His willingness to "lay down His life" qualifies Him as the GOOD SHEPHERD. Other shepherds would take a rod in hand and beat the marauders until they fled, but Jesus allowed Himself to be nailed to a rod, giving up his life so that the lives of his sheep could forever be spared. Now please understand – HE DID THAT VOLUNTARILY!

Now we understand the substitutionary nature of Christ's death. We believe that when He hung on the tree, He was dying in our place. Though He lived entirely separated from sin, He actually became sin for us. We deserved the cross, yet He carried it in our place. That's why Jesus' death is called "substitutionary." He was our substitute.

But not only was His death substitutionary, it was also VOLUNTARY. Jesus was not assassinated, He was not murdered. He willingly gave Himself up.

Remember the final words written about Jesus on the cross? It says, "He gave up His spirit" (Matt. 27:50). Nobody took it from Him. It wasn't snatched away – He gave it of His own accord.

If you have this mental image of Jesus being helplessly herded through a mock trial, hopelessly submitting to a public flogging and impotently hanging at Calvary, you need to know – that image is wrong! He was not powerless. He was not defenseless. The death of Jesus was not the result of the Pharisees getting the upper hand!

Remember in the Garden when Peter sliced off the Roman's ear? He was ready to defend Jesus to the point of his own death. But Jesus said,

Do you think I cannot call on my Father, and he will at once put at my disposal more than twelve legions of angels (Matt. 26:53).

By the way, a legion consisted of 6,000 men. If I multiply right, that's 72,000 angels. "*I can command 72,000 angels to come to my rescue – and any one could handle the job alone. They're not taking my life, Peter. I'm giving it.*"

Pilate was confused too. He said, "Don't you realize I have power either to free you or to crucify you?" (John 19:10b). Jesus replied, "You have no power except what was given you from above" (John 19:11a).

In fact, only when Jesus decreed, "The hour has come," (Mark 14:41) were his enemies able to arrest Him and crucify Him. Only then.

The Lord Jesus Christ was not the unfortunate victim of perilous circumstances. He was the empowered, voluntary substitute. Nails didn't hold Him to that tree – His love for the sheep held Him there. He willingly laid down His life for you and for me. That's why He says, "I AM THE GOOD SHEP-HERD. I have laid down my life for the sheep."

Let's go now to Hebrews 13. Jesus here is called not "The

Good Shepherd" but "THE GREAT SHEPHERD."

> May the God of peace, who through the blood of the eternal covenant brought back from the dead our Lord Jesus, that great Shepherd of the sheep, equip you with everything good for doing his will, and may he work in us what is pleasing to him, through Jesus Christ, to whom be glory for ever and ever. Amen (Heb. 13:20-21).

What a wonderful benediction! Now think with me: What qualified Jesus to be "The Good Shepherd?" Sure, His crucifixion. He "laid down His life for the sheep." That's His past work. It has already been fully accomplished.

But now He's called "The Great Shepherd." According to verse 20, what qualifies Jesus to assume *that* title? Sure, His resurrection. He was "brought back from the dead." Here's the thought: Jesus Christ, resurrected and victorious, functions in His present work as THE GREAT SHEPHERD.

What is His present work? As the Great Shepherd, Jesus has two assignments:

First, HE EQUIPS THE SUBMISSIVE SHEEP. Verse 21 says that he is to "equip you with everything good for doing his will." The present work of Jesus involves equipping those sheep who are following His lead to fully accomplish the will of God. And Paul makes it clear that Christ has already done that. For He has "blessed us in the heavenly realms with every spiritual blessing in Christ" (Eph. 1:3). Everything that we need for life and godliness is already ours through Jesus. There is nothing missing, no power withheld, no wisdom untapped, no authority held back. Because Jesus Christ lives, we have everything we need to follow Him.

But verse 21 also assures us that He's committed to the process. "May he work in us what is pleasing to him." He continually works in us and through us, mending what is broken, correcting what is faulty, shaping and molding us into a clear, unfogged reflection of Himself. Now notice, both verbs (both "equip" and "work") are in the present tense. So this is something that Jesus is now doing and, according to Philippians 1:6, something He will continue to do. For, "He who began in a good work in you, will carry it on to the day of completion." As we'll see later, our God finishes what He begins. He completes whatever He starts. His resurrection is proof that He certainly is able to do just that.

But there's a second work of the GREAT SHEPHERD. Not only does He equip the submissive sheep – He also RESTORES THE STRAYING SHEEP.

For you were like sheep going astray, but now you have returned to the Shepherd and Overseer of your souls (I Pet. 2:25).

Now in order to appreciate this work of Christ, we need to go back to our Palestinian shepherd. When evening arrives, the shepherd leads his flock to the communal pen. Remember? He then stands at the gate of the pen, examining and counting his sheep. But one is missing! Even if not 99 of 100 are safe, he'll leave the 99 and search and search and search until he finds that one lost sheep – calling his name, sounding his voice, searching under the thickets and in the caves. When he finally finds the sheep, he tenderly anoints the cuts and bruises with oil. Then he hoists the animal upon his shoulder and races toward the village, shouting, "I found him! I found him! My lost sheep is safe – I found him!"

Can you look back to a time in your life when you strayed? Sure you can. There's not a person reading these words who hasn't wandered. Now you didn't curse God; you didn't defame Christ – you just wandered. You started following your own voice, rather than the voice of the Shepherd. And in your rebellion, you got caught in the thicket of compromise. You found yourself perched on the precipice of destruction. I know what I'm talking about. I've been there. There have been many times when I have strayed from God's will. And you know what? Every time I strayed, He found me! Every time I blew it, He was there to restore me. That's the business of the SHEPHERD. That's His job! That's what shepherds do!

Now most of us picture God as a sanctimonious sourpuss – just waiting for us to step out of line so He can rap us across the knuckles with his staff! We picture Him dancing with glee when one of His children makes a mistake; because then He can let them have it! But that's not the heart of God! He's our Shepherd, and when we stray, He seeks to find us. And when he finds us, He bandages our wounds and massages us with the oil of mercy. Then He lovingly and carefully carries us back home.

Tony Campolo tells of the time he was speaking in Hawaii. He couldn't sleep, due to the time change, so he went to some greasy spoon at 3:00 in the morning to grab a bite to eat. It was the only place open, and, for a while, he was the only customer. But at 3:30, seven or eight streetwalkers came in and sat down. They sat in the booth next to Campolo, so he was able to listen in on their conversation. One of the prostitutes was named Agnes.

"Guess what?" Agnes said, "I'm 37 tomorrow!"

The other women said, "So what? What do you want us to do? Give you a party?"

146

"You kiddin'?" Agnes scoffed. "I ain't never had a birthday party in all my life!"

A few minutes later, Tony approached the manager and said,

"Are those girls here every night?"

"Yeah."

Tony said, "You know, I overheard Agnes saying that tomorrow is her birthday. What do you say we throw her a birthday party? I'll put up the money, if you'll let us do it here."

"That's a great idea," said the manager. "In fact, me and the wife will do the cake."

Tony said, "Great! I'll take care of the decorations!"

So Tony went out and bought crepe paper and bells and strung a banner that said, "Happy Birthday, Agnes!" He came in the next night and really dolled up the place! It was beautiful. The manager's wife had put the word out on the street, so by 3:00, Tony said, every prostitute in Honolulu was there. About 3:30 in came Agnes. Everyone yelled "SURPRISE!" And she couldn't believe it. She was stunned! Tony grabbed her arm, led her to the table of honor and said, "It's time for the cake!" They rolled out this huge birthday cake, with candles and "Happy Birthday Agnes" and they sang "Happy Birthday" – but Agnes still hadn't said a word. She just sat there in shocked silence. Someone told her to blow out the candles. But she just sat there. So one of the other women finally blew out the candles.

"Well, at least cut the cake," Tony insisted, "We want some cake!"

And the whole room started shouting, "We want

147

cake! We want cake!"

Suddenly, Agnes picked up her cake and said, "Please don't eat my cake. It's the only cake I've ever had, don't eat my cake. Please, can I keep my cake?"

Tony said, "Keep your cake."

She carefully backed out the door and slipped away into the darkness. Everyone in the room fell silent. Tony said,

"I think we need to pray for Agnes." He prayed, "Lord, Agnes has had a hard life. We don't know what she's been through to get to where she is, but she needs your love and your salvation."

The scene was electric! Tony said, "It was like church!" Those women were crying and shouting "Praise God!" "Thank you, Jesus!" Can you imagine? After the prayer, the manager pulled Tony aside and commented,

"I didn't know you were a preacher. What kind of church do you belong to?"

Tony said, "I belong to a church that throws birthday parties for hookers at 3:30 in the morning."

The manager didn't crack a smile. He said, "You know, I'd like to join a church like that."

I've got news for you, friend. There may not be many churches like that, but your Savior is like that. If you're straying, listen to me. No matter what you have done; no matter what you may have become – THE SHEPHERD LONGS TO RESTORE YOU. He wants to wrap His arms around you and decorate a cake and throw a huge party in your honor. In the meantime, He's tracking your every move, sounding that familiar voice, urging you to return to the fold. And He will not abandon the search until you are safely returned to the shelter of His care.

Never forget that, you who are the submissive sheep. Jesus came to seek and save the lost. He came not to serve the healthy, but to heal the sick. He left the 99 in the fold so that he could search for and find the solitary lost sheep. Jesus came to save the Agnes' of our world. Let's never fail to remember that.

I agree with William Barclay. Reflecting on this truth, he writes: "God is kinder than man." Isn't that true? We feel so removed from the filth of such people that we are almost offended at the thought of a birthday party for a prostitute!) Such people deserve, as Barclay puts it:

> . . . nothing but destruction. Not so God. Men may give up hope on a sinner. Not so God. God loves the folk who never stray away but in His heart there is a joy of joys when one is found and comes home; and it would be a thousand times easier to come back to God than to come home to the bleak criticism of men. (William Barclay, *The Gospel of Luke*, The Daily Study Bible, Edinburgh: The Saint Andrew Press, 1962, p. 208.)

How true. Howard Hendricks tells of a man who had been involved in an extended period of deep rebellion. The sin of his life was open to public scrutiny, and he languished beneath the hostility of those he had offended. But by God's grace, one day he was restored. Hendricks asked him how he felt during those days of rebellion. He said, "Howie, I felt like a person out in the ocean, drowning. I saw all these people on the shoreline, with life preservers, yelling, pointing fingers, accusing, and only one person dove in and swam out to me and said, 'Here, hold on. Let's go back together.'"

His is not an isolated incident. Just this morning I spoke with a man who, for several years, had tried desperately to live Christ's way, but failed. Etched into the lines of his face was the hurt of a broken man who couldn't understand why so many of his former "friends" had coldly turned away from him. His eyes filled with tears as he recounted the many lies, the oft-told slanders, the mean-spirited glances he endured. I tell you, my heart went out to him! Sure, he made some bad decisions. There is no doubt he was involved in sin. But as I looked into his tear-stained eyes, I saw a man who doesn't need my rebuke, but who needs my love! A brother who needs me to stop condemning his actions and start seeking to restore him!

How terrible to think that the flock of God is content to stand on the shore and toss out rebukes and judgments – while people are out there drowning – without hope and without help. How horrible to know that far too often the most critical, judgmental, non-forgiving people are believers. But not Jesus. He's the GREAT SHEPHERD. And He's committed to seeking and restoring stray sheep.

Let's go, finally, to I Peter 5. The Good Shepherd laid down His life – that's His past assignment. The Great Shepherd equips submissive sheep and restores straying sheep – that's His present responsibility. *But what about the future?* That's Peter's focus. And in the opening verses of Chapter 5, although he writes specifically to elders, I think his words can also be applied to any spiritual leader. So whether you are a teacher, a youth coach, a deacon or a parent – whatever your role or ministry – these words of counsel are for you:

To the elders among you, I appeal as a fellow elder, a witness

150

of Christ's sufferings and one who also will share in the glory to be revealed: Be shepherds of God's flock that is under your care, serving as overseers – not because you must, but because you are willing, as God wants you to be; not greedy for money, but eager to serve; not lording it over those entrusted to you, but being examples to the flock. And when the Chief Shepherd appears, you will receive the crown of glory that will never fade away (I Pet. 5:1-4).

You who serve in the Body of Christ serve as under-shepherds to Jesus our CHIEF SHEPHERD. And you are called to serve according to His example. You, like Jesus, are to know your sheep and they know you. You are to willingly lay down your life for the sheep. You are to equip the sheep who are willing and restore the sheep who are straying.

But be careful as you shepherd, for there are some very perilous pitfalls which must be avoided. Do you see them in the text?

"Not because you must, but because you are willing." That's the PITFALL OF INDOLENCE. True shepherds aren't lazy. True shepherds go the extra mile. True shepherds serve even when the timing is bad. True shepherds serve even when the Cowboys are on television. Look, if you don't like interruptions, if last minute requests cramp your style, then by all means, don't pick up the staff.

"Not greedy for money." That's the PITFALL OF GREED. Do what you do, not for what you can get out of it, but because it's the right thing to do. Don't ever let the green stuff turn your head.

"Not lording it over those entrusted you." That's the PIT-FALL OF PRIDE. Don't play king of the hill. Don't assume that you're irreplaceable. Don't expect people to cow-tow to your every whim and fancy. And no matter how successful you may be, remember: IT'S GOD'S FLOCK, not yours. No matter how many sheep you are called to shepherd, the fact is, you're still a sheep, too.

To those who are faithful, Peter promises "the crown of glory that will never fade away." You encourage the weak, you nourish the frail, you feed the hungry, you strengthen the weary – and one day, when Jesus returns – HIS GREAT AND FUTURE WORK IN YOUR LIFE WILL BE ONE OF REWARD. And you can take that to the bank. Your life of service will not be in vain. The coming King will bring with Him an extra crown just for you. Someday your deeds will be rewarded.

Isn't it good to know you've got a Shepherd? Isn't it good to know that He knows your name and where you are? Even when you stray?

Let me conclude with three practical statements of shepherd-ology.

#1: THE GOOD SHEPHERD BORE A CROSS. If you follow in His footsteps, you'll bear one too. But follow Him anyway.

I remember a game we used to play as kids. We'd blindfold one of the kids and have him run through a maze that we had designed. And he was to rely entirely on his partner to verbally direct him safely around or over the obstacles. He'd hear directions like, "Turn left, there's a tree coming!" Or, "Jump, there's a box in front of you." Now some kids just couldn't bring themselves to follow their partner's directions. So they would shuffle along, ever so slowly, even though their partner was right on target with his directions. Other kids would walk at a pretty good pace; still others would go like gangbusters.

All of us, though, had to continually fight the urge to tear off the blindfold in order to see what was ahead.

I have that same tendency in the spiritual walk. I know Paul said that we are "walk by faith, not by sight," (II Cor. 5:7) but it's tough to trust in Another's leading, even if He's the Shepherd. Solomon tells me that "He will direct my path," (Prov. 3:6) but there are times when I'm afraid what that path may bring.

I'll tell you what it'll bring. It'll bring a cross. The ways of the Shepherd are not always pleasant or easy. There will be seasons of doubt and fear. There are times when He will stretch you to your absolute limit. He may call you to trust a husband who has betrayed you, to restore a child who has shunned your leadership or to forgive a friend who has let you down. And you'll think, "I can't do it, Lord! I just can't do it!" But I challenge you: REFUSE TO PLAY IT SAFE. Don't allow your fears to sideline you. Don't try to avoid every unpleasant pathway. Instead, courageously pick up the cross of absolute trust and FOLLOW HIM.

#2 THE GREAT SHEPHERD CARRIES A CROOK. If you stray, He'll use it to bring you back. Return to the fold. Don't wander any longer.

Just like the woolie, we're foolish and prone to wander from the God we love. Contentment seems a cruel illusion, as we frantically search for alternative sources of happiness. Peace of mind is a torturing mirage of barrenness, so we run for what we think is higher ground. But despite our frantic pursuits, love and joy are unattainable. Purpose and meaning remain unreachable in a world gone mad. *But behind it all is the Lord.* And He never stops seeking His lost sheep.

Ernest Hemingway wrote a short story about a father who threw his son out of the house because of his son's sin. But as the years pass, the father's heart begins to change. He searches for his son, Paco, but Paco was not to be found. He searched and searched but to no avail. Years pass, and now Paco is a grown man. As a last ditch effort, the father put an ad in the paper. With big letters he wrote, "PACO, IF YOU WANT TO BE FORGIVEN, MEET ME IN THE TOWN SQUARE IN FRONT OF THE GOVERNMENT BUILDING AT 2:00." When the father arrived, there were nearly 1,000 Pacos standing hopefully in the town square.

Are you a "Paco?" Have you strayed from the fold? My friend, if you'll listen closely, you'll hear the voice of the Shepherd arising from the hills. If you look closely, you'll see Him standing at your side, oil in hand, ready to mend your broken soul. His voice is familiar. His staff is a cross. And He's saying, *"Paco, no matter what you have done, no matter what you may have become, if you want to be forgiven – meet me at the Cross."*

#3 THE CHIEF SHEPHERD WEARS A CROWN. If you remain faithful, you'll wear one too. Don't give up, your deeds will be rewarded.

Now the reward may not come in the manner and time in which you might expect it – but God is faithful. The reward will come.

The story is told of an elderly missionary couple returning home on a ship after many years of service in Africa. On the same ship was Teddy Roosevelt, who had just completed a successful big game hunt. As the ship docked in New York harbor, thousands of well-wishers and reporters lined the pier to welcome Roosevelt home. But not a single person was there to welcome the missionaries. As the couple rode to the hotel in a taxi, the man complained, "It just isn't right. We give 40 years of our lives to win souls in Africa and nobody knows or cares when we return. Yet the President goes over there for a few weeks to kill animals, and the whole world takes notice." But as the prayed together that night, the Lord seemed to say to them, "Do you know why you haven't received your reward yet, My children? It's because you are not home yet."

Scripture says,

> Let us not become weary in well-doing, for in the proper time we will reap a harvest if we do not give up (Gal. 6:9).
> Therefore . . . stand firm. Let nothing move you . . . your labor in the Lord is not in vain (I Cor. 15:58).
> Be faithful unto death, and I will give you a crown of life (Rev. 2:10).

Speaking of death, a day will come when you must pass through that dark valley. Let me ask you: "Are you ready? Do you know the Shepherd? And even more, does the Shepherd know you?" Jesus said, "*I am the gate. If a man enters by me, he will be saved – I will be His shepherd.*" That's the plan, folks. You come to Jesus, admit your sin and your need for salvation. And Scripture promises that "a broken and contrite heart, God will not despise."

Someday you and I will cross the dividing line and move to the other side. We'll traverse the shadowy valley. I can tell you with all assurance that the journey will be for me the most exciting adventure of my life. Yes, the path will be shadowy and dark. BUT I WILL NOT FEAR, FOR HE WILL BE WITH ME! How about you? Do you have that kind of assurance?

This is the kind of assurance that caused John McNeil to write:

> Someday, I will draw my feet into the bed for the last time and turn my face to the wall. And I will have to look at the gulf, but my Shepherd and I will look at it together. But I will fear no evil, for "he that cometh unto me I will in no wise cast out." I will hold onto that promise and dare to swing out over the wide gulf on the slender rope, knowing that it will not drop me, for it is rooted in God's imperishable love.

If you haven't taken hold of that rope, my friend, I urge you: TAKE HOLD!

The God Who Came Here

8

When the Divine Artist approached His easel and took the creative brush in hand, Earth rapidly began to take form. The work completed, He returned the brush to its place and looked upon a world of perfect harmony and beauty. And He said, "It is good." Then He took some dust in hand and sculpted the form of man; and when He blew into that form the breath of life, He said again, "It is good." Now during this time, God and Adam enjoyed a very unique relationship. God Himself would come to the Garden in the cool of the evening and walk and talk with Adam. For you see, in the beginning, God's creative canvas reflected perfect joy and solidarity between heaven and earth. There existed between Adam and His God an uncluttered purity. A dynamic oneness. But not for long. Eve blamed the snake, Adam blamed Eve; but the fact is, both of earth's original inhabitants disobeyed God's only command. Their betrayal of God's trust caused them to be expelled from His perfect canvas. Since that day, man has lived in desperate alienation and separation from God. This once beautiful relationship was broken, and a huge gap emerged, separating heaven from earth and God from man.

Now man has desperately tried to bridge the gap. He really has. But to no avail. There are numerous methods man has employed in an attempt to re-establish oneness with God. But when you boil them all down, there are really only two approaches to what we might call "self-salvation."

The first approach is built on the hope that God grades on the curve. So that if my life is better than, let's say, 65% of the population, then I'll get to heaven! Maybe by the skin of my teeth, but I'll get there! The thought is, "If I can do just a little bit more good than I do bad, then I'll slide right through those pearly gates!" But folks, "Curve-Theology" is a sham. You cannot do enough good to cancel out the bad. And if you try to beat the odds? You'll end up eternally busted. Because in God's classroom – it's Pass/Fail. You're either in or you're out. You're either saved or you are condemned.

The second, and equally common approach to "self-salvation," is built upon an understanding that, yes, I am sinful, but "If I can do enough religious things – if I can compensate for my sin by impressing God with my church attendance and my giving, by helping the poor and being kind to my dog – then God will let me in!" But think it through: Even if it *were* possible to compensate for sin through religious activities (and it's not! But if it were . . .), when would enough be enough? Seriously! If you are convinced that you can somehow restore your broken relationship with God on your own merits, just how many merit badges will it take to pull it off? What will

God accept as enough and what's the cut-off point? Do you see the problem?

No friend, we need to realize that there are some jobs we just can't do alone. Can you imagine a cardiac surgeon attempting to perform his own by-pass? Or a neurosurgeon trying to operate on his own brain? Or a quarterback trying to throw himself a pass? No! It's silly to even contemplate such an endeavor. Yet that's exactly what we do when we try, on our own, to restore our broken relationship with God.

What we need is a MEDIATOR. A go-between. A middleman. We need someone who can objectively and fairly represent both God and man, someone who can fully understand both the demands of God as well as man's foibles. We need someone to step into the middle of the fray and bring the two warring parties back together; to restore the harmony. That's THE MEANING OF MEDIATOR.

The word comes from the Greek, *mesites*, which in verb form means "to be in the middle of something." And although the word itself may not be familiar to us, the action of the mediator certainly is.

We read recently that because the United Mine Workers and the Pittston Coal Company have been unable on their own to resolve their differences and come to a mutually satisfactory agreement, Labor Secretary Elizabeth Dole has appointed what she called a "super-mediator" to intervene. An arbitrator. A go-between who, hopefully, will possess the necessary skills in negotiation to effect an agreeable solution and restore the peace in that troubled relationship.

In baseball, there are usually five or six men standing around the field, dressed in ugly black uniforms, whose job it is to represent both sides in the contest and assure that the game is played fairly. The umpire is supposed to be neutral.

He is to simply call the plays as he sees them. And although there are times when we'd like to choke the umpire, kick dust in his face or buy him a pair of glasses – if he weren't there to mediate, we acknowledge that most games would end in fisticuffs.

A marital counselor also functions as a mediator. He or she is called upon to help an aggravated husband and an irritated wife come to a place of peace. He is to do so without appearing to take sides, which is no small task, I assure you. But the marital mediator does his best work when both sides sense his fairness, yet feel continually nudged toward resolution.

So what is a mediator? A mediator is a go-between. He represents two opposing parties and helps bridge the gap between them, in an effort to lead them toward reconciliation. What makes this subject vital to the believer is that Scripture makes it clear that, apart from a spiritual mediator, God and man would continue to live in alienation and separation.

Job was the first to admit his need for a MEDIATOR. You remember Job. Although quite a righteous man, he endured enormous suffering and loss. In a single day, he lost all of his possessions, all 10 of his children, even his health. We find him in chapter 9 covered from head to toe with painful, itching, oozing skin-ulcers. And if that weren't bad enough, he had to endure the accusations of friends whom he thought had come to comfort him. Instead, they confused and irritated him.

In response to an especially blistering condemnation from his buddy Bildad, Job said:

Indeed, I know that this is true.
But how can a mortal be righteous before God?
Though one wished to dispute with him, he could not answer
    him one time out of a thousand.

160

His wisdom is profound, his power is vast.
Who has resisted him and come out unscathed?
How then can I dispute with him?
How can I find words to argue with him?
Though I were innocent (and I'm not) I could not answer him;
I could only plead with my Judge for mercy.
Even if I summoned him and he responded,
I do not believe he would give me a hearing.
He would crush me with a storm
   and multiply my wounds for no reason.
He would not let me regain my breath
   but would overwhelm me with misery (Job 9:2-4,14-18).

How miserable did it get, Job?

I still dread all my sufferings,
   for I know you (God) will not hold me innocent.
Since I am already found guilty,
   why should I struggle in vain?
Even if I washed myself with soap
   and my hands with washing soda,
   you would plunge me into a slime pit
   so that even my clothes would detest me.
He (*God*) is not a man like me that I might answer him,
   that we might confront each other in court.
If only there were someone to arbitrate between us (*a mediator*),
   to lay his hand upon us both,
   someone to remove God's rod from me.
Then I would speak up without fear of him,
   but as it now stands with me, I cannot (Job 9:28-35)

Do you hear the plea of Job's heart? *"If only there was a heavenly umpire who would intervene right now and help me plead my case before heaven. He could lay his hand on both of us and identify with both positions but then help us come to resolve. As it is, I feel totally alienated from God. I feel so alone, so forsaken and so very, very helpless."*

161

Have you been there? Have you ever felt as though God were far removed from you? That no matter how you struggled, heaven seemed unapproachable – and even if God were near, He certainly must not care! Are there times in your confusion when you wish you could just pull back the curtain of heaven and see Him for yourself? Even a brief glimpse would end most of the confusion, wouldn't it?

Well, not only was Job unable to pull back the curtain, neither could he find a middle-man, a go-between, to step in and plead His case before God. In fact, Job went to his grave yearning for a mediator. But there would be none. At least not in his lifetime. However, the mandate had been made: MAN NEEDS A MEDIATOR. For man without a mediator is forced to live in agonizing alienation and separation from God.

That's one reason God gave man THE LAW. He intended that the law mediate His mind to man. God understood the problems that this separation had caused, so He formulated an extensive rulebook. And when He gave THE LAW to man, through His messenger, Moses, here was His counsel: If you do the things contained in this Book, you will be blessed. You will enjoy long life, you will be prosperous, you will be successful in all you do. However, if you don't do these things, you will be cursed, you will be visited with turmoil and suffering (Deut. 30:9,10).

Later, when Joshua replaced Moses as the leader, God reinforced those earlier words when He said:

> Joshua, be careful to obey all the law my servant Moses gave you; do not turn from it to the right or to the left, that you may be successful wherever you go. Do not let this Book of the Law depart from your mouth; meditate on it day and night, so that you may be careful to do everything written in it. Then

you will be prosperous and successful (Josh. 1:7b,8).

Through the Law, God had carefully made His position known. He had clearly communicated His expectations to man. The problem was, the arrangement was one-sided. Man knew God's heart but was totally unable to communicate to God his heart. That's why the Hebrew writer said:

For if there had been nothing wrong with that first covenant, no place would have been sought for another. But God found fault with the people (Heb. 8:7,8a).

Why? Because the Law was an inadequate mediator. In what ways?

For one, *the Law not only informed man about sin, it actually increased man's sin.* Paul eloquently describes the problem in Romans 7. He writes,

I would not have known what sin was except through the Law. But sin, seizing the opportunity afforded by the commandment, produced in me every kind of covetous desire. I found that the very commandment that was intended to bring life actually brought death. For sin, seizing the opportunity afforded by the commandment deceived me, and through the commandment put me to death (Rom. 7:7b,8-11).

Isn't that the truth? The more I read those "Thou Shalt Not's," the more I want to try them out! How about you? Sure, that's human nature! We flesh-bound creatures are attracted to the forbidden. You see a sign that reads, "Don't eat in here," and just like that your stomach starts growling. What do you do when you see a "Wet Paint – Do Not Touch" sign? You touch it, just to make sure. And when the speed limit was 55, you probably drove 57. Now that it's been raised to 65, you're probably now driving 67. If the sign on the door says, "Sorry we're closed – Do Not Enter," you probably still try the latch anyway. Am I right?

There's something about the Law that makes man want to do what is forbidden. So the Old Covenant – The Law – was inadequate. Man needed more from God than just a long list of rules and regulations. He needed a mediator. He didn't need someone to frown and shake a finger in his face – he needed someone to intercede for him and remove his sin and give him the power to overcome.

According to the Law, that was supposed to be the job of the priest. The Old Testament priest was called by God to mediate man's sin. God knew that man was sinful, and He understood that a plan for forgiveness had to be put in place. As a result, He established the priestly order. And the primary responsibility of the priest was to offer sacrifices for sin (see Heb. 5:1). He was to carry the blood into the holy place and spill the blood on the altar, thereby making atonement.

But the problem was, the priests were sinful too. Even the high priest. So that because of his sin, his work as mediator put him in a very precarious position. Do you realize that when the high priest entered the Holy of Holies they tied a rope around his ankle? Do you know why? It's because if while in there he did something stupid, or if he entered into that place with sin in his heart – the magnificent, resplendent glory of God, which demands an environment of absolute purity, would instantly kill him on the spot. That's where the rope came in. If he died, while attempting to make atonement, they'd just drag him out! I don't know about you, but that rope wouldn't engender a great deal of confidence on my part concerning my high priest's ability to mediate sins!

So God, understanding the inadequacy of the Law and the

imperfection of the priests, said:

> The time is coming when
> I will make a new covenant
> with the house of Israel
> and with the house of Judah.
> This is the covenant I will make with the house of Israel
> after that time, declares the Lord.
> I will put my laws in their minds
> and write them on their hearts.
> I will be their God,
> and they will be my people.
> No longer will a man teach his neighbor,
> Or a man his brother, saying, "Know the Lord,"
> because they will all know me,
> from the least of them to the greatest.
> For I will forgive their wickedness
> and will remember their sins no more (Heb. 8:8b,10-12).

Then, in the fullness of time, God's promise was fulfilled.

When Christ came as high priest of the good things that are already here, he went through the greater and more perfect tabernacle that is not man-made, that is to say, not a part of this creation. He did not enter by means of the blood of goats and calves; but he entered the Most Holy Place once for all by his own blood having obtained eternal redemption. The blood of goats and bulls and the ashes of a heifer sprinkled on those who are ceremonially unclean sanctify them so that they are outwardly clean. How much more, then, will the blood of Christ, who through the eternal Spirit offered himself unblemished to God, cleanse our consciences from acts that lead to death, so that we may serve the living God!
For this reason Christ is the mediator of a new covenant, that those who are called may receive the promised eternal inheritance – now that he has died as a ransom to set them free from the sins (Heb. 9:11-15a).

Do you see what is being said? Because Jesus Christ

entered the Most Holy Place of God by means of His own blood, functioning in the role of Mediator-Priest, and because He entered in perfection, we don't have to offer sacrifices anymore. And we don't need a priest pastor or an elder to represent us before God either, because Jesus Christ mediated a New Covenant. And by this covenant He has opened wide the curtain of heaven so that you and I, and all who are named by Christ's name, through Christ can enter boldly into the presence of God!

Now just in case there is any confusion concerning the identity of this new Mediator, Paul, writing to his young protege, Timothy, identifies Him in unmistakable terms:

> For there is one God, and one mediator between God and men, *(Note that – there's only one. Who is He?)* the man Christ Jesus (I Tim. 2:5).

Picture it: On one side of the chasm is God. On the other, mankind. And if there is to ever be reconciliation, there must be a mediator. One who can fully identify with both parties and, in the process, bring them back into oneness. The Law couldn't do it. It told man what God wanted, but it failed to empower man to accomplish it. The priests tried but couldn't, because their own sins handicapped them. But Jesus, having been ordained before the foundation of the world, in the fullness of God's time, became that "ONE MEDIATOR BETWEEN GOD AND MAN."

WHAT WAS IT ABOUT JESUS THAT QUALIFIED HIM TO BE OUR MEDIATOR? What was it about Him that made Him different than all of those other priests? Here's where it gets exciting. Now understand: Jesus was commissioned to represent God to man, but also man to God. How could one person pull that off?

Well, in the prologue to John's Gospel, the Apostle tells us. Do you remember what He said? "The Word became flesh." (John 1:14a). That's how He pulled it off. Jesus, being fully God, came to planet earth and took on the flesh of man. We call that the INCARNATION. The root of the word is the Latin word, *carne*, which is translated "flesh." This reminds me of my favorite soup – chili con carne. It literally means, "Chili with flesh." That's the incarnation. God with flesh. And that's exactly what happened. And it had to. Jesus could not have functioned as the representative of man to God unless He knew what it was like to BE a man. In order to properly represent man, He had to take on flesh. SO JESUS BECAME, IN EVERY SENSE OF THE WORD, MAN.

But that brings up another problem. Scripture teaches:

Surely, I have been a sinner from birth (Psa. 51:5).
Even from birth the wicked go astray (Psa. 58:3).
We were by nature children of wrath (Eph. 2:13).

The very clear teaching of Scripture is that when I was conceived in my mother's womb, I was conceived with a nature that was bent toward rebellion against God. And that's true for all mankind. We have a sinful bent from birth and freely wander from the God Who made us.

Now here's the problem: If Jesus was conceived as a man and was born as a man (and He was) – and if part of His job was to represent God – how could He come to earth and become a man and yet at the same time remain free from the pollution of the sin nature in order to still be qualified to represent God? How is it that He could be born and grow to be a man and yet still avoid the plague that has marked all of humanity?

That's where virgin birth comes into play. If Jesus had

been conceived by both of human mother and a human father, he would have been fully man, but He would have been born with a sin nature – and therefore ill-equipped to mediate the mind of God.

However, if he had been ushered to earth on the wings of a white stallion, He would have affirmed His deity! No one would question His divinity! But then, no one would see him as a man, either. He would be, at best, a visitor. An alien in a foreign land.

The only way God could come to earth and take on flesh – and yet still exist in undiminished deity and absolute humanity – is through a virgin birth!

And when I say that Jesus was fully man, I mean FULLY MAN, so fully man that He made dirty diapers. He fell and scraped His knees, and when He did, they bled. At age 15, He may have had pimples and needed Clearasil. As he grew to manhood, he knew what it was to hold down a job. And because He was a carpenter, His hands were rough and scaly, His fingernails chipped and clogged with debris. He was a businessman. He knew what it was like to meet a payroll. To bid on a job and lose it. When He changed careers in mid-life, He often went without food. He had no place He could call home.

You need to understand that Jesus had the same physical needs and constraints that you and I have. He needed regular sleep. He required daily nourishment. He battled depression. He faced rejection. He feared failure. He was tempted by loose women. He sweat, and it probably didn't smell too hot! He snored, and it probably didn't sound too sweet!

And no, I'm not being irreverent, I'm being accurate. You may prefer to worship a God-In-A-Box – a Messiah that you can display on your mantel and polish when the preacher comes to call. You may prefer a sanitary manger scene. Your Jesus may be a sweat-less Jesus. He may be adorned with halos, a bright glow in the face and a soft, demure look in the eyes. But that's not the Jesus of the Bible. Now that kind of Jesus is easier to control, I grant you. That kind of Jesus you can stuff back in His box when you want to do your own thing. But the Jesus of Scripture was not a God-In-A-Box. He was fully human and absolutely divine.

And for the first, and only, time in all of human history, there existed in one body undiminished divinity and absolute humanity in perfect balance. And because of that, Jesus (and Jesus only) is the only One qualified to be our MEDIATOR.

So what was His task as Mediator? It was a two-fold task:

FIRST, HE WAS TO FAIRLY REPRESENT BOTH GOD AND MAN. And because He was both God AND Man, Jesus fulfilled that assignment to perfection. One commentator writes:

> To be of any use, a bridge across a chasm or river must be anchored on both sides. Christ has closed the gap between deity and humanity. He has crossed the grand canyon, so deep and wide, between heaven and earth. He has bridged the chasm that separated man from God. With one foot planted in eternity, he planted the other in time. He who was the eternal Son of God became the Son of Man. And across the bridge, the man Christ Jesus, we can come into the very presence of God, knowing that we are accepted because we have a Mediator. (Expositor's Bible Commentary – I Tim. 2:5).

SECOND, HE WAS TO FULLY RECONCILE MAN BACK TO HIS GOD. Now understand, in *this* case, only one of the parties was at fault. God didn't need to be reconciled to man; man needed to be reconciled to God. Man is the one who rebelled. Man is the renegade. Man is the disloyal offender. So Jesus' task was to reconcile man back to his God. HOW WOULD SUCH RECONCILIATION BE ACCOMPLISHED?

Well, God had determined centuries before that blood was the only acceptable payment for sin. So it was on the cross that Jesus reconciled man, voluntarily paying man's debt of sin by substituting His life in man's place. By dying on the cross, Jesus built a bridge to span the gap which man's sin had caused. And a sin-soaked world found reconciliation through a blood-stained Savior.

When I think of Jesus as the reconciling Mediator, my mind goes back to two scenes which played out during Jesus' last few hours before His death.

Scene One happened when Jesus strode into the temple area and found the money-changers ripping-off the out-of-town visitors who had come to Jerusalem for the Passover. He watched as merchants sold doves and lambs for three times their actual retail value! And He, in righteous indignation, shouted, "Get out of here! This is a house of prayer, and you've turned it into a den of thieves!" Make no mistake, friend. Jesus was no Casper Milquetoast. He was no wimp! Jesus was violently upset! Perhaps at no other time in Jesus's ministry did He so fully express and, therefore understand, God's wrath toward sin and His need to be the Reconciler.

Scene Two pictures our Savior on the cross. He has been nailed to the tree by His accusers. He's hanging between two known thieves. He listens as the crowd and the soldiers, and even one of his fellow condemned, revile and ridicule Him. Yet in the midst of the abuse, Jesus said,

Father, forgive them, For they know not what they are doing (Luke 23:34).

You don't see it in the English text, but in the Greek it's written in the imperfect active tense, conveying the idea of a continued past action. He didn't just say it once, He said it over and over again. "Father forgive them. Father, forgive them. Father, forgive them."

Never before has Jesus asked the Father to forgive anyone. He always did it Himself! In fact, that's what got Him into so much trouble! The Pharisees were constantly haranguing Him for claiming to forgive sin! When He healed someone, He didn't just heal them, He'd forgive them, too! He even said on one occasion,

> While I'm on earth, I have the authority to forgive sin (Mark 2:10).

So why is He now asking the Father to do the forgiving? Because He's not on earth right now. No, spiritually speaking, while Jesus was on the cross, He hung perilously suspended between heaven and earth. As with His own body, He bridges the gap between man and God.

Paul, in referring to the crucifixion, talks of the strange transferral that took place. He said,

> He who knew no sin, became sin on our behalf (II Cor. 5:21).

The blameless, sinless Lamb of God took upon himself, for a brief moment in time, the sins of the entire world. And in that moment, He could no longer be the sin-forgiver – He was the sin-bearer.

It was then that the Father turned His back, the sky went black and Jesus, in horrifying alienation from Heaven, cried out,

My God! My God, why have you forsaken Me? (Matt. 27:46).

It was in that moment, having already fully understood God's wrath, that He now fully experienced man's guilt. He felt the horrible separation, the aching alienation, the haunting silence of His holy Father. Then, His body fully spent, He cried,

It is finished (John 19:30).

And He breathed His last. But that final cry was not a cry of defeat. It was not a pronouncement of approaching death. It was a shout of eternal victory! *"I've done My job! Man's salvation has been provided! Sin is forever atoned! It is finished."* And in that moment, all of God's wrath was fully spent. His justice was satisfied. Sin's payment was paid in full. And when that happened, Jesus's task as Mediator was fulfilled. The bridge was built, the chasm spanned, the gulf enclosed. And instead of suspicion, there is now trust. Instead of alienation, there is oneness. Instead of fear, there is acceptance. Because of Jesus, I can now cross that bridge called Calvary and not only know the joy of forgiveness, but boldly and assuredly luxuriate in the very presence of God!

SELF-SALVATION is a myth. When you stand before God one day, He won't be interested in your morality or even your religiosity. He'll be interested in one thing – "ARE YOU COVERED BY THE BLOOD OF MY SON?" "Did you cross the bridge marked Calvary?" Your claim to eternal salvation is obtained only through Jesus.

I find two eternal truths powerfully illustrated in Jesus's role as Mediator.

FIRST, BECAUSE GOD BECAME MAN, HE UNDER-

STANDS OUR STRUGGLES.

As our Mediator, He knows exactly what we're going through. Scripture says,

> For we do not have a high priest who is unable to sympathize with our weaknesses, but we have one who has been tempted in every way, just as we are – yet was without sin. Let us then approach the throne of grace with confidence, so that we may receive the mercy and find grace to help us in our time of need (Heb. 4:15,16).

Isn't that good to know? He understands when you say, "Lord, I'm beat." Or, "Lord, I'm really hurting." Or, "Lord, I'm weak right now and I need You to help me." Or, "I feel so alone right now." He understands! He was a man! He knows what it's like to fail, to hurt, to lose someone you love, to face temptation, to be discouraged.

We don't serve a God Who has to wonder what it's like to be human. He knows. He came here, He lived, He suffered – and because of that, He knows exactly what you are facing. So tell Him about it! Not matter what "it" is, get "it" off your chest and lay "it" at His throne! Approach His presence with confidence! When you do, you'll find grace there. And mercy. And strength to carry on.

SECOND, BECAUSE HE WAS BOTH GOD AND MAN, HE BECAME MY SAVIOR. The go-between bridged the gap. He paid the price. And he did it out of love.

The story is told of a father named John. John was a good father. He loved his children, and he loved his wife. But his only son, a little boy, was very rebellious. John knew something had to be done in order to break his son's stubborn spirit. So one night at the dinner table, the little boy began yet another tirade and threw his food to the floor. John said, "Son, if you do that one more time, you're going to spend the night in the attic and you're going to go without any supper." Immediately, the boy picked up some more food and threw it down. John, true to his word, marched his son up the stairs to the attic.

About a half-hour later, John began to wonder if he had done the right thing. He said to his wife, "Honey, it's really dark up there. I think I need to go up and bring him down." His wife wisely said, "You can't do that. Even more important than your discipline is your word, and you said that you were going to make him stay up their all night. If you let him come down, you will teach him that you don't mean what you say." He knew she was right so he dropped the issue.

Long into the night, unable to sleep, he kept thinking of his son. Finally, he tiptoed to the kitchen, got some peanut butter and jelly and some bread and made some sandwiches. He went to the attic, opened the door and offered his son a sandwich. Then he laid down beside his son and the two fell asleep together, holding one another in appreciative, gracious love.

That's what Jesus did for you and me. He identified fully with our need. He did it because he loves us.

Being God, He understood the enormity of sin and rebellion. He fully acknowledged God's need for justice.

Being man, He understood the power of temptation and the allure of the flesh. The haunting need for forgiveness.

Being both God and man, He assumed the role of Mediator and built the bridge and spanned the chasm which had, since Eden, separated us.

Have you crossed that Bridge? It's toll free. The God Who came here paid your passage in full. Come on over.

Behold God's Lamb!

9

Although God created man for His pleasure, God's pleasure soon degenerated into intense pain. For the man into whom God had puffed the breath of life soon rebelled against His Maker. He sinned; and his sin polluted a relationship that was once pure and holy. Separation resulted. God sent man packing from His holy Garden; and throughout the ensuing years, man's sin became so blatant that God actually regretted creating man in the first place. And yet, from the very moment of man's sin, in fact, long before man had sinned – God had set into motion a plan. A plan whereby sinful man could find full pardon and absolute forgiveness of sin. The plan? God Himself would become man, and He would pay with His own life (indeed, His own blood) the price which man's sin demanded.

I like the way Jill Briscoe eloquently describes this in a little book entitled, "Prime Rib and Apple." She describes the moment when Eve took of the forbidden fruit and ate it. The character called "Prime Rib" is Eve and "Omnipotence" is God. She writes:

> Prime Rib (Eve) took the hand Omnipotence (God) had fashioned from her little piece of bone and with it plucked the piece of forbidden fruit. She placed it between the lips Omnipotence had framed to praise Him and absorbed into her system the poisons of independence, selfishness and death. And IMMEDIATELY JESUS PREPARED TO LEAVE FOR BETHLEHEM. (Jill Briscoe, *Prime Rib and Apple*: Grand Rapids: Zondervan Publishing House, 1976, p. 19.)

In fact, when Jesus arrived in Bethlehem, He made it quite clear why He had come. He said, "I did not come to be served, but to serve and to give my life as a ransom for many" (Mark 10:45). *"I came to do for you what you could never do alone. I came to redeem you. I came to purchase your forgiveness."*

That's why He went to CALVARY. Scripture emphatically states that "without the shedding of blood there is no forgiveness of sin" (Heb. 9:22). No forgiveness. God's methodology for saving people is blood. Your redemption is blood-bought. Your sins required bloodshed before you could receive God's forgiveness.

Now I realize there are many who don't understand. They hear us talk about Christ's blood and sing about His blood and commune together in remembrance of His blood and they think: "YUK! You Christians are a bunch of glorified cannibals!" And let's face it, Calvary was gruesome. The whole process of crucifixion was a messy, gory undertaking. But God's pre-ordained standard for forgiveness had to be fulfilled. Blood had to be shed. Why?

Well, tucked away in the Constitution of ancient Israel (Leviticus) we're told why. Listen to these words:

> For the life of a creature is in its blood, and I have given it to you to make atonement for yourselves on the altar; it is the blood that makes atonement for one's life (Lev. 17:11).

Blood makes atonement for sin. That is, it "reconciles" sin, it "covers over" sin. Why? Because blood is life! "The life . . . is in the blood." And when blood is poured out, a life is laid down; and only an act that severe could underscore the extreme view which God takes toward sin.

You see, God faced a dilemma in His relationship with man. God, being holy, just couldn't bow to our sin or pretend sin didn't exist – yet the heart of God couldn't just write man off either. It's as though God were saying, "I really want to bless my child. I want to fellowship with him and enjoy communion with him; but I can't as long as there is sin in his life! That sin has to be removed! And the only way sin can be removed is if there is a substitute, One who will shed the necessary blood so that sin can be forgiven."

And that's exactly what Jesus did for us. He died that we might have life. He spilled His blood that our sins might be covered.

That teaching is familiar to most of us, because that's the message of the Gospel. But what you may not realize is that long before Jesus arrived in Bethlehem, GOD HAD BEEN PREPARING HIS PEOPLE FOR BLOOD-BOUGHT REDEMPTION. In fact, throughout the whole of the Old Testament, a *scarlet thread* can be found, weaving its way from the Garden all the way to Mt. Calvary.

Contrary to popular opinion, blood sacrifice did not begin

at Passover. As I said, blood-bought redemption can be traced all the way back to the Garden. You may remember that in Genesis 3, we're told that when Adam and Eve sinned, God Himself clothed Adam and Eve with animal skins. Now in order to do that, an animal – perhaps a lamb (we don't know) – had to shed his blood so that their sins could be properly covered.

There were other patriarchal sacrifices as well. Remember Abel's sacrifice? It was more acceptable to God than Cain's. Why? Because it involved blood. Again, an animal – perhaps a lamb – shed his life so that Abel could make an acceptable sacrifice to God.

Then, in Genesis 22, we come to a very tender moment in the life of Abraham. You remember the story. Abraham waited for nearly 100 years before God finally gave him the son He had promised. That boy brought so much joy into their home that he and Sarah named him, "Laughter." Isaac. But one day, the Lord came to Abraham, and said,

> "Abraham!" "Here I am," he replied. Then God said, "Take your son, your only son Isaac, whom you love, and go to the region of Moriah. Sacrifice him there as a burnt offering on one of the mountains I will tell you about." (Gen. 22:1b,2).

Parent, put yourself in Abraham's place. After decades of coping with the heartache of infertility, Abraham finally has a son, and God now wants to take that son away? Yet, amazingly . . . .

> Early the next morning Abraham got up and saddled his donkey. He took with him two of his servants and his son Isaac. When he had cut enough wood for the burnt offering, he set out for the place God had told him about. On the third day Abraham looked up and saw the place in the distance. He said

to his servants, "Stay here with the donkey while I and the boy go over there. We will worship and then we will come back to you." Abraham took the wood for the burnt offering and placed it on his son Isaac, and he himself carried the fire and the knife (Gen. 22:3-6a).

Isaac was no pre-schooler, folks. He was big enough to carry wood, wasn't he? And as father and son climbed that mountain, Isaac, who had gone with his father on many sacrifices, was confused.

As the two of them went on together, Isaac spoke up and said to his father Abraham, "Father?" "Yes, my son?" Abraham replied. "The fire and wood are here," Isaac said, "but where is the Lamb for the burnt offering?" (Gen. 22:6b,7).

By the way, that's the first time in Scripture a LAMB was specifically mentioned in Scripture as the preferred animal of sacrifice. And Isaac says, "Dad, we forgot something! We've got everything but the lamb! Where's the lamb?"

God himself will provide the lamb, my son (Gen. 22:8a).

You know the rest of the story. Abraham tied Isaac to the altar, and raised the knife into the air, fully prepared to thrust it into his son's heart – when suddenly an angel called out, "Abraham! Abraham!" I picture Abraham thinking, "Oh, I'm so glad you called! Why did you wait so long?" The angel said,

"Do not lay a hand on the boy," he said. "Do not do anything to him. Now I know that you fear God, because you have not withheld from me your son, your only son." Abraham looked up and there in a thicket he saw a ram caught by its horns. He went over and took the ram and sacrificed it as a burnt offering instead of his son (Gen. 22:12,13).

What a momentous occasion in Abraham's life! And even more, what powerful imagery of an even greater substitute who was yet to come! Another "only son" Who would not be spared, but Who, as the PRECIOUS LAMB OF GOD WOULD BE PROVIDED BY GOD AS THE BLOOD-SACRIFICE FOR ALL OF MANKIND. That's what the Lord had in mind when He pulled Abraham aside and said,

> Through your offspring all nations on earth will be blessed (Gen. 22:18a).

As we turn our attention to Exodus 12, we see that as great as that moment on Moriah may have been, no event more powerfully pointed to the coming Lamb of God than did the Jewish Passover. Here's the historical setting: Israel had been held captive in Egypt for 430 years. Moses had been commissioned by God to free them from captivity and lead them to the Promised Land. But Pharaoh had so far stubbornly refused to let the people go. Even after nine horrible plagues, he still refused. The tenth and final plague was the worst of all. If Pharaoh still refused to release the people, the Death Angel would pass over Egypt and every firstborn son in the land would die, while the first born children of the Israelites would live. How would the Angel know which homes were Jewish and which homes were Egyptian? God comes to Moses and explains:

> Tell the whole community of Israel that on the tenth day of this month each man is to take a lamb for his family, one for each household.

Mark that. Every Jewish family was to secure a lamb. And not just any lamb . . . .

The animals you choose must be year-old males without defect (Exod. 12:3,5a).

Again, this is another picture looking ahead to the coming Lamb of God, Who would be, in fact, a Lamb without spot or blemish. Remember what was said about Him? That He was "tempted in every way, just as we are – yet was without sin (without blemish)." The unblemished lamb of Passover was a symbol which pointed ahead to the coming Christ.

Take care of them until the fourteenth day of the month, when all the people of the community of Israel must slaughter them at twilight. Then they are to take some of the blood and put it on the sides and tops of the doorframes of the houses where they eat the lambs (Exod. 12:6,7).

Why were they to do that?

On that same night I will pass through Egypt and strike down every firstborn – both men and animals – and I will bring judgment on all the gods of Egypt; I am the Lord. The blood will be a sign for you on the houses where you are; and when I see the blood I will pass over you. No destructive plague will touch you when I strike Egypt (Exod. 12:12,13).

When the Death Angel would pass, bringing the last plague upon Egypt, only those homes with blood on the doorframes would be passed over. Hence, the event's name. You see, the *BLOOD OF THE LAMB WAS THEIR SALVATION!* Now they didn't understand how that could be. There certainly was no logical reason any intelligent person would knowingly smear blood on his door jamb thinking that the blood could save his son's life. But God told them to do it – so they did it! And the only homes that didn't know death were the homes that had blood on their doors – just as God had said.

After having been set free from Egypt, the Israelites traveled to the base of Mt. Sinai. There they received the Law of God which would govern their nation, much of which has been preserved for us in the book of Leviticus. And a very central part of that Law had to do with the SACRIFICE. What I want you to see is that from this point forward, whenever a sinful Jew wanted to restore fellowship with God and find forgiveness for sin, he had to perform a sacrifice. An innocent lamb had to be selected and slaughtered and sacrificed.

> When a leader sins...and does what is forbidden in any of the commands of the Lord his God, he is guilty (Lev. 4:22).

Sin has occurred, restitution is required. What must he do to find forgiveness?

First, "he must bring as his offering a male goat without defect" (Lev. 4:23). He must secure an unblemished animal. Sometimes the animal would be a bull, occasionally a dove or a pigeon, most often either a goat (as in this passage) or a lamb.

Second, he is to "bring it." Bring it where? To the tabernacle! Which means, literally, *"The House of God."* He had to walk into the very presence of the glory of God with known sin in his life. Can you imagine? The only way he could do that was if he had under his arm a lamb. Then and only then could he step into the holy place and symbolically place his hands on the lamb.

That's the third thing that must be done. "He is to lay his hand on the goat's head." He leaned all of his weight on the lamb, saying in effect: "I transfer *MY* guilt and *MY* sin to this animal. This lamb is my blood-substitute."

Then, he was to "slaughter it at the place where the burnt offering is slaughtered before the Lord. It is a sin offering" (Lev. 4:24).

Finally, He is to

> ... take some of the blood of the sin offering with his finger and put it on the horns of the altar of burnt offering and pour out the rest of the blood at the base of the altar. He shall burn all the fat on the altar as he burned the fat of the fellowship offering. In this way the priest will make atonement for the man's sin, and he will be forgiven (Lev. 4:25,26).

Can you imagine living like that? We are so removed from anything so gruesome, but it was central to Jewish culture. It was so common that their everyday clothes were permanently blood-stained because of their many trips to the tabernacle. The only way to find forgiveness was through the blood, remember? Therefore, throughout the history of the Jews, literally hundreds upon hundreds of lambs were slaughtered at the altar. Every day, from dawn until dusk, the priests offered sacrifices. There were daily sacrifices, yearly sacrifices, festal sacrifices, festival sacrifices – millions of gallons of blood, literally, were poured out on those altars.

Yet even so, their sins were not really forgiven. At least not in the sense of a permanent forgiveness. They were just sort of ROLLED BACK! Even on the Day of Atonement, (Yom Kippur), Israel's national day of forgiveness – when they would sprinkle blood on the scapegoat and send him running wildly in the wilderness, symbolically removing the sins of the entire nation – sin was not permanently removed. And the people knew that. They knew it was just a symbol of the GREAT LAMB OF GOD Who would one day come and take away all sin forever!

But it wouldn't happen in their lifetime. So every day . . . day in and day out, week in and week out, year in and year out . . . they trudged to the tabernacle with their lamb tucked under their arm. That's just the way life was. You sin? You go find an animal, then you go to the priest, place your hands on the animal, slaughter the animal, catch his blood and then pour it out on the altar. Two days later, you sin again? You find another animal and another priest, place your hands on the animal, slaughter the animal, catch the blood and pour it on the altar. But then that night you sin again! So you find another animal . . . And that happened over and over and over again!

That's why Isaiah's words came to mean so much to the Jew. The verses of Isaiah 53 are so familiar to us that they've nearly lost their meaning! But to the Jew, they meant everything! They were tired of always having their sin before them. They were weary from so much sacrifice. They were sick of seeing so much bloodshed. To those weary hearts, Isaiah's words of prophecy provided much-needed hope:

> But he was pierced for our transgressions, he was crushed for our iniquities (Isa. 53:5a).

They had been piercing and crushing animals for years! But now there would come a "he" who would be pierced and crushed, not another "it."

> We all, like sheep, have gone astray, each of us has turned to his own way; and the Lord has laid on him the iniquity of us all (Isa. 53:6).

Do you see that? On "Him." Isaiah, with perfect 20-20 prophetic vision, told about a different kind of transferral.

Instead of transferring a man's sins to some lamb, or an entire nation's sins to some scapegoat, one day, God would transfer the sins of all mankind – past, present and future – to the shoulders of a "Him!" But this "Him," instead of just rolling back sin, this coming "lamb" would take the sin away forever! His sacrifice, His blood would provide PERMANENT forgiveness.

He was oppressed and afflicted, yet he did not open his mouth; he was led like a lamb to the slaughter (Isa. 53:7a).

He would be a pure, spotless Lamb, but a different kind of sacrificial lamb than had ever been slaughtered. This Lamb would remove the guilt of all sin in one fell swoop!

What a wonderful promise! But I want you to see that it got worse before it got better. After Isaiah put down his pen, 700 years passed – and still no lamb. In fact, when Malachi finished his prophecy, there was not another word from heaven for over 400 years. It was as though there would *never* be another word from the Lord.

During this silence, a number of religious societies were formed. Perhaps the most famous group called themselves "Pharisees." And because they too were so weary of the sacrifices, they tried their best to live above sin. They thought, "*If we take the Law and if we clarify it, then we'll understand it better and, as a result, sin much less. Then we won't have to go to the tabernacle and do the sacrifice as often.*" But what resulted was the exact reverse. The more intricate clarifications resulted in more potential for deviation and, as a result, more sin – not less. And with more sin came more sacrifices. At the turn of the first century, there were so many sacrifices that blood flowed from the tabernacle like water from a spigot.

But then came a stranger from the wilderness. They called him "The Baptizer." He wore camel hair and ate locusts and wild honey. And he traveled the countryside telling of a new kingdom. There would come after him One who was so great ... so holy ... that John wouldn't even be worthy to tie his shoe laces!

And then, the GREAT ONE appeared. When John saw Him, his mind was immediately transported back to Isaiah 53. And he cried out, "Behold! The Lamb of God, who takes away the sin of the world."

Could it be? Could it be that finally He has come? The One who is going to put an end to this sacrificial madness? "YES," John says. "It's the Lamb! He's here! The fullness of time has arrived. The Lamb has come. And He's going to take away all sin ... once and for all!"

Jesus, God's only Son, out of obedience to the Father and love for mankind, willingly emptied Himself and became a little lamb – The Lamb! But even though everyone had been looking for Him, when He finally came, so few seemed to understand. The religious crowd tried to trip Him up, and when they couldn't do that, they determined to eliminate Him. Crowds laughed at Him, scoffers mocked Him, His detractors ridiculed Him, His own family scorned Him. The soldiers at Pilate's Praetorium taunted Him. They blindfolded and hit Him, saying, "Tell us, King, who was it who hit you?" He stood naked before them, their spit mixed with His blood which streamed down his face.

Then came Calvary. Jesus carried His own instrument of death to Golgotha. His tired, abused body took the form of a cross as nails were driven into His palms, piercing them as the iron grips deeply into the wood. His cross was then lifted between two thieves and dropped with a thud into its prepared hole.

Meanwhile, the disciples cowered in the shadows. One of the thieves cried out for mercy. The crowd of spectators shouted, "Come down from the cross! Then we'll believe you, King!" But there was no rescue, there was no miracle. Only a shout of agony which rumbled across the horizon like the roaring thunder as Jesus, His body wracked with pain, cried out, "MY GOD, WHY HAVE YOU FORSAKEN ME?" (Mark 15:34). A bit later He whispered, "It is finished" (John 19:30). And thus spoken, He breathed His last. And when he died, His death seemed such a senseless tragedy that nature itself convulsed; the ground shook as in an earthquake; tombs cracked open; the solar system shuddered; the sun hid; and the sky went black!

But wait a minute! Why the shock? Why the surprise? From the beginning of time, God had promised a Lamb. Finally, at history's perfect moment, the Lamb arrived. And He shed His blood, laying down His life for man's sin. Isn't that what He was supposed to do? Wasn't that His job? Of course it was! Listen! As bad as it got on Golgotha, and it got really bad, the cross was not an accident – it was the Lamb's ultimate assignment.

Do you remember what Peter said on Pentecost? "This man, Jesus, was handed over to you by God's set purpose and foreknowledge" (Acts 2:23). Wow! The cross was no accident. It was not some tragic surprise. It was God's plan. It was His pre-determined decision. Isaiah said, "It was the Lord's will to crush Him."

The cross was sketched into God's plan from the beginning. From the moment Eve ate the fruit, the shadow of the cross began to loom across the horizon. Thus, when Jesus lifted His head and said, "It is finished!", it was not a cry of defeat. It was not a pronouncement of approaching death. It was a shout of eternal victory!

The same Jesus who died on the cross planted the tree from which the beams were carved. He placed the ore, the very ore used to cast the nails which held his hands in place, into Earth's belly. He knew of His death before He took His first breath! From infancy, He knew His destiny. He knew He was God's Lamb. And He set His face like a flint toward Golgotha.

That's why He rebuked Peter for slicing off the soldier's ear. That's why Pilate failed to intimidate Him. That's why the ropes which cuffed his wrists were unnecessary. That's why no guards were needed to keep Him on that tree. He wasn't going anywhere! He had a job to do! A plan to fulfill! And even if there had never been a Judas, no trial, no soldiers and no Pilate – Jesus would have climbed the cross and nailed Himself to that tree if He had to. BECAUSE HE WAS GOD'S LAMB! And the Lamb had to be sacrificed!

DO YOU SEE HOW IT ALL TIES TOGETHER?

Isaac, years before, asked his daddy a simple question. He said, "Daddy, where is the lamb?" It was answered at Bethany, near the Jordan when a gruff Prophet of Righteousness cried, "Behold the Lamb of God!"

Every year at PASSOVER, each family took a lamb to the temple to be killed. This happened at mid-day in order that all the preparations could be completed by Sabbath. But on this particular year, something was different. At the same time when thousands of lambs were being slaughtered in the center of the temple area – just outside the city, on a little knoll, THE LAMB OF GOD WAS BEING SLAUGHTERED ON A

PIECE OF WOOD. That's why Paul accurately called Jesus, "The Passover Lamb who has been sacrificed" (I Cor. 5:6,7). And because of His sacrifice, no other sacrifice is needed. Because God's Lamb willingly shouldered the most gruesome of all assignments, those daily, weekly, yearly trips to the tabernacle, with a yearling lamb in tow, are no longer required. The Hebrew writer looks back to those sacrifices and assures us with these words:

> The law is only a shadow of the good things that are coming – not the realities themselves. For this reason it can never, by the same sacrifices repeated endlessly year after year, make perfect those who draw near to worship. If it could, would they not have stopped being offered? For the worshippers would have been cleansed once for all and would no longer have felt guilty for their sins. But those sacrifices are an annual reminder of sins (Heb. 10:1-3).

Can you imagine living like that? A man would sin and immediately a massive wall of separation would stand between him and God. So he'd make a sacrifice and snatch just a glimpse of God's glory, but then it would shut up again because of another sin. So he'd get another lamb and pour the blood out so the wall would open, only to see it slam shut again. Why?

> Because it is impossible for the blood of bulls and goats to take away sins (Heb. 10:4).

That's why the Great Lamb had to come! Nothing else could satisfy God's wrath. Only Him. Only His pure, unblemished blood would suffice.

> Therefore, when Christ (God's Lamb) came into the world, he said: "Sacrifice and offering you did not desire, but a body

you prepared for me; with burnt offerings and sin offerings you were not pleased." Then I said, "Here I am – it is written about me in the scroll – I have come to do your will, O God." And by that will, we have been made holy through the sacrifice of the body of Jesus Christ once for all (Heb. 10:5-7, 10).

The wall has been demolished. God's glory is ours to behold. The Lamb laid down his life for our sins. That's why verse 14 says, "There is no longer any sacrifice for sin." Glory be to God's Lamb! We have been fully and entirely and eternally redeemed! No more lambs are required!

But wait a minute! I left out a very important part of this story! God's Lamb didn't stay dead, did He? No! Three days later, that limp, frail, lifeless figure of Calvary became the glorious, eternal victor over sin – as Jesus bodily broke the chains of death and the grave and burst from that tomb gloriously alive! The sinless, perfect Lamb not only fulfilled the purchase price for mankind's deliverance on Friday, but by Sunday, He had gloriously resurrected from the dead – never to die again! And now, He's in heaven, preparing a place for you and me, so that where He is now, there we may be also. And when God's heavenly calendar has been completed, God's Lamb will return and we shall see Him face to face!

I mention that because the only other place in the New Testament where the Lamb is mentioned, other than those already discussed, is the book of Revelation. And He's mentioned there no less than 29 times – and always with a view of victory!

My favorite section is in Revelation 5. Listen to these words:

Then I saw a Lamb, looking as if it had been slain, standing in the center of the throne, encircled by the four living creatures and the elders. He had seven horns and seven eyes, which are the seven spirits of God sent out into all the earth. He came and took the scroll from the right hand of him who sat on the throne. And when he had taken it, the four living creatures and the twenty-four elders fell down before the Lamb. Each one had a harp and they were holding golden bowls full of incense, which are the prayers of the saints. And they sang a new song: "You are worthy to take the scroll and to open its seals, because you were slain, and with your blood you purchased men for God from every tribe and language and people and nation."

Then I looked and heard the voice of many angels, numbering thousands upon thousands, and ten thousand times ten thousand. They encircled the throne and the living creatures and the elders. In a loud voice they sang: "Worthy is the Lamb, who was slain, to receive power and wealth and wisdom and strength and honor and glory and praise!"

Then I heard every creature in heaven and on earth and under the earth and on the sea, and all that is in them, singing: "To him who sits on the throne and to the Lamb be praise and honor and glory and power, for ever and ever!" (Rev. 5:6-9, 11-13).

Did you read that closely? "Every creature" will sing that song! That includes you and me. One day we will join the innumerable host of heaven around the throne of the Lamb, and together we will raise our voices in rapturous doxology, singing: "Worthy, worthy is the Lamb!"

So that nothing of the impact of these truths is lost, I want to turn to the words of the Apostle Paul. In Ephesians 1, Paul mentions, in a long list of spiritual blessings which are ours in Christ, the two most wondrous results which come from Jesus the Lamb. Look at these words:

"In Him (The Lamb) we have redemption through his blood, the forgiveness of sins, in accordance with the riches of God's grace" (Eph. 1:7). There they are. In Christ, God's

191

Lamb, we enjoy two unparalleled blessings: REDEMPTION and FORGIVENESS OF SIN.

Redemption means "to purchase by the payment of a price." And that's exactly what the Lamb did. We deserved to die because of our sin. But Jesus came and He paid in full the price we deserved to pay. Truly "the Lord laid upon Him the iniquity of us all" (Isa. 53:6b).

What was the payment price? "His blood." Peter put it like this:

> For you know that it was not with perishable things such as silver or gold that you were redeemed from the empty way of life handed down to you from your forefathers, but with the precious blood of Christ, a lamb without blemish or defect (I Pet. 1:18,19).

The Lamb was lifted up on a cross to pay for your redemption. *So how do you receive that payment as your own?* Just like the Jew of old, you must lay your hands on the Lamb. You must personally appropriate Him into your life. You must take all that you are – the gunk, the garbage, all that you've ever said or done – and lean heavily on Jesus. When you do that, you transfer your guilt to the Lamb.

Once that happens, you can look guilt straight in the face and acknowledge it. You can freely admit the whole stinking mess, but then point to the cross and say, "But He's taken care of it. I have been redeemed!"

There's a second benefit. Not only did the Lamb provide redemption, but He also purchased "the forgiveness of sins." In the original language this phrase is written in the imperfect active indicative. I mention that only because the imperfect active looks back to a past event which has resulted in a continual future action. Because of our redemption in Christ, because of the past event of Calvary, because of the Lamb's shed blood – not only could I claim forgiveness on the day I obeyed Jesus Christ, but I can continue to claim His forgiveness even now . . . and I will always be able to do so, even to the day of eternity.

Forgiveness. Certainly this is one of the most central truths of our salvation. It's definitely one of the most blessed.

Remember what David wrote after he was forgiven? After having lived for nearly a year in open rebellion and compromise, after having endured the drastic impact of his sin – the loss of his health, the decline of his nation, the disruption of his family – he repented. Sometime after that, he looked back on the whole sordid affair and wrote these words:

Blessed is he whose transgressions are forgiven, whose sins are covered. Blessed is the man whose sin the Lord does not count against him (Psa. 32:1,2).

The word "blessed" in the Hebrew is in the plural form. It literally reads, "Happy many times over" is the person who has been forgiven! "Happy, happy, happy, happy, happy" is the one whose sin the Lord does not count against him! Do you get the feeling maybe David was pleased about something? And why not? His sins were removed from him! His rebellion would not be held against him! How wonderful! I tell you, you'd be happy too!

David had been living in self-indulgence for over a year. He did whatever he pleased, but nothing he did pleased him. He went for whatever he wanted, but nothing he wanted seemed to satisfy. He chased happiness, but happiness seemed to fly away with the wind – until, that is, he received forgiveness.

Perhaps you are squirming right now because you are

presently where David once was. You've been doing your own thing, yet you've never been more miserable in all your life. You've tried to ignore the pain, but your burden is growing more and more cumbersome. Do you know why? It's because we were created to live in harmonious fellowship with our Creator. Whenever sin comes into the picture, fellowship is cut off. And when fellowship with God is cut off, misery inevitably results.

Augustine said, "Thou has created us for Thyself, and our hearts are restless until they find their rest in Thee." And we know that! And we yearn for the peace that comes from right standing before God. But here's the struggle: You've been living in compromise and rebellion for a long time, even though you desperately want to make your life count again. You wonder: Can it ever be the same? Can it be as it once was? If you're a child of God, and if you will simply acknowledge your sin as sin and confess it before Him, you can claim God's forgiveness through the blood of the Lamb. GUARANTEED.

But don't take my word for it! The Apostle John said it:

If we confess our sins, he is faithful and just and will forgive us our sins and purify us from all unrighteousness (I John 1:9).

No exception clauses, no fine print at the bottom of the page, no if's, and's or but's. That tells me something. It tells me that no matter what you have done, no matter what you have become, you can be forgiven. Go ahead! Devise the most heinous sin imaginable! Even that sin can be covered by the shed blood of the Lamb.

Do you struggle with that? Inevitably, when I teach on forgiveness, someone will say, "But Steve, you don't know what I've done. I've done some horrible stuff." I like the way Steve Brown responds to that comment. He says, "Do you really believe Jesus died on the cross for popcorn?" Really! Do you think He spilled out his blood for nothing but little white lies and four-letter words? I want you to know that God knows exactly how bad you are and how bad I am, and no matter how bad it is – IT'S FORGIVEN.

And not only is it forgiven, but let me tell you what God does with our sin when He forgives it. He does three things:

As far as the east is from the west, so far has he removed our transgressions from us (Psa. 103:12).

When God forgives our sin, He separates us from our sin as far as the east is from the west. And friend, that's a "fur piece!" If you start heading west and keep going west – you will never get to east; and if you head east and keep going east – will never get to west. And that's exactly God's point. When He forgives your sin, He removes it far away from you.

But there's more. God also promises to:

Tread our sins underfoot and hurl all our iniquities into the depths of the sea (Micah 7:19b).

He'll trample our sins, then He'll put them where no one can dredge them up again – He'll put them in the depths of the sea.

But there's one more thing God does with forgiven sin. In Isaiah 43:25 He promises, "I will remember your sins no more." When God forgives a sin, He banishes that sin from His mind, never to be remembered by Him again. Never. Isn't that remarkable? God doesn't just forgive – He forgets. He erases the board. He destroys the evidence. He burns the microfilm. He refuses to keep a record of my wrongs.

Now you'll remember them. And so will I. The "ghost of sins past" will haunt you, count on it. He'll try to trip you up and immobilize you. He'll remind you of that horrid lie, that business trip you took, that compromise which marked your life, that time you exploded with rage, that time your jealousy reached out and hurt someone you really do love. You will come under attack by the "GHOST OF SINS PAST."

SO WHO YA' GONNA CALL?

Forget the GHOSTBUSTERS. You call the Lamb. You call on a God Who has a mercifully horrible memory. Thanks to the Lamb, our God is a graciously forgetful God.

One day I will stand before the throne of God. Frankly I'm going to be quite apprehensive because there's a lot in my life I'm not proud of. I'll probably stammer and stutter and clear my throat a lot as I try to cover my bases. I'll say, "God, I'm sorry about all those evil thoughts, and I'm sorry for what I did . . . what I didn't do. God, forgive me for the garbage of my life." Then He'll pull out the recordbook and say, "Steve, I don't know what you're talking about. You see, there's blood all over your pages. I can't read a thing." Then the Lamb will lean over His shoulder and say, "Father, it's because Steve belongs to Me. The blood proves that he is Mine." Then the Father will say, "Well, come on in, Steve. Enter into the joy of My heaven."

What have you done with God's Lamb? Have you received His payment for your sins? The payment was made in full. There is no need for another sacrifice. The ultimate sacrifice has already been accomplished at Calvary. What you need to do is put your hands on the Lamb and accept His payment for your sin.

And if you have received His payment, then you need to tune up your voice! Because one of these days, He's going to split the heavens asunder, and you and I will find ourselves surrounded by the heavenly hosts, singing, "Worthy! Worthy is the Lamb that was slain!" HALLELUJAH!

He Is Alpha and Omega
10

If there is one thing you can count on never changing, it's
that things inevitably will change. And never has that been
more true than it is today. Because today, *CHANGE ITSELF
IS CHANGING*. It's coming faster and faster and faster. You
learn some new bit of information today? Don't even bother
to write it down. Tomorrow it will be carted away to
the museum and placed alongside other articles of antiquity . . . like the electric typewriter. New technologies abound.
Knowledge is expanding at mega-proportions. There are too
many opportunities and so little time to investigate them.

Life in the nineties could accurately be described as life in
the white-water rapids of change. And all of us, whether we
like it or not, are being swept downstream – internally horrified by the constantly changing landscape. Some of us try to

master the rapids, straining desperately to keep pace. Others stand on the shore, watching the world rush by, leaving us behind in hopeless bewilderment.

Some time ago, I was invited, along with several other professional, business and community leaders from across our state to examine the question, *"What will life be like in the year 2002?"* Our assignment was to examine the trends which will dominate life as we enter the next century. Each was to address the topic from his own perspective, and when the parts were added to form the whole, the changes we discussed were, to me, absolutely mind-boggling.

We spoke of the population explosion. I was intrigued to learn that it was not until 1850 that our world reached one billion people. By 1930, that number doubled. By 1960, the figure reached three billion. We've already hit five billion, and, by the end of the century, statisticians tell us earth's population will soar to seven billion.

We talked about the ecological impact of such growth. For example, waste disposal will be big business in the year 2002 – we will reach capacity in our landfills and find that there is no more land to fill; the disposal of toxic and nuclear waste will continue to demand creative and thoughtful solutions; the problem of acid rain will proliferate; the depletion of the ozone and the resultant warming trend will continue to dominate the agenda of those concerned about our ecological health.

We discussed the problem of world hunger and our growing inability to address it. We talked about the seemingly unwinnable war on drugs and the impact drug usage will have on future generations. We talked about the shrinking global village and a future one world government. We discussed the aging of America – the fact that by the year 2000, the majority of Americans will be 50 years of age or older. We talked about an increasing tendency to look to government for answers to our social problems, while at the same time being gripped with a cynicism that government is just as helpless to find the solutions as we.

Then we talked about the explosion of information. Someone mentioned that if we could measure knowledge by space, then all of man's knowledge from the beginning of time to 1845 could be measured in one inch. From 1845-1945, it would grow to three inches. From 1945-today? It would extend beyond the height of the Washington Monument!

We talked about that overload and agreed that it will only continue to worsen as our technology makes more and more information available to us. There is no doubt that the industrial age has passed the baton to the information age, but the human of the 21st century will find himself increasingly unable to keep up with the growing pile of knowledge which will demand his attention and digestion.

As I listened to this fascinating discussion, I concluded that, on a personal, individual, psychological level, two results will inevitably occur: *An abdication of personal responsibility coupled with a gnawing sense of absolute helplessness.* As information explodes, as the rapids of change reach tidal wave proportions, as the marketplace becomes global, as environmental concerns and human rights issues multiply – the individual will feel less and less capable of making a difference. He will grow less and less confident that there is indeed a solution and that he could actually take part in it. Man, in the year 2002, will grow increasingly hopeless and frighteningly helpless.

As a result, though the superstructure of humanity will continue to expand, the internal support system will systematically crumble. How will it happen?

For one, substance abuse will proliferate. The only means

201

of escape from the maddening, frightening world arena will be one's chemical of choice.

Sexual and physical child abuse will continue to skyrocket, as man's inability to control his environment will drive him to control someone who can't resist his authority.

Divorce rates will soar, and homes will be divided at epidemic proportions as faithfulness to a commitment will seem pointless and archaic.

Violent crimes such as murder and rape, as well as gang warfare, will systematically turn the street corners of America into a seething battleground of hopelessness.

Volunteerism will decline, as less and less of us will sense any ability to effect change in a culture gone mad.

As hopelessness and helplessness increase, anxieties will proliferate, alienation and isolation will reign!

Sounds terribly exciting, doesn't it? Sounds like an ideal world in which to raise kids, am I right? Let me be frank: I tend to be an optimist, but I left that meeting unusually sober and frightened. I thought, "This world is going to hell in a handbag, and there's not a thing we can do about it."

I boarded the plane for home, totally consumed with my fears. But as the plane took on altitude, I looked out the cockpit window and I saw the lights of the city grow increasingly dim and minute. *It was then that I remembered the Creator.* And I remembered that He Who made it all has promised to maintain it all. That He Who was on the Throne in the Beginning will remain on the Throne until the End. I remembered that He holds all things together by the power of His hand, and that there is nothing on our world's agenda which extends beyond the scope of His power. That there is no change which has ever frightened Him, no technological advance which serves to threaten Him. No, everything we think might happen and that which we could never dream will happen – He already knows and is in absolute control.

Calmed by that assurance, it was then that I quietly formed with my lips a name. A name that could only be applied to Jesus. A name that no one but He could rightfully assume. I whispered, "Jesus, You alone are *THE ALPHA and THE OMEGA*, Who is and Who was and Who is to come, the Almighty."

Now many of the names applied to Jesus could rightly also be applied to others – such as Servant, Lord, Master or even King. But this title, *ALPHA and OMEGA*, belongs exclusively to Him. No other is deserving of such noble ascription. No other dares assume it in reference to himself.

Let's take a brief tour of Scripture and examine together the usages of this glorious title. First, let's examine the testimony of the Old Testament. And although the literal rendering of the title is not found here, the essence of the expression is.

Be silent before you, you islands!
Let the nations renew their strength!
Let them come forward and speak;
let us meet together at the place of judgment.
Who has stirred up one from the east,
calling him in righteousness to his service?
He hands nations over to him
and subdues kings before him.
He turns them to dust with his sword,
to windblown chaff with his bow.
He pursues them and moves on unscathed,
by a path his feet have not traveled before.
Who has done this and carried it through,
calling forth the generations from the beginning?
I, the Lord – *with the first of them
and with the last – I am he* (Isa. 41:1-4, emphasis mine).

A bit later, the Lord reiterates the same thought:

This is what the Lord says –
Israel's King and Redeemer, the Lord Almighty;
I am the first and the last; apart from me there is no God.
Who then is like me? Let him proclaim it.
Let him declare and lay out before me what has happened since I
established my ancient people,
and what is yet to come –
yes, let him foretell what will come.
Do not tremble, do not be afraid. Did I not proclaim this and
foretell it long ago?
You are my witnesses. Is there any God besides me?
No, there is no other Rock; I know not one (Isa. 44:6-8, emphasis
mine).

What a thought! There is no other who is like our God. No,
not even one. One more word from Isaiah:

Listen to me, O Jacob,
Israel, whom I have called:
I am he;
I am the first and I am the last.
My own hand laid the foundations of the earth,
any my right hand spread out the heavens;
when I summon them,
they all stand up together (Isa. 48:12-13).

Marvin Vincent, in his fine volume, *Word Studies In The
New Testament*, tells us that the ancient rabbis, in commenting and instructing from this passage, would often use the
phrase, "from *aleph* to *tau*" to capture the thought, "aleph"
being the first letter in the Hebrew alphabet, and "tau" being
the last. From first to last, from "A" to "Z," from "aleph" to
"tau." It's a claim to absolute inclusivity!

When we move to the New Testament, the Apostle John, in
Revelation 1, records for us the very words of Jesus concerning His identity. And it's my conviction that Jesus, having
received his early training in the synagogue, agreed with the

analysis of the rabbis concerning the claims found in Isaiah and simply transferred the same thought from the Hebrew alphabet to the Greek alphabet, thus assuming a new name.

"I am the Alpha and the Omega," says the Lord God, "who is, and who was, and who is come, the Almighty." (Rev. 1:8).

"Alpha" is the first letter of the Greek alphabet, and "omega" the last. Jesus is saying, *"Remember the God Who spoke to Isaiah? I am He. I am the One Who is the First and the Last. The Beginning and the End. The initial and the ultimate. The tall and the short of it. The length and the breadth of it. I am everything from soup to nuts, from ying to yang, from aleph to tau, from A to Z."* That's the thought. And not only that, but *"I am also the God Who is (that's present), and the God Who was (that's past) and the God Who is to come (that's future.) I am the all-encompassing, ever-present God."*

Think of it. Before the stars, before Moses, before Adam – He was there. Before time, before matter, before space – He was there. And when this world hears the final trumpet blast signaling the finale of earth's history – He will still be there!

But Revelation 1:8 is not the only time Jesus assumed this name:

He said to me: "It is done. I am the Alpha and the Omega, the Beginning and the End. To him who is thirsty I will give to drink without cost from the spring of the water of life. He who overcomes will inherit all this, and I will be his God and he will be my son." (Rev. 21:6,7).

Will you please consider the enormity of this title? In our world, we have so deified man and so humanized God that we can scarcely tell the difference between them. But Scripture is never foggy about the Lord. He is unapologetically presented as God over all. Everything that is, is because of Him. And everything that isn't, isn't because of Him. And the movement of life, the moment by moment flow of earth's history, moves solely by the direction of His hand. And one day, THE DAY already scrawled into the calendar of God, a new heaven and a new earth will emerge. And a loud voice will say...

> Now the dwelling of God is with men, and he will live with them. They will be his people, and God himself will be with them and be their God. He will wipe every tear from their eyes. There will be no more death or mourning or crying or pain, for the old order of things has passed away (Rev. 21:3b,4).

Among Jesus' final words is yet another claim to this august title:

> Behold, I am coming soon! My reward is with me, and I will give to everyone according to what he has done. I am the Alpha and the Omega, the First and the Last, the Beginning and the End (Rev. 22:12,13).

Let's pause a moment and track the meaning of the term. There are two basic concepts which help form the backdrop for our understanding: The Hebrew concept, formulated by the word of God to Isaiah, and the Greek concept, spoken from the lips of Jesus Himself.

The Hebrew concept emphasized God's *COMMITMENT TO COMPLETION*. Thus, when God told the people, through Isaiah, that He was *"THE FIRST and THE LAST,"* He was committing Himself to complete the task He had begun years before under the stars with Abraham. He was committing Himself to the completion of that covenant. It was as if He was saying, *"I, who open, will close. I, who begin, will end. I, who start, will finish."*

Joshua is a great illustration of that. By the time we come

to the prologue of the Old Testament book which bears his name, Joshua has shouldered a very awesome assignment. Moses, the charismatic leader of the Exodus, has died. The man who led His people from bondage, who fed them with bread from heaven, who met with God and delivered to the people the law of God, who could speak to a rock causing water to gush forth – Moses, the mighty, beloved leader of Israel, is dead. Can you imagine the despair of the people? They're standing at the edge of Canaan. All they have to do is cross over, fight the battles and claim the land as their own! But then Moses up and dies on them!

Now the selection for Moses' replacement had already been arranged. The job would fall to Joshua. But can you imagine how he must have felt? How could he ever hope to follow such a powerful man of God as Moses?

So God pulled Joshua aside and said to him, "Moses my servant is dead." Now understand, He is Alpha and Omega. So there's no panic in God's voice. No sense of shock or surprise. He's merely making an announcement. *"Moses is dead. Just as I planned, just as I promised, he is gone."*

Moses my servant is dead. Now then, you and all these people, get ready to cross the Jordan River into the land I am about to give to them – to the Israelites. I will give you every place where you set your foot, as I promised Moses. Notice, "I will give it to you." And the territory is still the same as I described to Moses. Your territory will extend from the desert and from Lebanon to the great river, the Euphrates – all the Hittite country – and to the Great Sea on the west. Joshua, rest assured, nothing of my plan has been altered. No one will be able to stand up against you all the days of your life. As I was with Moses, so I will be with you; I will never leave you or forsake you (Josh. 1:2-5).

That final phrase is literally rendered, "I will never abandon you, and I will never loosen My grip from you. I will be wherever you are." Perhaps you are in need of that very assurance. Maybe you've lost a loved one through death. Perhaps you're facing the death of a marriage. Or a romance. Or the death of your career. Listen, child of God: He is *ALPHA and OMEGA!* The God of completion. And He will not leave you in the lurch! He'll not remove His hand from your life! He is present and available, and everything that is happening right now is happening under His absolute control. And you can rest assured, He will bring it to completion.

I like the way A. W. Tozer puts it: "When a man of God dies, nothing of God dies." Isn't that good to know? Sure, Moses was dead, but there was Joshua, ready to shoulder the responsibility – and through his leadership, Israel conquered her new land. She received God's promise!

I'm sure Joshua thought: "How can I do it? I don't have what it takes!" But the God of COMPLETION came to his rescue. He said, *"As I was with Moses, so I will be with you. Moses is dead, but Joshua, I am still on the throne."* Can you get a rope around that truth? You do and IT WILL TOTALLY REVOLUTIONIZE YOUR LIFE! Jesus is present. Always. The job He begins, He is faithful to complete. Always.

Now the Greek concept of *ALPHA* and *OMEGA* emphasized GOD'S *ABSOLUTE CONTROL*. His ever-present power. Look at Jesus' claim again:

I am the Alpha and the Omega (Rev. 1:8a).

Fritz Rienecker, a noted Greek scholar, writes:
"This phrase is seen to express not eternity only, but infinitude, the boundless life which embraces all while it transcends all." And isn't that what Jesus claims? Look at it again:

"I am the Alpha and the Omega," says the Lord God, "who is, and who was, and who is to come, the Almighty." (Rev. 1:8b).

I picture Jesus saying, "I am the ever-present, almighty God! Whatever you may be facing, whenever it is that you face it – I AM THERE! And I am greater than your need! I'm not merely ancient news conjured up from the dusty confines of antiquity! I am not One who merely was! I was, but I still am – and I will forever be!"

About three years ago, a young woman in our church had a routine doctor's exam scheduled several weeks in advance. It happened that her appointment was only a few days before the family's planned vacation. She almost rescheduled because she didn't want the bother, what with packing and cancelling the mail and all that. But she went anyway, and the doctor discovered a leaking cyst. If it had burst, as it surely would have while on vacation, she would have bled to death!

Now that will either scare the pants off of you, or it will fill you with peace to know that ALPHA and OMEGA knows all about cysts. He never had a frightful moment over the whole deal. He knew she wasn't going to cancel the appointment. He knew surgery would be performed. The whole deal, although quite shocking to her family and friends, was not a surprise to God.

When I was a teenager, I had a friend who was killed in a car accident. His death sent shockwaves through our little town. Hundreds of teenagers crowded into that tiny funeral chapel, and I can still remember the words of the minister. He said, "I will not say that God had anything to do with this tragedy. I will not say that God was involved in this, for my God is a God of love. He had nothing to do with this!" And even as a teenager, I thought: "If God isn't involved, who is? If God isn't in control, who is? If God is as shocked and surprised by this tragedy – if He is as powerless as I am, then He's not God!"

NO MATTER WHAT COMES YOUR WAY – and I exclude nothing – no matter what, it passes first through the nail-scarred hands of Jesus, our Alpha and Omega. (He knows everything that comes your way.)The One who is and was and is to come – the Almighty!

Scan that claim again:

I am the Alpha and the Omega, the First and the Last, the Beginning and the End (Rev. 22:13).

He is First (*protos*) in that nothing came before Him. He is Last (*eschatos*) in that nothing will come after Him. All things are enclosed in the parenthesis of Jesus. But He is also the Beginning (*arkei*) and the End (*telos*). The word arkei means "beginning as in source or origin." Jesus is the Beginning in that He is the source, the origin of ALL THINGS. Those aren't my words. That's from John.

Remember how he began His gospel?

In the beginning was the Word (Jesus), and the Word was with God, and the Word was God (John 1:1).

Go back, way back. Back before there was such a thing as time. Back before there was matter. And you'll find Jesus there. Jesus didn't start out as a babe in a manger. No, that baby in the manger once held the universe in place. He died on a cross of wood, yet He designed the hill on which it stood. But John continues:

Through him *all things* were made; without him nothing was made that has been made (John 1:3, emphasis mine).

As I read that, I thought of Voyager. After more than a decade, that little satellite finally arrived at the outer edge of our solar system. Passing alongside Jupiter, Voyager snapped hundreds of snapshots, just as she had with the previous planets in her path. Planets that heretofore we were only able to dream about. As a result of Voyager's journey, we have discovered rings and red spots and black spots and moons which rotate in reverse – and a myriad of other facts that we never would have imagined! But Jesus not only imagined them, He made them! Voyager is a tremendous tribute to the achievement of man, but Voyager has chronicled merely a tiny patch in the vast mosaic of Alpha's handiwork. And as she continues her flight toward galaxies unknown, be assured: there is not one star or planet or solar system that Christ did not first bring into being, that He does not monitor even now by the guidance of His protective hand. Be assured: Jesus is *THE BEGINNING!*

But He is also *THE END!* It is He who will close the door on this planet as we know it. He is the end in that all that we are, all that we could ever hope to be is rooted, ultimately, in Him. This is why Christians throughout the ages have said, *"If you don't have Jesus, you have nothing. You have no sense of beginning, no concept of the ultimate, consummating goal. Life apart from Jesus is a joke, because He alone is ALPHA and OMEGA."*

Wow! I'm out of words. Once all that I have written has been written, what is there left to write? Let's allow Paul to write it. In Romans 11, Paul comes to the end of a glorious presentation of God by emphasizing His UNTRACKABLE GLORY. He writes:

Oh, the depth of the riches of the wisdom and knowledge of God! How unsearchable his judgments, and his paths beyond tracing out!

211

Here is the great intellect, the Apostle Paul, yet He doesn't even try to examine God. He says, "His glory is untrackable!" You try to release your mind in order to track God's mind, and you can't do it! Who has known the mind of the Lord? Or who has been his counselor? Who has ever given to God, that God should repay him? He is absolutely beyond us! His ways are above our ways; His thoughts are beyond our thoughts. There is no way we can hope to unravel the mystery of God's glory! For from him and through him and to him are all things. To him be the glory forever! Amen (Rom. 11:33-36).

William Barclay, in commenting on this passage, writes:

Here the seeking of the mind turns to the adoration of the heart. What more can be said if all things come from God, all things have their being through God and all things end in God? God gave man a mind, and it is man's duty to use that mind to think to the very limits of human thought. But it is also true that there are times when that mind can only go so far, and, when that limit is reached, all that is left is to accept and to adore.

Look at Paul's benediction once more:

For from him and through him and to him are all things. To him be the glory forever!

"FROM HIM" suggests that He is the source or origin of ALL THINGS. "THROUGH HIM" suggests that He is the channel or filter of ALL THINGS. "TO HIM" suggests that He is the goal or destiny of all things. We're back to it again: whatever you face, if you trace that thing all the way to its beginning, you will come to God. And that's true whether your thing is a tragedy or a victory, a loss or a gain, an ecstasy or an agony. After all, ALL THINGS are *ALL THINGS*, right?

Jesus is ALPHA and OMEGA. THE FIRST and THE

LAST. THE BEGINNING and THE END. He not only pio-
neers and creates and develops – He perfects and finishes and
completes. He is Lord of all history – its beginning, its end
and all that lies between.
SO WHAT? WHAT DIFFERENCE WILL ANY OF THIS
MAKE IN MY LIFE? I like the way H. G. Wells put it. He
was not a particularly religious man, but after having studied
the history of the human race and having observed human
life, he came to this conclusion:

Religion is the first thing and the last thing; and until a man
has found God and been found by God, he begins at no beginning, he works to no end. He may have his friendships, his
partial loyalties, his scraps of honor. But all these things fall
into place and life falls into place only with God.

How true. I know it's true because that's what happened in
my life. Life for me came together when I met ALPHA and
OMEGA. As I reflect on that, three powerful implications
speak to my heart:

1. AS ALPHA, JESUS WAS
LORD OVER MY BEGINNINGS.
THEREFORE MY PAST WAS NOT AN ACCIDENT.

Have you ever wished you were never born? Think before
you answer. Remember when you felt unwanted? Misunder-
stood? Maybe you never felt the security of a mother's love.
Maybe your Daddy died when you were just a kid and you
never knew the warmth of his embrace. Maybe your parents
were harsh, often attacking you with hurtful, stinging words.
It's easy to think, isn't it, that maybe you were just an ill-
timed accident. But because JESUS is ALPHA, I can tell you
with absolute assurance – you were not! There is no such

thing as an accidental birth. Your arrival on this planet was not a mistake. You didn't come at a bad time. Alpha knew who you were.

Maybe you're still not convinced. Perhaps you are a teenager. Do you feel freakish sometimes? Maybe you're 5'2", but wish you were 6'4". You've got red hair, but you wish it was blonde. You have freckles, and you hate freckles. You wear glasses, and you hate glasses!

But it's not just the adolescent who struggles with his or her appearance. How many adults are also dissatisfied with their basic appearance? Let me remind you of a truth you already know: ALPHA made you. He wove you together in your mother's womb. You are a prescription baby, designed by Alpha according to His divine specifications. And you are exactly as He wants you to be. The color of your hair, the shape of your face, the length of your torso – notwithstanding. None of it is an accident.

Do you know why we struggle so much with this? It's because we can only focus on what has been and what now is. We look at the pain that we have endured, the problems we have encountered, and we think, "What possible good could come from this? God, something went terribly wrong!" But if we could only see life from heaven . . . we would see the beautiful tapestry that God sees of the whole of our life. *"It's all under control, my child. Every color, even the dark, forbidding colors, blend together with the bright colors to form a beautiful expression of My glory!"*

Your challenge, and mine, is to accept our beginnings. To stop digging around in the past, trying to find some reason for the madness that you are enduring. To stop trying to find someone to blame for your heartache. To stop pointing the finger at an abusive mother, an absent father, an unfaithful mate. To stop saying, "If only . . . if only . . . if only." And instead, to put your trust in the only One who was before You were and Who will be long after you aren't.

But there's a second implication:

2. AS OMEGA, JESUS IS LORD OVER MY ENDINGS. THEREFORE, MY FUTURE IS NOT SPINNING OUT OF CONTROL.

Thomas Merton put it so well. He writes:

"My Lord God, I have no idea where I am going. I do not see the road ahead of me. I cannot know for certain where it will end.

Nor do I really know myself, and the fact that I think I am following Your will does not mean that I am actually doing so.

But I believe that the desire to please You does, in fact, please You. And I know that if I do this You will lead me by the right road, though I may know nothing about it.

Therefore, I will trust You always though I may seem to be lost and in the shadow of death.

I will not fear, for You are ever with me, and You will never leave me to face my perils alone."

Talk about hope! Do you find yourself in tears as you consider your future? Omega is in control of that future! And He holds the keys which will unlock a glorious, victorious reality in your life! One day, He'll take that key and He'll unlock a future of wondrous meaning and blessing! And don't you dare believe otherwise.

Philippians 1:6 says, "He who began a good work in you

will carry it on to completion." In other words, when God starts a project, He finishes it. And be assured, His hammer is still pounding away. His construction permits are still valid. As Omega, He will not quit until your soul is safely at home in the bosom of Abraham. Count on it.

Then finally,

3. AS ALPHA *AND* OMEGA, JESUS IS LORD OVER MY *TODAY*. THEREFORE, MY *PRESENT* CIRCUMSTANCES ARE NOT BEYOND THE SCOPE OF HIS MIGHTY POWER.

What are you facing right now that you can't figure out? I'm convinced everyone is struggling with something. Maybe it's a temptation, a physical pain, perhaps it's a failed marriage, or a child who's gone bad. Perhaps it's a dreaded disease, or maybe a nagging worry. Maybe it's sin.

Whatever, there's something in your life that seems to be raging totally out of control. It is not! WHEN YOUR LIFE SEEMS UPSIDE DOWN, WHEN YOUR THEORIES ABOUT LIFE LAY SHATTERED ON THE FLOOR, WHEN YOUR DREAMS ARE A SHAMBLES AND ALL HOPE IS GONE –*FIX YOUR EYES ON JESUS!* Lift your focus from the agony and the oppression and look firmly into the eyes of the Alpha and the Omega. If you do, do you know what you'll discover? You'll discover that He's not a bit confused about why you're here, what you are to do or where you are to be heading. Neither is He frustrated by any circumstance you face, whether good or bad, prosperous or calamitous, pleasant or painful. And none of it is bigger than He. After all, He's ALPHA AND OMEGA! And He can handle it! Whatever it is.

Our God is not locked into some time warp of the past. He is a God of all epochs and seasons. And as David put it,

Our times are in His hands (Psa. 31:15).

Did you read that? Read it again.
Our times are in His hands.

Whatever you are now facing, be assured, "Your times are in God's hands."
Isn't it remarkable? With all of the advancements of man, we still have so very few answers. We're born in one hospital only to die in another. We search in vain for meaning and purpose, playing hide-and-seek with death and pain. We can't seem to figure out how to love or be loved. We can't find a pill to cure aging. We still don't know how to feed the hungry, how to get along with our parents, how to stay out of war.

We struggle to find a safe harbor in order to maintain balance on a planet spinning wildly out of control. As the waves crash around us, we look for some cave to hide in, some rock to crawl under, in order to guard ourselves from what seems to be unavoidable disaster. But there is a way of escape. His name is Jesus Christ. And He is the Alpha and the Omega. And our times – past, present and future – our times are in His hands!

I Am ... The Resurrection and the Life

11

Francis Bacon called it "*A friend.*" But Job disagreed. He called it "*The King of terrors.*" Thomas Browne cynically referred to it as "*the cure for all diseases.*" A German Proverb defined it as "*The poor man's doctor.*" And Thomas Gray refers to it as "*The inevitable hour.*" George Eliot calls it "*The Great Reconciler.*" And John Keats? He named it "*The Unwilling Sleep.*" To what are these men referring? To DEATH. Death, what Samuel Johnson called "*Nature's signal of retreat.*"

My favorite definition comes from the pen of perhaps the most prolific author of all time – Anonymous. Mr. Anonymous says that death is what happens "when man is put to bed with a shovel."

I love what Churchill said about his own death. He said,

"I am ready to meet my Maker. But whether my Maker is prepared for the great ordeal of meeting me is another matter."

Harry Young, responding to the question, "What is your greatest fear?" replied,

Death. It's the one thing I know nothing about. I've got no control over it. I can't choose how, where or when it will happen. I guess those two things, not knowing what it's about and having no control over it, make it number one.

Most of us would agree with Harry. We too are frightened by the prospects of death. Death casts a long, foreboding shadow across the face of humanity. And man's control over that shadow is severely limited. Neither our technological advances nor our improved living conditions seem to make even the slightest dent in the death rate. As a result, man, frustrated by his inability to escape death's snare and failing to frontally address and therefore honestly cope with his nagging questions and haunting heartaches, pretends that death doesn't even exist. We put death out of our minds. We force the ugly reality of death behind closed doors. You've heard of a death-defying feat? We are a *death-denying* people.

Richard Doss points out the subtle ways we try to deny death. He writes,

If a person dies in a hospital, as generally people do today, it's announced that the patient expired, and the attending physician then signs a vital statistics form. The patient no longer remains a patient at this point. He becomes a loved one. The remains of the loved one are removed to the mortuary where the family arranges the memorial estate. After preparation, the loved one is placed in a slumber room, sometimes called a reposing room. If he's a member of a church, the minister announces from the pulpit in very ministerial tones, that Mr.

220

Jones has now gone home, or passed to his heavenly home. The newspaper says, "Mr. Jones, beloved father, has passed away." If you're so coarse as to mention in a matter-of-fact way that Mr. Jones died last week, your neighbors, in some cases, think you have poor taste and perhaps you're indiscreet and so we use softened language to try to deny the harshness of death's reality.

Rather than cope with death, we ignore it. Pascal said, *"Man spends his life trying to put death out of his mind."* But man's efforts are in vain. For, as Euripides, the Greek dramatist said, *"Death is the debt we all must pay."* Scripture says it like this: *"It is appointed to man once to die"* (Heb. 9:27a). Whether you choose to face it or not, you will die. If the Lord tarries, you must traverse "the valley of the shadow of death," (Psa. 23:4) and so must I.

Have you visited that valley recently? Perhaps a loved one recently walked down that shadowy corridor. You watched him slip away, and there was nothing you could do. You had to stay behind, watching him slowly but surely drift into the darkness. You strained for even the slightest glimpse of him, for any sign that at the end of the corridor was a bright, new home. But no sign came. Only a haunting, deafening silence.

Perhaps you were in the ICU. You sat for hours, listening as the machines beeped and whirred, pumping air and nourishment into your mother's tired frame. Maybe you stood alongside your sister, as that uninvited, unwanted tumor slowly but surely drained away her very life. Perhaps you were assigned the task of carrying one of the handles of your best friend's casket. Perhaps you clasped the cold, stiff hand of your own child, hoping against hope that somehow, someway the warmth of your hand could infuse new life into that empty body.

If you've been there, you know how it feels to be in the SHADOW. You know how the questions ricochet from every direction – "Why her?" "Why now?" Why not someone else?" But no answers are forthcoming in the Valley. All that is heard is the constant echo of our agonized cry, "Why? Why?"

There's something about death that leaves us feeling so helpless, so hopeless. Listen to the words of a distraught father describing the day his son died:

> The rays of a late morning South Carolina sun struck me full on the face as I stepped through the door of the hospital. The squint of my eyes, however, was not occasioned by the rays of the sun; it was the visible display of the anguish and despair that wracked my very life. I had spent several hours with my sobbing wife. Now I was about to keep the appointment that would prove to be the emotional climax of the day my world collapsed. On my way to the appointment I stopped at a diner to have a cup of coffee and to bolster my courage. I was oblivious to everything except the appointment that awaited me. Leaving the diner, I made my way to a large white house, located on a corner in Columbia, South Carolina. I followed the owner into a large room, where he soon left me alone. I slowly made my way across a thick rug on the floor to a table on the far side of the room. Upon that table was a white box. I stood before that white box for endless eternities before I finally summoned enough courage to look over the top and down into the white box at the lifeless body of my son. At that sight my world collapsed. I would have given up all of my academic and athletic awards. I would have given up the prestigious executive training program I was engaged in with one of the largest international oil companies. I would have given anything. For the first time in my life, I had come to a hurdle I could not clear. My world collapsed. (Adapted from message by Ray Stedman delivered on April 10, 1966)

Those identical emotions most certainly gripped the hearts

of Mary and Martha. Their beloved brother, Lazarus, is dying. He's walking down that shadowy corridor and as they watch him slip away into the darkness; the heartache, the tears, the conflict between trusting God and coping with grief – it's more than they can bear.

> Now a man named Lazarus was sick. He was from Bethany, the village of Mary and her sister Martha. This Mary, whose brother Lazarus now lay sick, was the same one who poured perfume on the Lord and wiped his feet with her hair (John 11:1,2).

In fact, Jesus had developed quite a friendship with this trio. He would often come to Bethany and stay in their home when He needed to take a break, when the pressures had become more than He could handle. So we're not surprised that they send for Him, saying, "Lord, the one you love is sick." (John 11:3b). Now they didn't specifically *ask* Jesus to come; but that was their intent. They wanted Jesus to come and heal their brother. Just like He had healed so many others in so many other places. But surprisingly, Jesus didn't just drop what he was doing and head for Bethany. Instead, He said, "This sickness will not end in death" (John 11:4a).

Now He didn't say Lazarus wouldn't die; just that death wouldn't be the last chapter in his story. But Jesus didn't stop there. He uttered words that are immeasurably difficult to swallow, especially if you are right now staring into the face of death or some other ongoing struggle. He said, "No, it is for God's glory so that God's Son may be glorified through it" (John 11:4b).

By the way, that's at least one answer to that "why" question you've been asking. You may not necessarily like this answer; you will most certainly wrestle against it; you may even attempt to reject it outright – but it remains an answer nonetheless. The painful truth is, it may just be that your disease, your suffering, your affliction is a vehicle allowed by God for the high and holy purpose of bringing ultimate glory to God. I'm not asking you to like that answer, but I do suggest you grow to accept it.

Some students of Scripture wonder if Jesus didn't go to Bethany because He didn't care. But verse 5 tells us that "Jesus loved" those people. Perhaps He didn't realize how sick Lazarus was! Oh yes He did. In fact, verse 11 suggests that He knew the very moment Lazarus died. No, Jesus delayed because He knew the reason all of this had happened. In fact, verse 6 tells us that *after* he learned of Lazarus' fate, He "stayed where he was two more days." Why? Because He knew the end of the story.

Child of God, no matter how slow God may seem, please understand: He is never late. Read that statement again. Now let it soak in. No matter how long you have waited for God to move into action, that extended delay is not due to divine tardiness.

Do you believe that? Or when you pray for God to intervene, yet you wait interminably for God to do something about that prayer, do you at times think that perhaps He is late? Listen, God is *never* late. Oh, He may seem slow. Primarily because we think He ought to do it when we think it ought to be done. We expect Him to operate according to our calendar. We read Him our agenda, we set the schedule, determine the deadline; but then, when He doesn't come through on time, our faith crumbles and our hearts become bitter.

But let me tell you something, when God is silent, it's not because He's apathetic. When He delays, it's not because He's disinterested. Not at all. It's just that God will not speak until He has something to say; and He will not move into action until He has something to do; and He will not do it until the moment He has decreed has finally arrived.

I'm reminded of the story of Albert Einstein, once featured as a speaker at a dinner given in his honor at Swarthmore College. When it was time to speak, he stood up and told the audience, "Ladies and Gentlemen, I am sorry, but I have nothing to say." And he sat down. Two seconds later, he came back to the microphone and said, "In case I do have something to say, I'll come back someday and say it." He sat back down and the meeting ended. Six months later he wired the president of the college and said, "I now have something to say." And another dinner was planned, and Einstein appeared and delivered a profound speech.

That's our God. He says, *My child, I have nothing to say right now, but when I do, I will speak. I have no need to intervene right now, but when I do, I will intervene. It is not now time for action, it's time for delay."*

I suppose there is no more difficult trial that we must endure than the trial of God's silence – the affliction of God's delay. But what He wants from us in those times of waiting is our patient assurance that when the time is right, He will work out ALL things to His glory and for our good. And, that in the final analysis, His work will be done right and it will, in fact, be done right on time.

In verse 15, Jesus mentions another answer to our WHY QUESTION. Why does God, at times, delay? Why doesn't He immediately move into action when we have a need?

For your sake I am glad I was not there, so that you may believe (John 11:15a).

Do you see what He's saying? He's saying, "I'm glad I

didn't rush over and heal him, because now you will see that no matter how bad it gets, I am still sufficient for every need."

Do you realize if God always gave you whatever you asked for that you would never grow in your faith? There would be no need for you to grow up. It would be Christmas morning 365 days a year, as our Santa-God dumps lavish gifts into the laps of His expectant children. But waiting makes you learn to trust, doesn't it? God's silence drives you to your knees. It is the crisis times of your life when God finally gets your undivided attention and when He can do His very best work.

This verse assures me that there is never a time when the events of my life are out of His control. Jesus was not worried, He was not panicking. He was absolutely confident in His supreme power – even over death. Do you know what that tells me? It tells me that:

GOD IS AT HIS BEST WHEN MY LIFE IS AT ITS WORST.

Picture the scene: Everyone around Him was in pain, but Jesus was at peace. The disciples were confused, but Jesus was confident. The family was gripped with grief, but Jesus was contemplating God's glory. To everyone in Bethany it seemed that death had the final word, that the final chapter of Lazarus' life had been written. But Jesus knew there would be a sequel.

You must believe this. It's true! GOD REALLY IS AT HIS BEST WHEN YOUR LIFE IS AT ITS WORST. He knows exactly what is happening in your life right now. And He knows how your story will end. Your situation is well within the scope of His power; there is not one fiber of His being that is in panic.

Now He may not resolve this thing WHEN you think it ought to be resolved, but, rest assured, He will resolve it. He is not going to leave you in the lurch. He will not leave you alone to fend for yourself. He will handle it. Your responsibility, and mine, is to patiently and trustfully wait.

Back to Bethany. Four days later, God's time for intervention has finally arrived. Jesus begins His journey toward the home of his good friends. Martha hears that He is coming, so she goes out to meet Him. And immediately, she says,

Lord, if you had been here, my brother would not have died (John 11:21).

Do you sense the pathos in those words? Where were you, Jesus? Why didn't you come? He was so sick, Jesus, and You are the only One who could have done something, but You didn't even come to his funeral. You're late, Jesus. If you'd been on time, my brother would still be alive.

Jesus knew that behind Martha's stinging rebuke was a very painful, heart-wrenching grief. So he let her say whatever was on her heart without one word of explanation. I see no hint of any defensiveness or any attempt to reposition His inactivity in a better light. Instead, I picture Him taking Martha's head in His hands and holding her to His breast as she sobbed deeply. Then I see Martha taking her apron and drying her tears, then taking a deep breath – and saying,

But I know that even now God will give you whatever you ask.

Picture Jesus gently lifting her gaze until her eyes met his.

227

Now listen as He says,

> Your brother will rise again. Martha answered, "I know he
> will rise again in the resurrection at the last day."

You see, she thought Jesus was just handing out the standard line that is heard at every funeral. You know, "He's at peace now." Or, "He's with the Lord." Or, "You'll see him again one day." Although all of those phrases are certainly true for the believer, that's not what Jesus was saying to Martha. She took His words as a conventional expression of comfort, but Jesus was telling her what He was about to do!

It's then that Jesus said it. He said to her what has been repeated at countless gravesides ever since:

> I am the resurrection and the life. He who believes in me will
> live, even though he dies; and whoever lives and believes in
> me will never die. Do you believe this? (John 11:25,26).

She said, "Yes, Lord, I believe that You are the Christ" (John 11:27a). But that's as far as her faith could go. After all, how can a person die and yet never die? How could she possibly understand such obvious double-talk? For the first time in human history God in the flesh is standing toe-to-toe with death, and He makes His mark in the sand. Jesus, for the first time, claims ultimate power over man's ultimate fear.

It was at Lazarus' tomb that Jesus threw down the gauntlet and set the stage for the enormous battle of Calvary. He stared into the dark recesses of that shadowy valley and said, *Martha, this is no problem for me. Death has finally met its match! I am the Resurrection and the Life. Martha, do you believe that?"*

Do you? Really! Do you believe that the itinerant, penniless preacher of Palestine is larger than death itself? Do you believe that? Oh, it's easy to believe it in church. You're safe there. And it's no big deal to believe it when you're surrounded by your Bible study group either. But what about when you're the one who is staring down that long, dark corridor, and it's your loved one who is slipping away? Or when it's you who has to make the trip? That's when this question really matters. When your life is reduced to the nubbies and all of your crutches are stripped away – will you still believe?

When Mary came along, she said the same thing to Jesus:

> Lord, if you had been here, my brother would not have died (John 11:32b).

Now Mary, being the more tender and fragile of the two women, obviously crushed by her sorrow, struck a deep, emotional chord in Jesus' heart.

> When Jesus saw her weeping, and the Jews who had come along with her also weeping, he was deeply moved in spirit and troubled (John 11:33).

The phrase "deeply moved," literally means, "to snort like a horse." And it connotes anger. Jesus, seeing their tears, got angry. Now understand, not at Mary. He wasn't mad because the people were grieving; it wasn't the tears which disturbed Him. Jesus was angered because He knew the story behind the story. He knew that behind Lazarus' death was the tyranny of Satan himself, the god of destruction, bringing sorrow and devastation to God's creation. He was angered that Satan for so long could have created such heartache.

Then He walked toward the cemetery, the place which had

been, to this point, the unchallenged domain of Satan; with divine ears, He listened to the groans of the corpses which were trapped in death's prison. Jesus heard Satan's evil cackle ricochet from cave to cave. And seeing Lazarus' tomb, hearing the cries of the people and knowing that behind it all was the work of Satan – HE WEPT (John 11:35). Here was God in the flesh. He knew that this thing would not end in death, but the grief and the sorrow and the havoc of Satan's destruction was more than He could bear, so He lost it. He was overcome with emotion, and He wept.

> Jesus, once more deeply moved, came to the tomb. It was a cave with a stone laid across the entrance. "Take away the stone," he said.
> "But, Lord," said Martha, the sister of the dead man, "by this time there is a bad odor, for he has been there four days."
> Then Jesus said, "Did I not tell you that if you believed, you would see the glory of God?"
> So they took away the stone. Then Jesus looked up and said, "Father, I thank you that you have heard me. I knew that you always hear me, but I said this for the benefit of the people standing here, that they may believe that you sent me."
> When he had said this, Jesus called in a loud voice, "Lazarus, come out!" (John 11:38-43).

Augustine was the first to say that if Jesus had not used Lazarus' name, the whole cemetery would have emptied! But it wasn't time for that, so He said, *"Lazarus, you're the only one right now. You . . . you (and only you) come out!"* And out he came! Imagine! He'd been dead and buried four days. But suddenly, his cold, decomposing body begins to warm up. There is a rustling of movement – and the crowd hears it, because they were stunned! There was not even the slightest peep from the astonished crowd of onlookers. All that could be heard was the rustling of fabric as Lazarus struggled to find the entrance while fully wrapped in his grave clothes. When he finally appeared, he looked like a mummy! I'm sure some of the crowd took off at that point. They couldn't handle it anymore!

But as soon as he stumbled into the daylight, Jesus said, "Take off the grave clothes and let him go" (John 11:44b). Can you imagine helping Lazarus with his wrappings? I wonder what it was like to look into the face of a man who had been beyond, and now he was back! WOW!

Oh, how amazing! The devil and his henchmen had chiseled into the stone of Lazarus' tomb two horribly haunting words, "The End." But Jesus said, "No, Martha! It's not even close to the End!" And He strode to Lazarus' tomb, shouted three words, and the Finger of God effortlessly erased "The End" and wrote instead, "TO BE CONTINUED." Hallelujah!

DO YOU BELIEVE THAT?

John Donne believed. In fact, the great sixteenth century poet and priest staked his very life on it. In his masterful work entitled, "Devotions," Donne wrote:

> Thou so disobedient a servant as I may be afraid to die,
> yet to so merciful a master as thou I cannot be afraid to come.

Some accused Donne of an obsession with death (32 of his 54 songs and sonnets center on the theme), but Donne considered death the Great Enemy. To illustrate his conception of death and resurrection, Donne used the analogy of a map. Spread out flat, a map, in two dimensions, radically separates east from west. The two directions appear irreconcilably distant. But curve that same map around a globe – a far more accurate representation – and the furthest eastern point actually touches the farthest western point. The two are contiguous. The same principle apples to life. Death, which appears to sever life, is actually a door opening the way to new life. Death and resurrection touch; the end is really just a beginning.

Believing that fully, Donne wrote these wonderfully assuring words:

Death be not proud, though some have called thee
Mighty and dreadful, for, thou art not so . . .
One short sleep past, we wake eternally,
And death shall be no more;
Death, thou shalt die."

His epitaph reads:

Our last day is our first day; our Saturday is our Sunday; our eve is our holy day; our sun setting is our morning; the day of our death is the first day of our eternal life.

Speaking of epitaphs, here is the epitaph that Benjamin Franklin, having written with his own hands, intended to have displayed at his grave.

The Body of
B. Franklin
Printer

Like the cover of an old Book,
Its Contents torn out
And stript of its Lettering and
Gilding

Lies here, Food for Worms.
But the Work shall not be lost;
For it will (as he believed) appear once
more,
In a new and more elegant Edition,
Revised and corrected,
By the Author.

How wonderful to carry such assurance to the grave! Assurance that the exit of death is also an entrance. That, in death, man merely leaves one place in order to enter another. And that's the hope Jesus came to provide!

DO YOU BELIEVE THAT? Sadly, not everyone does.

Robert Ingersoll didn't believe. That's why, when he died, the printed program at his funeral solemnly instructed,

There will be no singing.

That's the way many approach the specter of death – no singing, no comfort, no hope. For those who cannot bring themselves to believe that Jesus is indeed the Resurrection and the Life, death is a formidable foe. And all that is left for them to do, at the moment of death, is to simply put their loved one in the ground and allow him to become fodder for worms. Tears flow, angry words are expressed, hostilities are exchanged, because there is an inexplicable insanity that accompanies a death which knows no hope.

It may be difficult to comprehend, but at this very moment there are people who have just learned of the death of a family member. They are charged with the task of planning a funeral and a burial. Yet, because they do not believe, they have absolutely no hope to cling to beyond a beautiful casket, lots of lovely flowers and a water-tight vault. How horrible it would be to live like that. Even more, to die like that. Jesus says, *"You don't have to."* But the point is,

DO YOU BELIEVE? Do you?

The Apostle Paul believed. In fact, looking back on this event and the much greater event of Christ's own resurrection, Paul writes words of truth and hope for believers of every age. He begins by stating the fact:

> But if (since) it is preached that Christ has been raised from the dead, how can some of you say that there is no resurrection of the dead? (I Cor. 15:12).

That's what's being preached, folks. Jesus Christ conquered death and the grave, when three days after His own crucifixion, He popped right out of the tomb – alive! Never to die again! That's the message of the Gospel. Paul says, *"And it's a fact, friend, not a dream. He appeared to too many people for it to just be a hoax."* He had listed several of those "people" earlier in the chapter.

> He appeared to Peter, and then to the Twelve. After that, he appeared to more than five hundred of the brothers at the same time, most of whom are still living, though some have fallen asleep. Then he appeared to James, then to all the apostles, and last of all he appeared to me also, as to one abnormally born (I Cor. 15:5-8).

And that's just a partial list. Mark it down: Jesus Christ conquered the grave. Too many people saw him. Too many lives have been changed, including my own. That's what's being preached, folks – and it's the truth.

But then Paul shifts gears. He says, *"OK, just for the sake of argument, let's assume that Jesus DIDN'T rise from the dead! We know He did, but what if He didn't?"* Then he lists a number of truths that are also not true, if Jesus is still dead. Look at them:

> If there is no resurrection of the dead, then not even Christ has been raised. And if Christ has not been raised, our preaching is useless and so is your faith.
> More than that, we are then found to be false witnesses about God, for we have testified about God that he raised Christ from the dead.
> And if Christ has not been raised, your faith is futile, you are still in your sins.
> Then those also who have fallen asleep in Christ are lost (I Cor. 15:13-15, 17-18).

Then he concludes his argument with one of the classic understatements ever written:

> If only for this life we have hope in Christ, we are to be pitied more than all men (I Cor. 15:19).

That doesn't say the half of it! If He is dead, our hope, our faith, our reason for being is stripped away. All we have to look forward to is an eternity of nothingness.

But hold on, this entire argument hinges on a tiny little preposition – "IF." IF there is no resurrection, we're hosed. We're in big, big trouble. But there *is* a resurrection! Jesus *did* rise from the dead! Paul writes:

> But Christ has indeed been raised from the dead, the firstfruits of those who have fallen asleep (I Cor. 15:20).

And because He lives, we too shall live! That's our Blessed

Hope! And that hope is as sure as the breath you're inhaling this very moment.

Jesus said,

Truly, truly I say to you, he who believes in Me has eternal life (John 3:36).

Count on it – it's true! Believe it – it's a fact! And mark this: He said it in the present tense. If you are presently in Jesus Christ, you have in your possession, right now, the gift of eternal life. You don't have to hope that you will get it someday – you've already got it.

And because that's true, the very worst thing that could ever happen to you is that you will die physically. That's as bad as it can get! You'll have to lay aside a body that couldn't make it through eternity anyway. At the very best, you might live four score and ten on this earth. But the incredible truth of the Gospel, the blessed reality made possible through the RESURRECTION, our Savior Jesus, is that today I stand before you immortal! Though I may die physically, I'll never really die!

I agree with Paul. "Why should we be afraid though this earthly body be destroyed?" Indeed! I tell you, I'm glad mine's going to get destroyed. It's fouled up in so many ways; it's such a mess, I can't do a thing with it. But one day, I'm going to get a brand new body, one that is totally exempt from pain, sin, fear, death, tears and heartache! Oh that will be glory for me! And not for me only, but for all who long for His appearing.

HOW'S IT ALL GOING TO HAPPEN? Glad you asked. Paul answers you in remarkable detail:

Listen, I tell you a mystery: We will not all sleep, but we will all be changed – in a flash, in the twinkling of an eye, at the last trumpet. For the trumpet will sound, the dead will be raised imperishable, and we will be changed.

We'll have to be! We'll have to be clothed with an eternal garment, not just this old thing! Those who have died before us will be raised and clothed with their new garment. Then we'll be caught up and we'll be clothed in our new garment.

When the perishable has been clothed with the imperishable, and the mortal with immortality, then the saying that is written will come true: "Death has been swallowed up in victory."
"Where, O death, is your victory?
Where, O death, is your sting?"
The sting of death is sin, and the power of sin is the law. But thanks be to God! He gives us the victory through our Lord Jesus Christ.
Therefore, my dear brothers, stand firm. Let nothing move you. Always give yourselves fully to the work of the Lord, because you know that your labor in the Lord is not in vain (I Cor. 15:51-52, 54-58).

I wonder, DO YOU BELIEVE THAT?
Scripture says,

Now we know that if the earthly tent we live in is destroyed, we have a building from God, an eternal house in heaven, not built by human hands (II Cor. 5:1).

When this tent breathes its last, my soul will immediately inhabit a new building. A strong, eternal building. Do you believe that?
Scripture also says,

Therefore we are always confident and know that as long as

we are at home in the body we are away from the Lord (II Cor. 5:6).

This means that when we leave this body behind, we'll be with the Lord. Do you believe that? Do you believe that when you lay aside your worn-out body, that in the instant you die, you'll be ushered into the presence of God?

Every one of us, if Jesus tarries, will face death. Each one of us will, by ourselves, have to walk that shadowy corridor. But for the one who believes, there is a grand and glorious future to behold. For in Jesus, death has met its match. And because Jesus Christ lives, death holds no terror for the Christian. Grief? Yes. Terror? No.

Hardly a week passes that I don't look into the red, swollen, tear-filled eyes of one who is grieving. In those moments I thank God for the hope that is ours in Christ. For without that hope, I would have nothing to say. But because of that hope, I can say, with confidence: "It's good to know, isn't it, that one day all of our tears will be wiped away. And there will be no more pain, no more sorrow, no more death." I can say that because Jesus said it first. He said,

> I am the Resurrection and the Life. He who believes in Me
> will live even though he dies; and whoever lives and believes
> in Me will never die. DO YOU BELIEVE? (John 11:25-26).

Now the truth of the Resurrection isn't good news for everyone. All mankind will rise, please understand that. However, those who rise having never been related to Jesus Christ will rise, not to eternal life, but to eternal death. Jesus said,

> A time is coming when ALL who are in their graves will hear
> (my) voice and come out – those who have done good will

I AM THE RESURRECTION AND THE LIFE

rise to live, and those who have done evil will rise to be condemned.

Just before, He clarified the thing that needs done. He said:

I tell you the truth, whoever hears my word and believes him who sent me has eternal life (John 5:28,29,24a).

I put it like this: If you reject the life-giving power of Jesus, you will face eternal death. You will rise, but your resurrection will be a resurrection to eternal torment, misery and punishment. You will spend an eternity of death in Hell.

However, if you accept the life-giving power of Jesus, you will receive the gift of eternal life. If you are now a believer, you are in every sense of the word – immortal! If you are not, but you choose today to allow Jesus to save you, you can become instantly and eternally invincible. Then, when your life on earth comes to an end, you will be instantly ushered into the very presence of Jesus, nestled in His bosom – never again to face heartache, pain or loss of any kind.

In October of 1800, John Todd was born in Rutland, Vermont. Soon after, his parents moved to Killingworth, Connecticut. When John was six years old, both his parents died. A kind-hearted aunt in North Killingworth agreed to take John and give him a home. He was brought up by her and lived in her home until he left to study for the ministry. In middle life, his aunt became seriously ill and feared she would die. In distress she wrote John Todd a pitiful letter in which she asked what death would be like. Would it mean the end of everything, or is there beyond death a chance to continue living, loving and growing?

Here is the letter John Todd sent his aunt in reply:

It is now 35 years since I, as a little boy of six, was left quite alone in the world. You sent me word that you would give me a home and be a kind mother to me. I will never forget the day when I made the long journey of ten miles to your house in North Killingworth. I can still remember my disappointment when instead of coming for me yourself, you sent Caesar to fetch me.

I well remember my tears and anxiety as perched high on your horse and, clinging tight to Caesar, I rode off to my new home. Night fell before we finished the journey, and as it grew dark, I became lonely and afraid. "Do you think she'll go to bed before we get there?" I asked Caesar anxiously. "Oh, no," he said reassuringly. "She'll stay up for you. When we get out of this here woods, you'll see her candle shinin' in the window." Presently we did ride out into the clearing, and there, sure enough, was your candle. I remember you were waiting at the door, that you put your arms close about me and that you lifted me – a tired and bewildered little boy – down from the horse. You had a fire burning on the hearth, a hot supper waiting on the stove. After supper you took me to my room, heard me say my prayers and then sat beside me till I fell asleep.

You probably realize why I am recalling all of this to your memory. Someday soon God will send for you to take you to a new home. Don't fear the summons, the strange journey or the dark messenger of death. God can be trusted to do as much for you as you were kind enough to do for me so many years ago. At the end of the road you will find love and a welcome awaiting, and you will be safe in God's care. I shall watch you and pray for you till you are out of sight and then wait for the day when I shall make the journey myself and find my Savior and you waiting at the end of the road to greet me.

I ask, a final time, the question that has been woven throughout this chapter. No question deserves more careful attention and inspection than this:

DO YOU BELIEVE?

He Is the Way, the Truth and the Life
12

Have you ever faced a time in life when it seemed as though everything that once was so very good suddenly became so very bad? Riding the crest of success and prosperity, you lost your job, your business went belly-up. Perhaps it was the loss of your mate, either through death or divorce. Or maybe it was the loss of health. You thought it was a routine exam, but the doctor called you into his office and said, "I see something on your X-ray that concerns me." If you've been there, you understand what the disciples must have been feeling in the Upper Room the night Jesus was betrayed.

Four days earlier, Jesus was the toast of Palestine! He rode triumphantly into Jerusalem on the back of a young colt. His admirers laid palm branches in His path, and waved others wildly as He passed, and shouted, "Hosanna! Lord! Save us!"

As you might imagine, His disciples were ecstatic! Finally, after three and half years, Jesus is gaining political momentum! They surmised, "Our time has finally arrived!" But four days later, as they were sharing a meal with their Leader, He drops a bomb on them. In fact, several bombs. And all of their planning and scheming blew up in their faces.

What was it that He told them? He told them straight up that He was about to die. He had told them before, but this time He didn't soften the blow. He even told them the method of His death. He said, "I will be lifted up" (inferred, on a cross; (see John 12:32).

Then He told them that one of the Twelve was a traitor. And sure enough, that very night Judas slithered out into the night, hell-bent on betrayal.

Then, Jesus informs these men, who had left all to follow Him, that He will soon be leaving them.

My children, I will be with you only a little longer. You will look for me, and just as I told the Jews, so I tell you now: Where I am going, you cannot come. (*Now Peter, being Peter, wasn't going to give up that easily.*) Simon Peter asked him, "Lord, where are you going?" Jesus replied, "Where I am going, you cannot follow." Peter asked, "Lord, why can't I follow you now? I will lay down my life for you." (*"Lord, if this is some kind of loyalty test, I'm ready for it!"*) Then Jesus answered, "Will you really lay down your life for me? I tell you the truth, before the rooster crows, you will disown me three times!" (John 13:33, 36-38) (*"In less than 24 hours, Peter, you'll eat those words. You, My most vocal supporter, will deny that you ever knew Me."*)

Then Jesus turned His attention back to the Eleven and said:

Do not let your hearts be troubled (John 14:1a).

The Greek word translated "troubled" literally means disturbed, agitated, perplexed. Are you kidding, Jesus? In less than an hour, the disciples find out that You are going to die and there's not a thing they can do about it; that You will be betrayed by one of their very own; no less that You are leaving and they can't go with You; and that not even Peter will stay true to You. Yet You have the audacity to say, "Do not let your hearts be troubled?" Jesus, their hearts *were* troubled! They were confused, shocked, frightened by this terrifying turn of events. All of their dreams had turned to dust. How can You say that, Jesus? But that's exactly what He said:

> Do not let your hearts be troubled. Trust in God; trust also in Me (John 14:1).

By the way, that was a command. Jesus is not giving advice, He's not making a suggestion – He's saying, "Men, you've trusted Me in the past . . . trust Me now. You've believed Me in other equally troubling times . . . don't stop believing Me now."

Why *should* we trust You, Jesus? "BECAUSE I'VE GOT A PLAN!"

> In my Father's house are many rooms; if it were not so, I would have told you. I am going there to prepare a place for you (John 14:2).

"Men, I do have to die, but that's not the last chapter of my calling. I will live on! And while I'm away from you, I will be preparing a place for you – so that all of you, (yes, even you, Peter) will someday be reunited with Me. In fact . . ."

> And if I go and prepare a place for you, I will come back and

take you to be with me that you also may be where I am (John 14:3).

It occurs to me that that "place" must be some kind of a place! If Jesus created this beautiful planet in just six days, imagine the beauty of that place which, so far, has taken Him 2,000 years to prepare! But not only is He preparing for us a place; HE'S ALSO PREPARING US FOR THAT PLACE! He's not just building heaven, He's building you and me for heaven. So that when we go to be with Him, He will present us to the Father "without fault and with great joy." (Jude 24).

Jesus is saying, "MEN, DON'T GET UPSET ABOUT ALL OF THIS – I'VE GOT A PLAN. I'VE GOT A PLAN." In fact, He reassures them,

You know the way to the place where I am going. (John 14:4).

At this point, Thomas couldn't take it anymore! He's confused and he doesn't care who knows. So he blurts out all that pent-up confusion:

Lord, we don't know where you are going, so how can we know the way? (John 14:5b).

Unfortunately, Thomas has gotten a bad rap. Because of this and one other unfortunate incident, which has been recorded for all of eternity, we come to look at Thomas in a very discouraging light. In fact, seldom do we even call him, "Thomas." Most often, it's "Doubting Thomas." This poor fellow has a permanent blight on his record – and I don't think that's fair!

Do you know what I've discovered recently? I've discovered that Scripture nowhere infers that conversion completely erases our basic personalities. Just because you come to the Lord and find full forgiveness of sins and are transplanted into God's forever family doesn't mean that your inherent temperament will be immediately or even radically altered. Think of the Twelve: Philip had a calculator for a brain. Whenever Jesus wanted to do something, Philip was the one who immediately told him how much it would cost (along with at least three reasons why they couldn't afford it!). Now there was nothing wrong with that, nothing at all. It was entirely consistent with Philip's analytical, mathematical personality! Then there's Peter; no matter how closely he was attached to Jesus, Peter remained a strong-willed, impetuous daredevil. Don't forget – he's the one who tried water-walking. He's the one who sliced off the soldier's ear. Now James and John had a problem with a short fuse. Even after three years with Jesus, they struggled with unmanageable tempers. That's why He nicknamed them the "Sons of Thunder." And then there's Thomas. Thomas the skeptic. Thomas, who by his very nature, struggled with pessimism. It was just a part of who he was! And that part of him wasn't systematically and magically swept away just because he was now a follower of Jesus!

So we find Thomas honestly confused by all of this new information Jesus was laying on them. What I find intriguing about this scene is that Jesus wasn't put off by Thomas' doubts. He didn't put him down. No, Jesus knew that what Thomas needed was a reminder, not a rebuke.

Can you look back to a time in your life when you were discouraged? Chances are good what you needed was not some new information – certainly not a rebuke – you simply needed to be reminded of what you already knew to be true. But you desperately needed to hear somebody else say it.

That's much of the power of counseling. It's not so much the sharing of new information and insight, as it is reminding those who, in the panic of the moment, have begun to lose their stability. In the heat of the crisis, they have lost perspective. Thomas said, *"Jesus, I don't know where this WAY is! I'm afraid! Help me!"*

Then Jesus, with that great shepherd's heart, replied:

I am the way and the truth and the life. No one comes to the Father except through me (John 14:6).

Can you imagine such a statement? At this point, Jesus' entire flock could be numbered on little more than two hands. Within hours, He will be led out of the city and nailed to a cross. Yet He dared to say, "I am the way, the truth and the life. No man comes to the Father except through Me." What a bold, sweeping statement!

It occurs to me that we allow Jesus to say things we would refuse to allow others to say. We honor Him for words that would cause dishonor for any other who would speak them. What attracts us to Jesus would repel us from anyone else. The truth is: no one else – no religious leader, no political leader, no media celebrity – could ever say what Jesus said.

Not one of the great world religious founders said it. Not Mohammed, not Buddha, not even Confucius. Only Jesus.

None of the great political leaders said it either. Alexander the Great tried to become king of the world. But not even he dared say, "I am the way." Nor did Napoleon. Or Hitler. And what about George Washington, the father of the most blessed nation on earth? Not even he said, "I am the truth." Abraham Lincoln glued our country back together; Franklin Roosevelt forged the New Deal; Ronald Reagan engineered the Reagan

Revolution. But as loved and esteemed as these men are, if any one of these men had claimed to be "the life," we would have considered them blasphemers. We've grown to expect wildly boastful sentiments from our celebrities. That wasn't always the case. We were shocked, for example, when Cassius Clay looked into the cameras and screamed, "I am the Greatest!" But we're used to it now. Roseanne Barr claims to be the funniest woman in America. Joan Kennedy maintains she is one of the most fascinating women anywhere. Jim Brown still asserts that he is the greatest running back in football history and that, given a chance, could still outrun those young, grossly overpaid whippersnappers. We've grown accustomed to the outrageous, egotistical statements of our sports and entertainment celebrities. But we would never permit them to say, "No one comes to the Father, except through me."

Jim Jones came dangerously close. I watched the documentary on his life again recently. I can't explain it, but, for some reason, I am strangely haunted by what happened in the People's Temple. As I watched the actor who portrayed Jones and became mesmerized by his gripping portrayal, every time he said something like, "I am God," "I am your Father," "Worship me" or, "My children, I will save you," my stomach churned. Jim Jones said things no one else dared to say. And for 10 years, about 1000 people believed him. They trusted him so implicitly that they willingly drank his tainted Kool-Aid in an unbelievable display of loyalty. But not even Jones could, with undeniable authority and unquestioned integrity, say, "I am the way, the truth and the life."

Shirley MacLaine has twisted Jesus' words. She says, "You are the way." Shirley and her ilk are pandering to the secularistic, prideful, self-sufficient mind set of our day. And

247

as a result, she's got quite a following! But she's dead wrong. She encourages us to command our cosmic energy and come to full potential by tapping into the god that is within us, whatever that means. Her movement is called "The New Age," and it's sweeping across our nation. Man is his own god, and therefore, an end unto himself. So who needs Jesus? Listen, Shirley MacLaine not only went out on a limb with this garbage – the poor lady is out of her tree!

Isn't it amazing that only the Lord Jesus Christ has been permitted in all of history to make this statement? And instead of being repulsed, turned-off and irritated, multiplied millions have said, "Jesus, I believe You are the way. I believe You are the truth. And I believe You are the life." Not A way, or A truth or A life. But THE way, THE truth and THE life. Only Jesus said it, and only of Jesus is it true. Let's take a closer look at this name, perhaps the most comprehensive name of Jesus in all Scripture.

First, Jesus said: "I AM THE WAY."

The original term means, "a road or path" and it suggests the idea of a journey. The thought is, *As you journey through life, preparing for the next life, I am the road that will take you there.*

Oliver Wendell Holmes once boarded a train but was unable to find his ticket. After watching him fumble through his pockets in growing dismay, the conductor said, "That's all right, Mr. Holmes. I'm sure you have your ticket somewhere. If you don't find it, just mail it into the railroad. We'll trust you." Looking the conductor straight in the eye, Holmes replied, "Young man, that's not my problem. I don't care about giving my ticket to the railroad. I just want to find out where in the blazes I'm going!"

That's our world. We're hurried and pressured; life is hectic and fast-paced – but we have no idea where we are going.

There is way which seems right to man, but the end thereof is the way of death (Prov. 14:12).

Solomon was right: There are so many options we can take, so many voices clamoring for our attention, so many opportunities seeking our allegiance. And as a result, we're CONFUSED. We're bombarded by a myriad of choices and theories and philosophies, and because there is no consensus concerning which way is right and which way is wrong, Man, perplexed, wonders, "Which way should I go? What path should I take?"

Jesus says,

"I AM THE WAY. There is no other path, no other road that can lead you to your desired destination. Only Me. You want to see the Father? Come through Me. You want to get to heaven? Take My road. But understand, I am not merely the Map which charts the way; neither am I the Guide who can show you the way. I AM THE WAY! I'm the gate you must come through. I'm the door you must open. I'm the path that you must take."

In Jesus' first public address, He informs us that not only is He the *only* path that leads to the Father, but that it's only on His path that we will escape destruction. Look at what He said:

Enter through the narrow gate. For wide is the gate and broad is the road that leads to destruction, and many enter through it. But small is the gate and narrow the road that leads to life, and only a few find it (Matt. 7:13-14).

Can you sense the urgency in His words? He's saying, "*Enter* that gate. Don't just stand and look at it – ENTER IT!"

249

But make sure when you do that you enter the correct gate. You see, there are only two gates. One leads to destruction, the other leads to life. There's no in-between. No third alternative. It's destruction or life. And everyone will enter one of the two. It's like a true/false exam. It's either/or. No room for discussion. It's one or the other. What's frustrating is that the most popular gate will fool many people into thinking that it is also the RIGHT gate. But Jesus says, *"No, that's the wrong gate. Public opinion cannot impact the rightness of your decision. You come the narrow way."*

Does this kind of talk surprise you? Are you shocked that the meek, mild, gentle Jesus could be so narrow, so unbendingly rigid? You bet this plan is narrow. It's focused entirely upon the person of Jesus Christ and one's personal relationship with Him. PERIOD. If you want to see the Father; if you want to escape destruction – there's only one path to take. One gate to enter. And that's Jesus Christ.

Now I realize that goes cross-grained to everything you're hearing these days. Things like: "It doesn't matter what you believe as long as you're sincere." Or, "One religion is just as good as another." Or, "We're all just taking different roads leading to the same place."

Oh really? That's not what Jesus said. You see, the problem with such lofty sentimentality is that even though it sounds so right, it's so terribly wrong. It's incredible to me that truth in every other area of life is by necessity narrow. And we're glad it is.

Take music, for example. What if your favorite music group sang a song, and the pianist decided to play it in "C," while the tenor sang it in "F" and the bass sang it in "D-flat?" It would be awful! And no matter how sincere the hearts of the musicians, the noise would result in irreversible nerve damage in 17 seconds flat! Truth is narrow in music. If it says "B-flat," you play a "B-flat." If it's 4/4 time, you play it in 4/4 time. You don't mess around with what's written. There is an absolute narrowness in music.

And what about athletics? When a halfback is streaking down the sidelines and inadvertently steps out of bounds, the referee doesn't say, "Well, it really doesn't matter which side of the line you're on! One side is good as another!" Hey, it matters. It matters so much these days that they now employ replay officials, whose primary job is to make certain that what was decided on the field is indeed what happened. Truth is narrow in athletic competition. Seconds count. Inches can determine the difference between a champion and a chump.

And if you're like me, you want narrowness on an airplane too. Would you be caught dead on a plane with a pilot who ignored directions from his traffic controller? PROBABLY. Would you board a plane piloted by someone who thought one runway was as good as another, or who got his operating license through mail order? Oh, he may be sincere! He may really think he knows which is the best course to take, but I wouldn't want to be on his plane and you wouldn't either.

All across the board: whether it's medicine, engineering, computer science, food preparation – whatever – the way is narrow. It's exact. There is no room for compromise.

So why should it be any different when we come to the subject of eternal life? The same standard of rigidity applies. Jesus says, "*I am the way. No man comes to the Father except through Me. ALL OTHER SUPPOSED WAYS ARE MERELY DEAD ENDS.*"

But He doesn't stop there! He also says, "I AM THE TRUTH."

Talk about practical! If Jesus is right, if He really is the

Truth, then man's search for truth is ended. Certainly there has been no more fierce search in all the world than the search for truth. Nor has there been a more unproductive search than the search for truth. Someone has said, "*Truth is the scarcest commodity in the whole world.*" And I think he's right.

It's not that we lack "Seekers." There are plenty of voices out there, more than eager to give you their version of "the truth." We're inundated with self-help books designed to help you discover what is "truth" for you. Daytime television is blanketed with talk show panelists who proudly boast of their new-found truth. With so many voices, it's easy to assume that truth is something to be found. We believe the lie that truth must be sought.

And just like at the County Fair, we move from booth to booth, tasting and sampling the various offerings, hoping somehow to come away with the real thing.

We're like a moped driver I read about recently. A Corvette pulled up to a stop light, and beside him was a moped. The driver of the moped said, "Good looking car! Mind if I take a peek?" So he opened the passenger door, and the guy leaned in, looked it over. The light turned green, the Corvette driver slammed the door shut and slammed the pedal to the floor, showing off a little bit. All of a sudden, the moped zoomed right past him! The Corvette driver was embarrassed, so he put the pedal to the metal and left the moped in his dust. But again, the moped zoomed past him, went a few yards ahead, stopped, turned a 360 on a dime, then fell over on the ground. The guy in the Corvette stopped and said,

"Are you OK?"
The moped driver said, "I'm fine."

The guy in the Corvette said, "Well, is there anything I can do?"

To which the moped driver replied, "Yeh, you can open your door and unleash my suspenders."

We're just like that poor fellow, aren't we? We're being drug through life by our sensual, naturalistic society, believing whatever it wants to teach us, going wherever it wants us to go, traveling at whatever speed it wants to take us.

Paul warned us about that. He said that apart from the truth we are:

> Tossed back and forth by the waves, and blown here and there by every wind of teaching and by the cunning and craftiness of men in their deceitful scheming (Eph. 4:14).

And isn't that exactly what happens? We get jerked around, because we don't know where to find this thing called "TRUTH." But Jesus says, "*Look: Truth is not something you find, it's Someone you trust. I AM THE TRUTH! The fullness of TRUTH in human form.*" Notice, He didn't say, "I contain truth." Or, "I came to teach truth." He said, "*I AM TRUTH. The search is ended. There is no need to look any further. I am here.*"

The problem is, you can look truth right in the eyes and still not see it. You want an example of that? Pontius Pilate. In John 18, Jesus is on trial before Pilate, the Roman Governor. Now picture it in your mind: standing before Pilate is TRUTH INCARNATE.

> "You are a king, then!" said Pilate.
> Jesus answered, "You are right in saying I am a king. In fact, for this reason I was born, and for this I came into the world, to testify to the truth. Everyone on the side of truth listens to

me."
"What is truth?" Pilate asked (John 18:37,38a).

Can you imagine? A fully-educated, highly-intelligent
Roman official looking at truth right in the eyes! Yet he
throws his hands in the air and wonders, "What is truth?"
Why, he could reach out and touch truth! Winston Churchill
once said: "Every now and then someone will bump into the
truth. Usually he picks himself up and goes on." That's Pilate.
And multiplied millions of other earthlings, too.

I WONDER, WHAT PATHS HAVE YOU TAKEN IN
YOUR SEARCH FOR TRUTH?

Many have taken the path of education. That was Lyndon
Johnson's conclusion. He believed that the hope of society
rested in a properly educated people; and if enough opportunities could be made available, our nation would become the
Great Society he envisioned. But listen, friend, as wonderful
and helpful as your education may be – if nothing else – you
know that it is no panacea for our world's ills. Never has
America been better educated. Yet never has America been
more morally bankrupt. You see, education cannot do one
very important thing. Education cannot lead you to the truth.
That happens only through faith in Jesus Christ.

I just finished reading a fascinating book entitled, *Intellectuals* by Dr. Paul Johnson (Paul Johnson, *Intellectuals*, Harper
and Row, 1988). Johnson's basic premise is that the highly
touted historians and philosophers of humanity were wholly
inadequate and inconsistent in their search for truth. Their
words and philosophies may sound quite noble – in fact, most
are still religiously observed even to this day. But the fact is,

the intellectuals themselves failed to conform to their own philosophies. Johnson discusses such philosophical masters as Rousseau, Marx, Tolstoy, Sartre, Bertrand Russell, Lillian Hellman and others. Let me give you a brief sketch of his research:

It may surprise you to learn, for example, that Rousseau, the father of the "Back to Nature" movement, progressive education and the omnipotent state was a hypochondriac and masochistic exhibitionist, with a monstrous ego. He treated his mistress of 33 years abominably, often ridiculing her in front of guests. He allowed the patroness of his youth to die in poverty at a time when he had more than ample means to support her. Four children born by his mistress were abandoned to an orphanage. Rousseau was a writer of unmatched brilliance, yet was fatally unbalanced in the fleshing out of his humanitarian views. His life is best summed up by the woman who, he said, was his only love, Sophie d'Houdetot. She delivered this verdict: "He was ugly enough to frighten me and love did not make him more attractive. But he was a pathetic figure and I treated him with gentleness and kindness. He was an interesting madman"[1] (Johnson, p. 27).

Consider Karl Marx. Johnson writes, "Karl Marx had more impact on actual events, as well as on the minds of men and women, than any other intellectual in modern times" (Johnson, p. 52).The proletarian champion despised revolutionary leaders from the working class, was vicious in his attacks on associates who offended him and was rather anti-semitic. He spent his entire life mooching off family and friends. Due to his improvidence, his wife and children lived in squalor much of the time. When his wife's health failed, Marx took a servant as his concubine, then refused to acknowledge or in any way assist the child of this union.

Tolstoy fancied himself as called by God to effect a "moral transformation of society." He saw himself as part of what he called an apostolic succession of intellectuals – a heady list of leading world figures including both Moses and Isaiah. He seemed driven to fulfill this supposed moral destiny. However, much of Tolstoy's insatiable drive toward moral issues was due to an overwhelming (and valid) sense of guilt. For one, he ran up massive debts and was a chronic gambler. But perhaps his most blatant sins were sexual. He considered himself "highly sexed." A number of diary entries attest to his lustful tendencies: "Must have a woman. Sensuality gives me not a moment's peace" (4 May 1853). "Terrible lust amounting to a physical illness" (6 June 1856). In an effort to satiate his hunger for sex, Tolstoy resorted to brothels, and, as a result, was treated a number of times for venereal disease. He fathered a son by a serf-girl who worked at his country estate; but like the others, "never acknowledged the child was his, or paid the slightest attention to him. What is even more remarkable is that, at a time when he was publicly preaching the absolute necessity to educate the peasants, and indeed ran schools for their children on his estate, he made no effort to ensure that his own illegitimate son even learned how to read and write" (Johnson, p. 116).

Johnson writes:

> We have looked at a number of individual cases of those who sought to counsel humanity. We have examined their moral and judgmental qualifications for this task. In particular, we have examined their attitude toward truth, the way in which they seek for and evaluate evidence, their response not just to humanity in general but to human beings in particular; the way they treat their friends, colleagues, servants and above all their own families. What conclusions should be drawn? The belief seems to be spreading that intellectuals are no wiser as

mentors, or worthier as exemplars, than the witch doctors or priests of old. I share that skepticism. A dozen people picked at random on the street are at least as likely to offer sensible views on moral and political matters as a cross-section of the intelligentsia. Above all, we must at all times remember what intellectuals habitually forget: that people matter more than concepts and must come first (Johnson, p. 342).

I wonder if the public humanitarianism of the intellectual is a form of compensation. Grand declarations of esteem and affection for the masses camouflage a wretched inability to deal decently with individuals. At the heart of intellectualism lies the absence of an objective moral code.

No, the answer is not education. It was Calvin Coolidge who said, "The world is full of educated derelicts." Nor is the answer intellectualism. Sweeping philosophical idealism does not truth make.

But wait a minute! Church attendance is no guarantee of truth, either. That's a path many religious people take. But there's one major problem with this approach: your perfect attendance record won't get you one inch closer to truth. Nor will increased Bible knowledge necessarily guarantee that you'll discover truth. Yes, you read that last line correctly. No, it's not a misprint.

In Kalinovka, Russia, attendance at a Sunday School picked up after the priest started handing out candy to the peasant children. One of the most faithful was a pug-nosed boy who recited Scripture for even more candy. He would pocket the rewards and flee for the fields. The priest took a liking to the chubby boy and persuaded him to attend church school. By offering other inducements, the priest managed to teach the boy the four Gospels. He won a special prize for learning all four Gospels by heart and reciting them non-stop in church one day. That's Matthew, Mark, Luke and John – by heart. Over 60 years later this man died and on his tombstone appears the name Nikita Kruschev. He could quote Matthew, Mark, Luke and John by heart! But it never made its way into his heart.

Just like Kruschev, just like Marx, just like Pilate – exposure to truth doesn't guarantee that you will find truth. Because truth is not something you find – it's Someone you trust. Jesus said, *"That Someone is Me. I didn't come to merely showcase truth, I'm not here to reveal truth – I AM TRUTH! And no one comes to the Father except through Me."*

Finally, Jesus said, "I AM THE LIFE." Contrary to popular opinion, Christianity is not a system of philosophy, nor is it a ritual of rules. It's not a code of ethics, nor is it a set of laws to be obeyed. Christianity is simply and primarily the impartation of life. It points to One who originated life, Who gives full, abundant life freely to all Who seek Him and Who supplied, through Calvary, eternal spiritual life. Jesus says, *"I am that Life-force! You want life? I can give it to you."*

I want to suggest that Jesus gives life on three different fronts:

FIRST, HE IS THE SOURCE OF PHYSICAL LIFE.

Jesus, as Creator, brought into being all Life. But not only did He create Life, He sustains it by the constant monitoring of His hand. Life was begun by Christ, and it continues in Christ. The air we breathe, the water we drink, the food we eat – it's all sourced in Him. You remove the sustaining power and influence of Jesus Christ from this world, and she would not survive even the smallest, infinitesimal second. Life would not continue for even an instant. Take Jesus from this world, and you wouldn't even be able to suck in one more breath. Your heart would immediately stop beating, and you would die.

But not only is He the source of physical life: SECOND, HE IS THE SUSTENANCE OF ABUNDANT LIFE.

By that I mean that ultimate meaning and purpose in life is found only in Jesus. Jesus alone can lift us from the Abyss of Absurdity. But apart from Him, life is as described by Shakespeare's Macbeth, when he said:

> Life's but a walking shadow
> A poor player
> That struts and frets
> His hour upon the stage
> And then is heard no more.
> It is a tale told by an idiot,
> full of sound and fury, signifying
> nothing.

But none of us wants to live like that. So we are constantly trying to devise strategies for making life work, so that we can enjoy happiness and fulfillment and pleasure. But as I look at our world, it appears that never before in history has mankind been more frantic in its attempt to find purpose and direction in life – yet at the same time absolutely convinced there is no purpose in life. No meaning. No happiness to be found. Nevertheless, we keep trying!

It's like the old country song, "Looking for Love in All the Wrong Places." Man's problem is that he's looking for LIFE in all the wrong places. He's stuffing his life full of things that can never bring him the lasting fulfillment and empowerment that he is seeking.

Some try to fill up their lives with material possessions.

But Jesus said,

> Be on your guard against all kinds of greed: A man's life does not consist in the abundance of his possessions (Luke 12:15).

Others try to fill up their lives by waiting for the right person to come along. It may be an unhappy single person. Or a childless couple. It may be someone who longs for a close friend. Or a chance to move away from wherever you now are living. "When that happens, then I'll have life by the throat!" Scripture says, however, that it's foolish to connect happiness to your location or to look to some other person to bring you fulfillment.

Still others try to fill up their lives by waiting for their BIG DREAM to come true. That dream may be owning a business, or making your first million, or reaching an educational goal or having a baby. And as much as goals and dreams help us achieve, they will never bring lasting satisfaction. Now there is a burst of momentary pleasure when a goal is achieved, but not ultimate, lasting pleasure. The high just won't last. If you don't believe me, ask Freddie Prinz, or Andy Gibb, or John Belushi or Marilyn Monroe. The story line is the same. Whatever your dream, even when it is fulfilled, it won't ultimately and entirely fill up your life.

Jesus says, "THAT LIFE IS IN ME! IT *IS* ME!" Yet we all but ignore His call, seeking instead to find Life on our own terms, with a lusty hunger that drives us toward our own destruction.

We're like the wolves of the frozen tundra. Do you know how Eskimos kill wolves? It's rather gruesome, but I think I'll tell you about it anyway. First, the Eskimo coats his knife blade with animal blood and lets it freeze; then he applies another layer and yet another layer until the blade is completely concealed by frozen blood. Next, the hunter fixes his knife in the ground with the blade up. When a wolf follows his sensitive nose to the source of the scent and discovers the bait, he licks it. Tasting the fresh frozen blood, he begins to lick faster, more and more vigorously, lapping the blade until the keen edge is bare. Feverishly now, harder and harder the wolf licks the blade. So great becomes the craving for blood that the wolf does not notice the razor sharp sting of the naked blade on his own tongue. Nor does he recognize the instant at which his insatiable thirst is being satisfied by his own warm blood. His carnivorous appetite just craves more until the dawn finds him dead in the snow.

That's man. We can (and have) become so deeply entrenched in licking our own blood – trying to find meaning and purpose – that we are totally unaware that in the process, we are killing ourselves.

Here's the bottom line: Jesus is the only One who can bring meaning to life. He is THE LIFE!

Now, not only is Jesus the source of physical life and the sustenance of abundant life – THIRD, HE IS THE SUPPLI-ER OF SPIRITUAL LIFE. The world hears that and thinks, "Jesus is going to give me spiritual life? How can He give life? He couldn't even save His own neck!"

We're just like Japan at the end of World War II. In 1945, the conquering Allied powers met at Potsdam. Great Britain, the USA and the Soviet Union, as part of their decision at Potsdam, demanded unconditional surrender from Japan. That was the demand: Unconditional Surrender. They said, "If you do not surrender, there will be prompt, utter destruction. There will be a final blow. Your army, your homeland, your people will be mercilessly destroyed." You know what happened: the Japanese emporer and cabinet said, "We intend to fight to the finish." And all of us also know the aftermath. In the face of that horrific warning, they said, "There is no such power. There is no weapon capable of such dire devastation." But we know today that those bombs dropped on Hiroshima were only the beginning of an ever-increasing arsenal of absolute destruction.

You may wonder how it can be that an itinerant preacher from the first century could impact your life today, but the facts are: JESUS IS THE WAY, THE TRUTH AND THE LIFE. NO ONE WILL GO TO THE FATHER EXCEPT THROUGH HIM. He alone supplies spiritual life. And to obtain that life, to go through Him, demands your UNCON-DITIONAL SURRENDER.

With this august claim, Jesus throws down the gauntlet. He is THE way, THE truth and THE life. The ball is now in your court. Can you say right now that you know that WAY? That you hold that TRUTH? That you walk in that LIFE? Please examine your life. Look at the path you're on. Is it the ONE TRUE PATH, or is it just one of many? Have you embraced THE TRUTH, or are you still searching for truth? Have you found THE LIFE, or is life for you a sick, cruel joke? The answer to each of those needs is found in only one person – JESUS.

He Is Our Advocate

—— 13 ——

We've come to the end of our portrait. Now ours is by no means a complete portrait. As I mentioned at the outset, one commentator has counted more than 700 descriptive names and titles of Jesus in Scripture. So far we've studied 12. However, our intention was never to fully exhaust the vastness of Christ's glory, but to merely sketch the highlights of His identity and ministry.

As we come to a close in our study, it occurs to me that there may be those who might question the value of such a study. After all, what's wrong with just calling him Jesus?

I'm reminded of the story of a young minister who was in the habit of praying extremely long prayers, often employing words and phrases far beyond the grasp of his flock. He would sometimes begin by praying, "Oh Thou, the Omnipotent Father, The Living Word, The Transcendent Being, Thou who art our Omniscient Counselor and our Omnipresent Deliverer . . . " And he would just continue to drift on somewhere up in the ozone for what seemed like hours to his people! One morning, as the minister droned on interminably in especially somber tones, impressing no one but himself, a little Scottish woman in the choir decided to take matters into her own hands. She reached across the stage and, taking a firm grasp of his coat tail, yanked it and whispered not so quietly, "Jest call Him Father and ask Him for something."

I thought about that story, and I wondered if perhaps some readers might be thinking the same thing: "Steve, what's wrong with just calling Him, 'Jesus?'" Absolutely nothing. You'll find no argument here: There is not another name in all of history which compares to the beauty, power and simplicity of the name, Jesus. It's the first name of God that most of us spoke as toddlers. It's the name of God we love to sing about more than any other. It's the most common name used of Him in Scripture – having been used nearly 600 times. Above all, it's the name Mary was told by the angel to name Him at birth. "You are to give Him the name – Jesus" (Matt. 1:21).

So why can't we just call Him "Jesus, and forget about all of these other names?" Let me answer that by telling you another story. It's not original with me. I believe R. C. Sproul told it first:

A little boy was selling fish one day. He had a large sign above his make-shift stand which read, "Fresh Fish For Sale Today." A well-meaning businessman came up to the boy and said, "Son, anyone who's going to buy fish from you knows you're selling it today. You're not selling tomorrow, you're not selling it yesterday, you're selling it today." So the boy

HE IS OUR ADVOCATE

took his paint brush and covered up the word "today," which left the sign reading, "Fresh Fish For Sale." Another person came along, looked at the boy, looked at the sign and said, "You know, son, your sign is a little bit wordy. Anyone with half a brain knows you're selling fresh fish. After all, you wouldn't be lending it or renting it or giving it away." So the boy took his paint brush and covered up the phrase, "For Sale," which left the sign reading, "Fresh Fish." A salesman came by, looked at the boy and looked at his sign and said, "Listen, son, anyone with a sense of smell would know you're selling fresh fish. You can smell it half a mile down the road. You see, in advertising, son, the motto is 'streamline your words.'" So the boy took his paint brush and slashed the word "Fresh," which left the sign reading "Fish." Finally, a well-meaning elderly woman looked at the boy, looked at his sign and said, "Sonny, your sign is somewhat of an overstatement. Even with my poor eyesight, I can see that you've got fish." The boy, dejected, took his paint brush and covered up the word "fish." Then he looked at his sign, and out of frustration, he tore the sign down, ripped it up and threw it in the trash can because the sign no longer had anything to say.

Now while it's true that a study of Jesus' other names and titles will not in any fashion make Jesus more truthful than He already is, it is also true that they can add definition and enlightenment to our hearts.

The other names of Jesus are not at all superfluous. This is not fluff study, nor is it merely filler. Each title assigned to Him by others, each name assumed by Himself reflects and reveals powerful truth regarding His identity and His ministry.

And as beautiful and expressive as the name "Jesus" is, there is no one name, not even the name "Jesus," which can fully capture Him. In a very real sense, Jesus is THE UNNAMEABLE ONE! You take any one of Jesus' names – and if used entirely alone, to the exclusion of Jesus' other names – you come away with a very inadequate and, yes, even inaccurate portrait of our Savior. Trying to use any one of His names as a full and complete description of Jesus would be like trying to hit a major league home run with a whiffle ball bat.

I said at the outset that one of the best ways to come to know Jesus is to paint a mental portrait of Him using only the mosaic of His many names. I believe that now even more than at the outset. I am convinced that, unlike many studies we might pursue, a study of His names will enable us to know Jesus more intimately so that we can then imitate Him more perfectly. That has been the driving motivation behind this book. So far, we've seen Jesus presented as:

• THE LORD. The ultimate authority. The "boss" of the universe.

• But then we took that name a step further. We learned that not only is He THE LORD, but He is KING OF KINGS AND LORD OF LORDS! And as such, His power knows no limit, His authority is unquestioned, His rulership unrivaled.

• Then we saw Jesus presented as THE MESSIAH. The Promised One of God. The Hope of Israel. And we learned that, because He came the first time on time, He'll come again . . . right on schedule . . . just as He promised.

• We also turned to Jesus' own testimony concerning Himself. For example, He said in John 6, "I AM THE BREAD OF LIFE." "Only I can fill your hungering soul so completely that it will never hunger again." (John 6:35).

• In John 13 we saw Him stooping low to wash His disciples' feet. And we learned from His own lips that if the KING OF KINGS AND LORD OF LORDS could be a SERVANT, then we who are His followers must aspire to be the same.

• What an affront it must have been to Israel when He

claimed, "I AM THE TRUE VINE" (John 15:1). "Israel failed to produce the fruit the Father desired, so I have come and have replaced Israel as God's chosen Vine." Because of Israel's failure, I have become the solitary source of Spiritual Life. So what is the response He expects from those who would follow Him? He said, "Remain in me and you will bear much fruit" (John 15:5).

• Then He claimed, "I AM THE GOOD SHEPHERD" (John 10:11). And as our shepherd, He not only laid down His life for the sheep, but He remains to this day, fully committed to equipping His submissive sheep and restoring His straying sheep.

• We learned that Jesus is the only MEDIATOR between man and God. He's the only one in all of human history fully qualified to understand both the heart of God and the need of man.

• And who can forget the chapter where we traced the bloody path toward Calvary? We watched as Abraham nearly sacrificed his son, but at the last moment a substitute was provided. We grimaced at the thought of lambs being slaughtered in preparation for the Passover. We were horrified to recall the daily trips which were made to the Tabernacle, with lamb tucked under the arm, in hopes of finding forgiveness. This is why we rejoiced (along with all of Israel) when John the Baptist, seeing Jesus, cried out, "BEHOLD THE LAMB OF GOD WHO TAKES AWAY THE SIN OF THE WORLD!" (John 1:29).

• Remember what he said in Revelation 1? "I AM THE ALPHA AND THE OMEGA" (Rev. 1:8). "I am the all-inclusive God. I complete what I begin. I enclose all things in the parenthesis of My power. Neither the past, nor the present, nor even the future resides beyond the scope of My awesomeness!"

• And don't forget that dramatic moment when He looked deeply into the grieving, swollen, tear-stained eyes of Martha, and said, "I am the Resurrection and the Life. He who believes in Me will live even though He dies; and whoever lives and believes in Me will never die. Do you believe this?" (John 11:25,26).

• Then he said, "I AM THE WAY, THE TRUTH AND THE LIFE." (John 14;6). I am the path you must take if you would see heaven, the road you must choose if you would know eternal life."

There is one final name to add to our portrait. It is without question the least mentioned name of all those we have studied, but it is also most certainly among the most blessed. Picture in your mind not an infant Jesus, wrapped in swaddling clothes and lying in a manger; not a shepherd Jesus, with staff in hand and his flock in tow; nor a King Jesus, wearing a studded crown and sitting on a lofty throne. No, picture an attorney Jesus, fully clad in the regal robes of jurisprudence and approaching the bench of God's justice on our behalf.

Isn't that amazing? Despite the fact that for generations it has been considered fashionable to mock and castigate lawyers, Jesus is unapologetically presented in Scripture as the Attorney for our defense. He is our Barrister. Our Counselor. Literally, our ADVOCATE.

Webster defines an advocate as "a person who pleads another's cause." It carries the idea of a courtroom, complete with a judge and a jury, a counselor and his client. And the Counselor – the Advocate – not only provides important information to his client – helping him know how to testify, instructing concerning his legal rights – but he also pleads his client's case before those who are charged with rendering the final decision.

Ralph Waldo Emerson defines an advocate as,

Not the man who has an eye to every side and angle of contingency . . . but who throws himself on your part so heartily that he can get you out of a scrape.

That's Jesus. Truly He is our ADVOCATE.

Now the term translated ADVOCATE is actually a combination of two Greek words: *Para*, which means "*to be alongside something*," and *Kaleo*, which means "*to call*." When you put them together, *PARAKALEO* means "*to call someone alongside*." In the noun form, *PARAKLETE*, it means a companion or friend who is called alongside you to help and assist you. To plead your case. To defend you. That's Jesus. He is our Paraklete. Our Advocate.

Let's go once more to what are now well-worn verses in this study. Let's go to John 14. What I find interesting about the term "Advocate" is that the very first time it is used in Scripture, it is used not in reference to Jesus, but rather, it is used by Jesus in reference to Another.

Let's travel once again to a tiny upper room located on the outskirts of Jerusalem. No one but Jesus knew it at the time, but this was the final meal Jesus would share with His men before being dragged into a kangaroo court, convicted of a series of imagined charges and sentenced to the maximum penalty – execution. But the major panic of the night surrounded Jesus' announcement that He would be leaving. Although he assured them that He would return and take them to be where He is, that still didn't stem the tide of heartache.

So in verse 16, He reveals to His men one of the most exciting truths of the new covenant. He tells that He is going to send Someone Who would be with them in His absence. He said,

And I will ask the Father, and He will give you another Counselor (John 14:16a).

269

The word translated "counselor" in the NIV is the Greek word, *Paraklete*, Advocate. Jesus said, "I will send you an advocate. And not just any advocate. ANOTHER advocate." Now, unlike our rather mundane English language, the word "another" is expressed quite clearly in the Greek. The word of choice can either be "heteros," which means "another of a different kind," or it can be "allos," which means "another of the same kind." Jesus uses "allos." "I'm leaving," says Jesus, "but when I'm gone, I'm going to send you another Advocate, and not a different kind of Advocate – not some cheap imitation, not some lesser variety – but another Advocate of the exact same kind as me!" And exactly who was Jesus? Sure! GOD IN THE FLESH! Jesus is saying, "I am going to send to you another Advocate Who is every bit as much God as I am!"

WHO IS THIS ADVOCATE? "The Spirit of truth" (John 14:17). So we have two divine advocates, don't we? The Spirit AND the Son. And each one carries out a specific and eternally significant function. I describe their roles as follows:

THE SPIRIT IS OUR *EARTHLY* ADVOCATE, INTERCEDING *WITH* US THAT WE MIGHT *NOT* SIN!

THE SON IS OUR *HEAVENLY* ADVOCATE, INTERCEDING *FOR* US WHEN WE *DO* SIN!

Let's linger there for a few moments. First, let's examine the role of our EARTHLY ADVOCATE. As I read through John 13-17 (which is called Jesus' "Upper Room Discourse,") I discover that the Spirit fulfills that function in three very dramatic ways:

First, THE EARTHLY ADVOCATE TEACHES US ALL TRUTH. Jesus promised the Apostles,

> But the Counselor, the Holy Spirit, whom the Father will send in my name, will teach you all things . . . (John 14:26).

I take that "all" literally. In a similar manner, whatever spiritual truth you have learned, you have learned that truth from the mouth of God's Holy Spirit. He is THE TEACHER OF ETERNAL TRUTH. Your Sunday School teacher, your Bible Study group leader, your preacher may get the credit; but only the Spirit deserves it! So give Him the credit! He may use my vocal chords or my pen, but He is the Teacher! If you have learned anything at all of divine truth, it's because you have been instructed by the Spirit of God through the Sword of God's Spirit, the Word!

You see, I may be able to vocalize truth, but He alone can take TRUTH and drive it deeply into a person's heart. I can explain and disseminate information, but only the Spirit can permeate wrong habits and break down walls of resistance – thus, protecting the believer from sin.

But let's read on. Not only does our Earthly Advocate teach truth, HE ALSO REMINDS US OF TRUTH.

> . . . and will remind you of everything I have said to you (John 14:26b).

Has that ever happened to you? Maybe in a moment of distress or a time of extreme anxiety, you were tempted to just "Curse God and die." But then suddenly, in that moment of quiet desperation, your mind was immediately awash with truth like:

> My grace is sufficient for you, my power is made perfect in weakness (II Cor. 12:9a).

Or, "I will never leave you nor forsake you" (Heb. 13:5).

Or, "My peace I leave you. My peace I give to you. Do not let your hearts be troubled and do not be afraid" (John 14:27).

Do you know Who it was Who put that truth into your mind? The Spirit! Our Earthly Advocate!

Perhaps you were facing enormous temptation. But for some unexplainable reason, you were stopped short of succumbing to that sin. Why? Because flooding your mind came the warning of Paul, "Do not be deceived: God cannot be mocked. A man reaps whatever he sows" (Gal. 6:7).

If that's happened to you, don't call it coincidence; call it the divine assistance of your Earthly Advocate! In the moment when you need truth most, it is the Spirit Who races to your rescue and brings to your mind just the right truth for just the right need.

Now when we go ahead and sin anyway – despite His efforts to dissuade us – do you know Who it is Who refuses to let us get away with that sin scot-free? Do you know Who it is Who liberally administers the necessary conviction and guilt? You guessed it: Our Earthly Advocate! He is the One who administers guilt.

> But I tell you the truth: It is for your good that I am going away. Unless I go away, the Counselor will not come to you; but if I go, I will send him to you. When he comes, he will convict the world of guilt in regard to sin (John 16:7,8a).

Why does He do that? Because His role is to keep us from

sin! And in that role, He teaches all truth, He reminds us of truth already learned, and, when we sin, He promptly and vigorously applies the necessary guilt.

Oh, there is so much more to the ministry of the Spirit. As our Earthly Advocate, He regenerates those who are lost, He encourages the downtrodden, He helps the suffering to pray, He guides and He empowers. All thi s is with a view toward keeping us from sin.

BUT THERE IS ONE THING THAT THE SPIRIT CAN-NOT DO! He cannot remove guilt. He cannot solicit pardon in the divine court of God's holy justice. That's Jesus' job.

But let's move on: While it's true that the Spirit is our Earthly Advocate, interceding *with* us that we might not sin, THE SON IS OUR *HEAVENLY* ADVOCATE, INTERCEDING *FOR* US WHEN WE *DO* SIN!

The Apostle John is the one who used that term in connection with Jesus, and even he used it only once. It's found in I John 2. Let's consider his words. Now by the time we come to I John, the Apostle is the sole surviving member of Jesus' original band of disciples. He is now quite old and is living in exile on an island named Patmos. His writing style reflects his new status as elder statesmen of the church:

> My dear children, I write this to you so that you will not sin (I John 2:1a).

"That's my hope, little children. My hope for you is that you would not sin." Have you ever done that with your kids? "Honey, I hope that you will never have to face some of the things your mom and I faced." "I hope you do better with life than I did." Who hasn't said that to their progeny? That's typical "parent-talk" if I've ever heard it! We all want better for

273

our children than we had ourselves. And here is John, the "grand-daddy of the church" saying, "I really hope that you will put life together in perfection." But John was also pragmatic enough to know that wouldn't happen. So he said, "But if anybody does sin," (I John 2:1b), and realistically, we probably will, "we have one who speaks to the father in our defense."

Now the phrase, "one who speaks in our defense," is only one word in the Greek. Can you guess what that word is? Right. *Paraklete*. Advocate. In fact that's how it is rendered in the KJV, "We have an Advocate."

But notice, this Advocate speaks directly to the Father. The Holy Spirit works on earth, interceding with us that we might not sin. But this Advocate works in heaven, speaking "to the Father," so that when we sin, and we most assuredly will, He speaks to the Father on our behalf.

OK, John, who is this Heavenly Advocate? "Jesus Christ, the Righteous One" (I John 2:1d).

This is the only place in all of Scripture where Jesus is identified as our DEFENSE ATTORNEY. When sin comes into my life, I have an Advocate who will represent me before the awesome throne of God, Who will speak on my behalf and appeal to the Father for forgiveness.

Why is Jesus the only One Who can fulfill that role? Read on:

> He is the atoning sacrifice for our sins, and not only for ours but also for the sins of the whole world (I John 2:2).

The word "atonement" is an interesting term in the Greek. It means, simply, "satisfaction." What does that have to do with forgiveness? Everything. You see, when sin occurs, God's law is broken. And the Law of God clearly declares,

"The soul who sins will die" (Ezek. 18:20). Why is the penalty for sin so stiff? Because God's justice is at stake. Man's rebellion pierces the heart of God and transgresses His holy Law. So God, although madly in love with man and desirous of a restored relationship with him, is also equally driven to affirm His divine justice. And justice demands that a penalty be paid for man's sin.

Do you see God's problem? As James Kennedy puts it, "God is just and must punish sin, but He is merciful and doesn't want to punish it." We could accurately call this THE DIVINE DILEMMA.

And this dilemma is perfectly illustrated in a story told by the British theologian P. T. Forsythe. He tells of the revolutionary activities of a man named Shamel who was fighting against the Czarist regime in Russia about 1870. His was a guerrilla group, including not only the fighting men but also their families and livestock. His organization was his own tight little universe, with law fundamental to its own existence. Then one day, stealing broke out in the camp and his organization began to fall apart in mutual suspicion. So Shamel laid down the law and announced the penalty: The penalty for stealing would be a hundred lashes. Before long, the thief was caught. It was Shamel's own mother. Now he had the problem of law and love. (That's God's dilemma, too.) For his little universe to survive, the law must stand. In no society can stealing be treated with indifference. At the same time, he loved his mother and could not face the fact that she would bear a hundred lashes. So Shamel shut himself in his tent for three days trying to find a solution. Finally, he came out with his mind made up; his mother, for the sake of the law and the whole society, must receive the lashes. But before three blows had fallen, Shamel could take it no longer.

He removed the shirt from his own back, crouched before the stump and received, in his mother's place, the full measure of every blow. The price had to be paid in full, but the price had been paid by him. His law stood firm; but then again, so did his love.

That's exactly what happened at Calvary, isn't it?

He who knew no sin, became sin for us (II Cor. 5:21).

All *we* like sheep have gone astray, but the Lord laid on *Him* the iniquity of us all (Isa. 53:6, emphasis mine).

He himself bore our sins on His body on the tree that we might die to sin and live to righteousness (I Pet. 2:24).

God solved His divine dilemma by exercising the full extent of His wrath upon His own Son at Calvary. And because Jesus is the unblemished Lamb Who fully paid the price tag for sin, He alone, as "The Righteous One," can approach the presence of God and plead our case before the heavenly bar of God's justice.

Now understand, He doesn't plead our innocence. No, he readily acknowledges our guilt. He knows full well the grief our sin has caused. So He doesn't plea bargain, He doesn't plead temporary insanity, He doesn't try to make our sin appear less sinful than it is. No, He fully acknowledges our iniquity, but then He presents before the court His own blood as the grounds for acquittal. And on that basis, and that basis alone, the case is dismissed, the charges dropped and the sin forgiven.

I find two very compelling reasons you and I are in need of an Advocate. Let me give them to you. Why do we need an Advocate?

First, and this is almost too painfully obvious to mention,

IT'S BECAUSE WE CONTINUE TO SIN. And that "we" includes everyone of us.

Scripture clearly affirms that "all have sinned and come short of the glory of God" (Rom. 3:23). Is that a problem for you? Do you struggle with the fact that you not only are now but will continue to be a sinner? Well, look at verse 8 of the previous chapter:

"If we claim to be without sin, we deceive ourselves and the truth is not in us" (I John 1:8). Wow! That's pretty plain! You don't need any Greek word studies to figure out what that means! Whether you choose to admit it or not, whether you try to hide it or not – the fact is, you are a sinner! And so am I! It's a good thing we have an Advocate, isn't it?

Perhaps you're wondering, "How do I get in contact with the Advocate when I need Him? How is it that I can get in touch with Him and retain His services?" That's verse 9:

If we confess our sins, he is faithful and just and will forgive us our sins and purify us from all unrighteousness (I John 1:9).

Now that goes cross-grained to our nature, doesn't it? I don't know about you, but when I'm caught in some sin, the last thing I want to do is CONFESS it! I either try to JUSTI-FY IT, or I try to HIDE IT. Don't you?

Sure you do. We all do. When we are caught in some sin, our first response is JUSTIFICATION. We try to justify our sin by pointing to a body of information that we are convinced will somehow magically transform the rightness of our wrong.

For example, we point to an absentee father or a harsh mother. "It's not my fault," we say. "If mom and dad had been what they should've been, I wouldn't be in this mess!" Or,

277

"It's my job! Things are so stressful down there! That's why I started taking those pills! That's why I am constantly on edge with my family!" Or, "It's my wife! If she had met my needs the way I need them to be met, then I wouldn't have gone out on her!" A teenager might say, "It's my parents! If they weren't so strict, I wouldn't be so rebellious!"

It's like a cartoon I heard about years ago. Pictured was a group of Danish Knights sitting at a round table in medieval times. The knight in charge of the meeting finally says to the rest of the knights, "Then we're agreed. There's nothing rotten in Denmark. Something is rotten everywhere else."

It's so easy to think that, isn't it? Stop trying to justify your sin! Come clean with it! Admit it! Own up to the fact that you're not nearly as lily-white as you've been pretending! Confess that sin in your life, and when you do, you will release the cleansing power of your Heavenly Advocate – who will immediately and persuasively plead your case before the Father! And forgiveness will be yours! Guaranteed!

Now if we don't succeed at justifying our sin, we go to Plan B. If we can't justify it, WE TRY TO HIDE IT! When are we ever going to learn that hiding our sin doesn't make it go away? It doesn't, you know. It only postpones (and in most cases, intensifies) the inevitable.

Need a case (or cases) in point? Great! How about Adam and Eve? Remember when they sinned? They immediately tried to hide their shame with loin cloth and fig leaves. And then, when God came down for their evening stroll, where was Adam? You guessed it. He was hiding. But YOU CAN RUN, BUT YOU CAN'T HIDE FROM THE FATHER! So they were removed from the Garden.

Remember what Cain did with his brother's body after he

murdered Abel? He hid it! But God knew what had happened, so Cain was banished into aloneness.

Remember what Moses did with the Egyptian after he killed him? He hid him! But God knew where the body was, and Moses was run out of Egypt on a rail.

David tried to hide his sin with Bathsheba by granting her husband a three-day pass. When that didn't work, he saw to it that Uriah was placed in the most intense, most vulnerable unit of Israel's fighting machine. But even with that intricate plan, God knew what had happened and David paid dearly.

I say it to our shame, I'm afraid, but we've learned well from our forefathers, haven't we? We too hide our sins. We try to hide the truth from ourselves, and we do our best to hide the truth from others. As Mark Twain put it: "We're like the moon. We have a dark side we don't want anybody to see."

A few years ago, newspapers carried the tragic story of the murder of eight-year old Chris Dilullo. The death actually occurred in 1984 when it was reported that Chris drowned in the lake at a country club while hunting for golf balls. His three friends told police that he had slipped in the pond, and they thought he was playing a trick on them. But they were hiding a secret. Almost two years later, the 15-year old who pushed Chris into the water finally confessed his guilt to a friend. That two-year period of darkness took an incredible toll on all three of the boys. The paper reported:

> Since the drowning, all three witnesses have suffered emotional instability, according to their parents, police and their own stories. Their distraught parents say the boys are withdrawn and have nightmares. They are no longer friends.
>
> The paper went on to say that one of the boys began crying frequently after Chris' death and had to sleep with his mother

... Once he cut his head when he ran full speed into a dumpster.

The second boy was fired from a job because he would stay home from work on days when he felt "angry and disgusted" about telling a lie to protect a friend.

The third boy started hearing voices and seeing visions and barely talked to his parents.

He later entered a hospital for emotionally-disturbed children.

What a powerful reminder that sin cannot be hidden. Now we adults are much more adept at handling *our* secrets. But the toll can be just as severe. There is the loneliness of cover-up. The emotional expenditure of keeping the lid on. The fear of discovery. The torment that haunts you day and night as you wonder what will happen if someone finds out ... TO LIVE LIKE THAT IS TO LIVE IMPRISONED BY ONE'S OWN FOOLISH PRIDE.

John Powell writes:

When you repress those things which you don't want to live with, you don't really solve the problem – because you don't bury the problem dead, you bury it alive. It remains alive and active inside of you.

Think about that for a moment. Isn't that the truth? It certainly is in my life, especially when it comes to hidden, unconfessed sin. There have been times when I have slipped into a difficult time of depression. Or perhaps I couldn't really put my finger on it, but something unexplainable was sapping me of my energy and emotional strength. There are those who might have suggested that I visit a Christian counselor – perhaps even some psychotherapy. But in each case, do you know what I needed most? Not some little white pill, not another book to read or tape to play – what I needed most was to go to the Lord and confess my sin and ask for forgiveness. Then what I needed was to go to the person I had offended and confess my sin and ask for his/her forgiveness.

Scripture is fundamentally clear on the connection between confessed sin and emotional well-being.

James said, "Confess your sins, and you will be healed" (James 5:16).

And here, John says, "Confess your sins, and He will be faithful to cleanse you and purify you of all unrighteousness" (I John 1:9).

My point? Don't try to justify your sin, don't try to hide it – CONFESS IT! And when you do, the Heavenly Advocate Himself will take your case to the very highest court. And on the basis of his shed blood, He will purchase for you ultimate and complete forgiveness! Why do we need an Advocate? Because we continue to sin.

But there's another reason we need our Heavenly Advocate: We need Him BECAUSE WE HAVE AN ACCUSER.

Did you know in Revelation 12, Satan is called, "The accuser of the brethren?" (Rev. 12:10). Now please understand, because of the death, burial and resurrection of Jesus Christ, Satan is a defeated enemy. But boy, is he ever enraged! Someone has said, "The dragon has been slain, but his tail still swishes."

And if he can use that swishing tail to disrupt your walk with God or even to turn you away from Christ in shame and remorse, then he has succeeded in his despicable agenda. That's why, as he moves through heaven, he stops off at God's throne just long enough to accuse you of every sin in the book. He is constantly pointing the finger in your direction and saying things like, "Do you know what he's been doing?" And much of what he says about us is true! It's a good thing we have an Advocate, isn't it? Just think: If Jesus weren't there to come to our defense, the Father would have to listen to all that garbage. But as it is, Jesus, our Heavenly Advocate, stands in our defense and says, "Satan, you stuff a sock in it! My blood has already covered that sin!" Oh! How wonderful! The accusation which we deserve to have shouted across the skyline of heaven, Jesus silences without so much as a satanic whimper in reply.

Perhaps that's the scene David had in mind when he wrote,

You are my hiding place. You will protect me from trouble and surround me with songs of deliverance (Psa. 32:7).

The authorities are still not sure why it happened. By all external measurements, the takeoff from Detroit's Metro airport should have been routine. Winds were moderate, the pilots were veterans, and the plane had been in service once already that day. Yet from the moment the aircraft lifted off runway 3-C it was clear something horrible was about to happen. Eyewitnesses watched in horror as the heavily-loaded plane staggered into the sky, failed to gain altitude, grazed an Avis car-rental building, then slammed into a four-lane highway, exploding on impact. The crash of Flight 255 was the second worst in U.S. history. One-hundred fifty-six people died in the resulting inferno; the blaze was so enormous, the heat so intense, no survivors were expected to be found. Yet, miraculously, rescuers found little four-year old Cecilia Cichan – badly burned, but alive!

How is it that she survived while all the other passengers were killed? One reason: her mother sheltered her from the blast with her own body. Her charred remains became the hiding place little Cecilia needed to sustain life.

So also Jesus . . . He died that we might live. He willingly used His body to protect us from the blast of God's wrath. Truly He is our hiding place!

You see, there is no way that you and I can get clean by ourselves. There is no way we can escape the fire alone! We've got too much garbage! Too much debris! Too much filth! It's high time we quit justifying it and hiding it. It's high time we confess it. It's high time we said, "Lord, I'm guilty. I'm wrong. Please, forgive me." And when we do that, "He is faithful and just and will forgive us our sin" and He will plead our case before the Father and secure for us what we could never secure alone – the eternal salvation of our souls.

Thanks be to God for Jesus Christ, our Heavenly Advocate!

Well, our portrait is now complete. The features of our Savior have been clearly and powerfully communicated. So what do you do with what you now know? As you examine the brush strokes and gaze at His likeness, how do you respond? I'll tell you how I responded. When I completed this chapter, I shut the door to my prayer closet and I wept. Not tears of sorrow, but tears of gratitude and joy for what God, through Jesus Christ, has done for me. And I offered to Him my life – all over again. It was, for me, a private moment of re-commitment. I said, "Lord, I don't have much to offer You, but what I have, I freely give."

There comes a time in everyone's life when you need to reaffirm your original commitments. Perhaps that's your need right now. Perhaps you need to sit quietly in His presence and contemplate the general course of your life were it not for Christ. Perhaps you need to say, "Lord, if I had to live it all over again, I'd still live my life for You."

Go ahead. Enter into the Master's presence. Let Him speak

to your heart, as you speak your heart to Him. "Let Jesus paint a Masterpiece of your life that reflects a portrait of Him."

AMEN.